T0341077

THE LONG UNWINDING ROAD

THE LONG UNWINDING ROAD

A Journey Through the Heart of Wales

MARC P. JONES

2024

© Marc P. Jones, 2024

All rights reserved. No part of this book may be reproduced in any material form (including photocopying or storing it in any medium by electronic means and whether or not transiently or incidentally to some other use of this publication) without the written permission of the copyright owner. Applications for the copyright owner's written permission to reproduce any part of this publication should be addressed to Calon, University Registry, King Edward VII Avenue, Cardiff CF10 3NS.

www.uwp.co.uk

British Library Cataloguing-in-Publication Data
A catalogue record for this book is available from the British Library.

ISBN: 978-1-915279-58-3

The right of Marc P. Jones to be identified as author of this work has been asserted in accordance with sections 77 and 79 of the Copyright, Designs and Patents Act 1988.

Cover artwork by David Wardle
Typeset by Agnes Graves
Printed by CPI Group (UK) Ltd, Croydon CR0 4YY

The publisher acknowledges the financial support of the Books Council of Wales.

*For Andrea, who changed everything,
and for Paul, who was always there*

AUTHOR'S NOTE

Throughout this book, one of the unavoidable themes is the use of place names and the challenge for the writer in deciding which forms are the most appropriate to use. Welcome and positive moves have given prominence to the native forms of some of our best-known places, such as the world-renowned Brecon Beacons. These are now increasingly referred to as Bannau Brycheiniog and Snowdonia bears the name Eryri to the world, although it's true the world may need a little time to catch up. In this book, I use the English names simply because this is how I have always known them and how my relationship with these wonderful places was introduced many years ago.

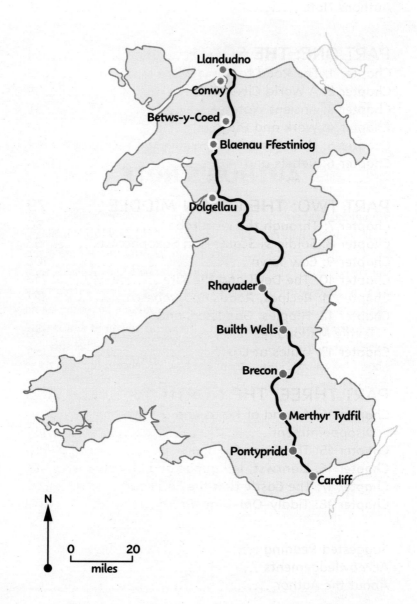

Llandudno

Conwy

Betws-y-Coed

Blaenau Ffestiniog

Dolgellau

Rhayader

Builth Wells

Brecon

Merthyr Tydfil

Pontypridd

Cardiff

N

0   20
    miles

CONTENTS

Part One
THE
SOUTH

CHAPTER 1

THE ROAD TO SOMEWHERE

In the greyed-out 1970s of my Cardiff childhood, while bloody-nosed friends armed with sticks and water pistols ran around arguing over who was Starsky and who was Hutch, I could zone out in a second. This left me usually as the one taking the role of the 'perp' whose main job was to hide, usually in the back of my father's Morris Marina that had a rear window missing.

My curiosity and imagination didn't only get in the way of playground games – it drove my teachers crazy too, and their main communications with me often began with a drawn-out sigh. My early books in a house full of them were atlases, often in childish cartoon style, portraying Inuits in wide icy wastes and shield-carrying tribesmen in the plains of Africa.

I then fell in love with Hergé's Tintin and Snowy as they solved mysteries in the most exotic parts of the planet. Any ideas I had of seeing the world were sown without any reference to the country I was growing up in, which of course was far too confined for my wild imagination.

Brought up in the inner suburbs just to the east of the centre of Cardiff, the travel fantasist in me saw the A48, or Newport Road eastwards, as my only way out. To my naïve thinking, this had to be the most important road because it ultimately led to London, where everything that mattered happened. Like *Swap Shop*, John Noakes, or even the Bay City Rollers, no doubt living it up like kings away from their own home town.

The A48 also regularly carried us on the first part of our summer holidays, with my brother and I packed tightly around pillows and sleeping bags and beach kits, somehow still managing to breathe in the back of the aforementioned Marina. The car had been handed down to my dad by my aunt, the one careless owner, and I can still remember the stench of her sixty-a-day habit ingrained in the vinyl seats we would peel painfully off in the summer heat.

Cornwall or Devon were the destinations of choice then. From Cardiff, that meant going along the Newport Road all the way across the Severn Bridge until we could turn south and spend hours in a trickle of like-minded holiday goers, turning travel games into arguments, breathing in the grey pumping exhausts of the cars around us and generally thinking the whole trip was a bad idea.

Despite these travails, and my father clearly wishing he could be anywhere else, the thought of heading north out of Cardiff didn't even arrive in the family psyche. In fairness this was usually because the holidays themselves, once the hellish journey had been completed, were joyous. Early morning play with the kids in the next caravan, late nights in a pub beer garden where my dad let me sip his warm beer, and the boundless energy that seemed to arrive like a caffeine overdose when we took sight of a beach. We dined like kings and played like fools, and there was never a moment of rain. That's how I see it now, so why in heaven would we have gone anywhere else? What could the road north do for us that the road east and south couldn't?

The first time I would have travelled to the outer planets of North Wales (as I saw it at the time) was on a Howardian High School trip to Snowdonia. It's difficult to explain to a modern eleven-year-old who has probably had a wider world opened out to them on family vacations how life-changing this was, but I can still conjure up the memories of the gigantic green slopes appearing to swallow the school bus at the Horseshoe Pass.

Everywhere we looked, there was something we'd never seen before. A glistening, dark blue lake following us for what seemed like hours, birds the size of aeroplanes, a mountain so high you couldn't see the top. It was almost a science-fiction landscape and we just drove deeper and deeper into it and a million miles further away from the grey streets of our neighbourhoods at home.

Of course, there's always someone who's done it before, and for me that was my bus buddy Francis, who managed to come up with a fact for everything outside the window based on his family holidays, which, if he was to be believed, seemed to be wild expeditions into the heart of darkness, discovering ancient lost cities somewhere near Aberystwyth.

'There's crocodiles in that lake,' he said assuredly. 'That's why Mrs Manning won't let us go in it.' Or, 'That's the fifth highest mountain in the world' as we all stared silently at the looming rock-strewn ridge threatening to topple down on top of us.

Whether we believed Francis or not, and some of the more timid children did, the imprint of this place on our minds, certainly mine, has been indelible.

What is perhaps more interesting now in retrospect is that we saw it as a trip into the wildest unknown and not to another part of the country we all came from. That we were still in Wales wasn't a consideration because, to us in the mid-seventies, Wales was just another name for Cardiff. It seemed not that there wasn't any more to it, it was just that it was where we were.

Welsh identity didn't stamp itself hard on me until later, in fact ironically when I left the country to live abroad for many years; but maybe to many people of my age, growing up in Caernarfon, or Swansea, or Fishguard or Rhayader, being Welsh was perhaps a more obvious element of who they were.

Rhys, who I have known for many years, grew up in Bangor on the northern Gwynedd coast in the shadow of Snowdonia, and his sense of the nation as a boy was the mirror reverse of mine.

His summer holidays were spent on his grandparents' farm just a dozen miles or so from home, where he would be out all day with the farm dog, exploring the riverbanks, the fields and the ancient woodland at the foot of the mountain.

To him, North Wales was the heart of the world, a much more natural world than mine, and the thought of a capital city way down in the south didn't even cross his mind. The south to Rhys was rather pointless.

'I used to think there were no trees down there. All I saw on the television was rows and rows of tiny houses, mines and dirty streets,' he told me when we reminisced recently. 'My father hated the idea of the south and called it "Purgatory" whenever he mentioned it. If the rugby was on the telly he'd say, "Coming to us live from Purgatory" as we sat around laughing at the hellish place we had in our minds.'

One thing we had in common is that Rhys's family holidays were also in the east. They would head along the north coast to Rhyl or Pwllheli and fall in with families of Liverpudlians and Mancunians who came west for the holiday camps and the sparkling sea.

So both of us had that same off-key note ringing in our young heads. That where we came from bore no similarity to the rest of the nation, and we were as blind to it as we could possibly be. The whole stretch of the country from the mining valleys of the south, up through the glorious Brecon Beacons, the gateway to Mid Wales, and then on to the southern foothills of Snowdonia, was as vacant in spirit to me as it was to Rhys in reverse.

That school trip to Snowdonia in the scorched earth summer of 1976 changed that, and it started on the road out of Cardiff. Thirty kids in a bus with no air conditioning, already high on pop and two-thirds of their way through a packed lunch of crisps and spam by the time they got to Pontypridd, meant an uncomfortable time for many, not least the driver, who was already the subject of satirical nicknames sung loudly by the cooler kids at the back. One of whom would vomit over his brand-new school-trip trainers around Merthyr.

The rest of that journey now escapes me as I try to claw it back in memory, but in the years since, every time I head north, I get a tiny thrill knowing I'm retracing steps I first did in awe over forty years ago.

I must have spent many solid months on 'the road north' since. In the commuter logjam each morning from Pontypridd down to Cardiff, or on the beautiful stretch that acts as an unofficial motorcycle racetrack between Merthyr and Brecon. I've been stuck for seemingly ages behind a monster tractor at the agricultural superhighway around Builth Wells, and pulled over just to bask in the still glory of the foothills of Snowdonia. There's the newer stretch that cuts off Dolgellau from the rest of the world, and then almost endlessly hugs the banks of the glorious River Conwy before settling into a pencil-straight final stretch ripping through the more gently sloping landscape to the sea at Llandudno.

All this along one road. The A470.

We talk about it now as the only road in Wales that directly links the north to the south. But 'directly' is a notion with some flexibility. Travelling the whole road requires some map-reading skills and no little frustration as it disappears in front of you, reappears a mile away from you, and moves inelegantly from dual carriageway to tractor track just as you seem to get the hang of it.

Depending on which way you approach it, it starts or ends at the glorious Victorian North Shore of Llandudno, and then does the same (starts or ends) at Cardiff Bay. Two polar opposites of what Wales is, right there. Llandudno is a Victorian architect's vision of what leisure and respite from the pressures of the world should be. A glorious sweeping crescent of a shore fronted by 'grand-dame' hotels that look and feel as though the nineteenth century in all its elegance and charm can still be experienced today. Cardiff Bay, however, around 180 miles down the fragmented road to the south, is all chrome, glass and graffiti. A vision of contemporary living and leisure standards mixed with financial services companies, government and hen nights.

I say 180 miles, but no matter how many times I travel the route, I never seem to record the same mileage. I've done it in 182 miles and somehow, following the exact same route, I've recorded 187. A ghostly five miles erased from my experience, as though on that lonely road from Rhayader to Llanidloes in the broad Welsh midlands, I was abducted by aliens and placed back a while to go through that stretch again as an unwitting part of some interplanetary practical joke game show.

Those 180 miles or so of road are hugely significant. Not only is it the only road that stretches throughout Wales, tying north to south, but it is also the only direct method of getting there. By a combination of difficult geography, economics and governmental apathy over many years, there is no rail link through the country. To get from Cardiff to Llandudno by train requires a couple of changes, and entry into England; the same is true if you want to get from Cardiff to Aberystwyth in the west of the country.

Often, we are told that it's impossible to engineer such a single line, that the mountains and the lakes present too great a logistical problem to overcome, an argument paying no attention of course to rail lines on far more difficult terrain elsewhere in the world, even elsewhere in the UK, come to think of it.

The question 'What about flying?' presents a chance to get really riled up. At the time of writing, a previously occasional route between Cardiff and Anglesey, which was closed during the coronavirus pandemic of 2020 and has not since re-opened, is causing arguments in the Senedd about whether there are important socio-economic and cultural links to be maintained and serviced between the north and south of the nation, or just economic costs to be saved.

Clearly then, with no available alternatives, the A470 remains the one Welsh route that wholly traverses the nation, the one physical tie that binds the country together geographically. In itself it's just a link between north and south, but I wonder if it also makes it easier for children growing up in those regions to know each other's life experience better, or whether the north and south remain as apart as they were in my own youth.

Having returned for a short while from living in Asia, where distances are measured in thousands of kilometres and diverse cultures thrive in its millions of peoples, the thought arises as to whether I could take that short 180-mile Welsh road journey once again and find more on the trip that brings us together than demonstrates how far apart we are.

I started thinking through that grand, overarching, aspirational theme for the trip up the A470 and I wondered what was there before it. How did we end up with this one road right through the middle of the country?

It's no surprise that it's a mad amalgamation of many smaller roads stuck together, not with the goal of linking the North Wales and South Wales coasts, but instead and in much smaller degrees of linking the myriad farms, villages, and market towns within which everyday life carried on without thought to a wider world.

In truth the full A470 is only just over forty years old. All those old roads and lanes had their own individual character until, with some rising nationalism in the 1970s, a campaign gained momentum in the *Western Mail* newspaper for a single route to link north and south.

Eventually this was taken up by the then Welsh Office and the A470 was christened in 1979. In that same year the people of Wales voted overwhelmingly to reject self-determination, or at least a much-diluted form of it, but hey, they did get a road through the country with a single name.

The route was in no way in great condition throughout, and with single-lane traffic here, a dual carriageway there, and many miles of it hedge-bordered and potholed, the A470 from its birth was something of a Frankenstein's monster. A road put together from parts, not all serving or even suiting their purpose.

It could be argued that, in 1979, nothing had changed. If you drove the length of the country, you were still on those same roads, but at least it had the smell of something new and dynamic. After years of non-investment in transport infrastructure, it at least looked to the apathetic eye as though government was doing something. From their perspective, it was cheaper than building a rail link, far more socially acceptable than driving a motorway through the Welsh countryside, and it put off the argument that Wales was being neglected by London for a few years more.

Arguments over the importance and quality of the road are by no means new. In fact, if we went back in time to the early days of heavy industry in the Rhondda valleys, and the production of iron around the 1760s, we find a hero in the shape of Anthony Bacon, a notable industrialist and, for the purposes of this book, more importantly a huge critic of the South Wales transport network of his time. Or, more accurately, the lack of it.

In *The History of Merthyr Tydfil* written in 1867 by Charles Wilkins, it is noted that Bacon, in sending his forged iron down to Cardiff, was hindered by the deteriorating state of the canals and the lack of an alternative. In parliament, a Monmouthshire MP was asked, when the state of the road was raised, how he travelled: 'In gutters!' the sitting member replied.

Bacon sent his iron down the valley in those gutters and, after losing contracts and shipping windows due to the time the journey took, took matters into his own hands. Cleverly, he did this by hosting a feast for the local farmers in the Merthyr Vale. By supplying a grand and rather excessive quantity of ale, he lulled the landowners and farmers into a 'comfortable' state and, after receiving grand (and much sated) thanks from each, managed to persuade them to contribute funds for improvements to the road south.

Waking up the next day with red faces and pounding heads, the farmers found they had overnight become investors in infrastructure. It was to their benefit too of course, as their own packhorses made the journey south on the new road (completed in 1767) in far greater comfort and with far less strain on their bodies, meaning less rest time and higher prices for the farm produce which was arriving far fresher.

Effectively, it can be argued that we have this road now because Anthony Bacon knew how to put on a really good spread.

Since then, the state of the A470 has remained variable and some part of the route is seemingly being worked on by road gangs daily. This doesn't seem to hold back its appeal to the motorist, though.

In 2014 the petrol giant Shell surveyed two thousand motorists to find their favourite UK road, and the stretches of the A470 that travel between Snowdonia and the Brecon Beacons came out on top. Motorists from all over the UK described it as the perfect road for the great British tradition of the Sunday afternoon drive.

You may well ask why this particular road should be worthy of its own book, when there are almost a quarter of a million miles of roads in the UK, each just a method of getting from A to B. Why, then, would the A470 be any more significant than the A1, the Great North Road from London to Edinburgh, arguably Britain's main artery, or the A303 which passes Stonehenge and across the ancient west of England?

I think it's because no other road in the country carries such a responsibility and also provides such an opportunity. It's exactly *because* the A470 is the only 'direct' road through the heart of Wales that it's so important and why it's such a focus around which Wales and Welshness establishes itself in people's lives.

The typical (almost stereotypical) images of Wales are many, so there is a widespread assumption in the external world that the Welsh are all the same.

I can remember at a dinner in Hong Kong being sat between an Australian and a Singaporean and, after sharing where we were all from, the Australian immediately remarked that I must love Tom Jones. There then followed a discussion between my two fellow diners, to my exclusion, about who Tom Jones was. There was this sense, albeit unspoken, that because I was Welsh there would be an immediate kinship and love between me and the singer.

To an extent this is of little concern, and I'll not make it a debate if someone suggests that me being Welsh means of course that I can sing beautifully (I can't) or know *Under Milk Wood* off by heart (I don't) or have a romantic interest in sheep (I don't).

Much of this is typical 'hello' banter when you meet someone abroad for the first time, but it becomes a bit more of a worry when the stereotypes are raised by the Welsh *of* the Welsh.

One time some Welsh friends and I in Asia were sharing a bar with a very friendly couple of Canadians who were looking forward to holidaying in Wales and were asking where they could go. One of our party offered some remarkably off-tune advice: 'Don't go to Swansea whatever you do – it's a shithole.'

I was shocked. I've been all around the world and never heard anyone from any country be so negative about their homeland, and it just perfectly served the point that Wales has a problem in sharing a common pride.

On another occasion, in Germany to watch the Welsh football team, I remember seeing fights breaking out between fans of rival Welsh clubs in the streets. Bangor City fans were throwing chairs and bottles at Wrexham fans while a completely bemused and open-mouthed group of Germany supporters watched nearby.

'Do you guys hate each other?!' one of them asked me as I slumped in disappointment.

A lot of this comes from an inward-looking perspective, a sense that if you're not the biggest fish in the pond, you'd better be a smarter minnow than the one swimming alongside you.

It's that same perspective that both Rhys and I had as young boys growing up in a small corner of the country with no vision of what was beyond our own neighbourhoods. To an extent that may have been tolerable, if not understandable, in the mid-seventies, but since then surely Wales has become a far more world-aware nation than it used to be. Where once, as with the drunken Merthyr farmers of the eighteenth century, there were communities who lived, worked and died within a ten-mile radius of the same village, we now have bigger and more multicultural cities and towns than H. V. Morton saw in his 1932 work, *In Search of Wales*.

Henry Vollam Morton was one of that remarkable generation of early twentieth-century travel writers, including Edith Wharton, Daisy Bates and Freya Stark, who it could be argued created the genre of travel reportage, a genre that now fills shelves in bookstores and libraries. I've read and reread his *In Search of Wales* many times but, as I visit home for a short while, it draws me in again and presents a question I can't resist trying to answer.

What will I see if I open my eyes wide to Wales today? Morton was a Lancastrian who had cut his teeth as a journalist writing in depth about London, wider England, Scotland and Ireland before venturing into Wales. I grew up here and maybe I can look at the nation through a twenty-first-century prism, with reflections from my own past that may explain a little more of who we are now, in a post-Morton world.

The A470 gives me the opportunity to travel the entire length of the country, my borrowed classic Vespa scooter Gwendoline permitting, to see the places that dot it and explore the national themes from more localised perspectives.

Throughout the journey there will be key aspects that continue to drive wedges between what some people consider as Welshness. Principal amongst these elephants in the room is the language. 'Do you speak Welsh?' remains the most separating question any group of Welsh people gathered can be asked.

The exact number of Welsh speakers is never perfectly arrived at by statisticians, with numbers being skewed by people answering surveys in many ways. In the last Annual Population Survey of 2019, the number of Welsh speakers using Welsh as either a first or second and fluent language was given as 29 per cent. In my youth it would have been significantly less, and much effort has been made by successive recent Welsh governments to promote the language, but the unspoken question for many is, 'If you don't speak Welsh... are you Welsh enough?'

This is a pertinent question in my own home, where I, not a native Welsh speaker, live with my stepdaughter, fluent in Welsh having been educated throughout her schooling in the medium of Welsh. There are some in Wales who would instantly judge that she is more Welsh than I. This despite me, my parents and grandparents all being born in Wales. Everybody has a right to define themselves as they wish. I'm clear on that. But can I define myself as Welsh to the satisfaction of others? Or do I even have to? It's a complex issue with many aspects for sure, and one that I want to resolve now for my own sense of belonging.

This, and other cultural divisions, are fascinating, not least in the fact that in the twenty-first century they still exist. One thing I do know, however, from many years travelling around Wales, is that it remains one of the most beautiful countries I have ever seen – and I think this is something that all Welsh people would certainly find common ground on.

So on this journey up through the heart of Wales, I'll leave Cardiff and head through Pontypridd and Merthyr, the old industrial powerhouses, out into the beauty and splendour of Mid Wales. Then I'll travel across the Brecon Beacons and out into the agricultural heartland around Builth Wells, and onwards to take in the wonderful wildlife around Rhayader. I'll enter the southern edge of Snowdonia, pass on through the UNESCO Heritage Site of the slate north, on to the outdoor sports paradise of Betws-y-Coed and out again along the bright blue river at Conwy, finally meeting the sea at Llandudno.

Gwendoline and I have a trip ahead and all these places, and the people within them, are to be found on the same long and unwinding road, the A470.

CHAPTER 2
A WORLD CITY?

Cardiff was a world city a century before it awoke to its wonderful potential, sometime in the mid-1990s, to declare itself a Welsh one. As a boy I had seen it as something of a slumbering place, but of course that was a narrow view. Its past had already defined it as a thriving international centre of trade bringing migrants from far shores that drove an economy based on sweat and toil.

It's hard today to sense that backdrop of time and imagine that thrusting city of industry, as Gwendoline and I ride around the edge of a still-water bay, surrounded by the homogenous chrome and glass of a bored architect's Friday afternoon musings.

The wind hurls itself off the bay here and blasts against the buildings that arc around the gentrified waterfront. It's not even a warm breeze, but instead a full-bodied gust that lifts my coffee cup up and deposits its contents over the wooden decking I've stopped on.

It's very early on an autumn morning and despite this being one of the city's business districts, with commercial offices and government buildings aplenty, there's almost no one around. I was able to bring Gwendoline right up to the railings on a walkway around the bay and I leave her here after her successful completion of the first sixteen miles of the journey, from my home to the start point of the A470.

Most of the buildings that edge onto the water now are barely twenty or more years old. Glass and chrome homes for the white collars who moved in once the ugly industrial past had been swept under the carpet and the muddy tidal bay had been flooded to form a lake.

Regeneration is the casual watchword here. Maintaining its watchful eye on the present is the Senedd, the Welsh government building opened in 2006 that reminds me of a cross between a greenhouse and a flat-roofed pub.

Only a couple of the older dockside buildings that birthed Cardiff's wealth and status well over a century ago remain now. One of those is the elegant red-brick Pierhead Building, site of the original headquarters of the Bute Docks Company, standing as a gothic echo of similar constructions in other nineteenth-century industrial powerhouses like Manchester and Glasgow. It looks like something from the side of a train set. While it's completely incongruous in its pedestrianised surroundings, it deserves a nod for its attempts to maintain an aura of dignity on a strip otherwise devoid of character.

Cardiff Bay has taken a strange path to how it looks today. From the grime and salt of Great Britain's largest exporting port in the reign of Victoria, up to its vital place in post-war industrial regeneration of South Wales, then on to neglect, poverty and crime as the docks diminished. Now, the bay lounges in its role as Cardiff's two-for-one discount playground. Six beers for a tenner and try to use the bins provided.

Looking for something and somewhere to take the chill out of the air and trying to put the pavement-covering residue of last night's hen nights behind me, I walk across Roald Dahl Plass. An eye-shaped boardwalk that stretches about a hundred and fifty yards from the water's edge and as far as the dramatic and rather wonderful Wales Millennium Centre that stands as the cornerstone of the newly regenerated bay, and is by far the most appealing building in the neighbourhood. Being far more dramatic than the car-showroom look of the Senedd, this opera house and concert venue stands as excellence in architectural modernity, with a sweeping high arc roof and a warm and elegant copper facing that reflects light across the boardwalk and forms the backdrop to every picture you see of the new bay.

It's said that to aid the construction, the single biggest private donation to the arts in the UK, of around £20 million, was made by South African businessman Donald Gordon and there's no doubt, as I walk alongside it this morning, that while the docks lost so much in the transition away from industry, there are at least some gains to be celebrated too.

If we are to consider the Ordnance Survey an authority on such things, this boardwalk, the Pierhead Building and the opera house are sited directly on the southern end of the A470 and will be the witnesses to the start of the journey that Gwendoline and I will shortly embark on.

When I was growing up, this was a very, very different place. Characterised as rough, poor, dark, underinvested, it was also Cardiff's most multi-ethnic community, warm-hearted and alive. My parents would often warn me not to go down 'The docks' as it was generally known, but the truth was that the area, for all its visibly neglected ills, held so much interest for anyone with an eye for exploration.

Outside of Cardiff, the area became known for much of the last century as 'Tiger Bay', but that only ever really referred to a few streets, and the wider docklands or 'Butetown' was much bigger and often darker than the legend suggested.

In 2022, where once were some of the city's most dangerous pubs, now sit coffee shops selling crushed avocado breakfasts. Where once were vast numbers of huge ships pulling in and out of the docks daily on the tides with their cargoes of coal, now lies a vast artificial lake fit for the occasional bobbing yacht or the tourist waterbus that sails up and down the River Taff that empties here.

And where once a whole community worked the docks or the shops, pubs and laundries that serviced them, shiny offices now hold office workers, many of them travelling in by car from the suburbs and the wider South Wales. The inevitable changes that in time all communities face, that bring necessary economic growth and wealth, are perhaps seen in starkest form here. The Cardiff of today isn't the result of a binary switch from tradition to modernism of course, but the effects of the simple roll of time that confronts us all. 'New happens', so to speak.

The change (or marketing project) from 'The docks' to Cardiff Bay was also, in part, a 'Welshification' of the area. The dragon flag now flies from at least some buildings or can be seen in a few shop windows, creating a vague sense of a wider nation theme where previously this could have been a dockland in any industrial city in Britain.

But that's largely because Cardiff itself didn't present itself as particularly Welsh throughout most of my life. It's only in the last forty years that the notion of Cardiff as the capital city and principal face of Wales to the rest of the United Kingdom has become apparent, to me at least.

In fact, when I was growing up, Cardiff barely figured in a wider British culture at all. If for any reason it featured on national television, such as a news report, or perhaps Cardiff City on *Match of the Day*, it made for the main conversation in school the next day. 'Did you see *That's Life* last night? They were asking people on Queen Street about flared trousers! Honestly!'

Cardiff has a bigger part in the play that is the UK now. From a barely seen extra in the mid-twentieth century, the city now at least has a speaking part and is often in the spotlight as the venue for major international sporting or entertainment events, or as a magnet for shoppers to its impressive centre. Its bar and restaurant culture is now also one of Britain's finest and the weekends are awash with hen and stag parties battling for dining and drinking space with concert goers, conference delegates and family fun seekers.

The city centre where that all takes place is a mile up Bute Street from where I walk now, still in the old docks area alongside the empty skeletons of some of the most impressive Edwardian buildings of the age. Leaving the water's edge behind, I walk from regeneration to decline in only a few steps.

On Bute Street, I find the high pillars, gargoyles and carved arched doorways of long-shut-down banks, insurance houses and shipping agents: a depressing sight. It is a deplorable state that these stunning architectural treasures now find themselves in. Many have been empty for years, with caved-in windows, boarded-up doorways and filthy stonework. Yet somehow the character remains. Solidity, strength, reliability. All the hallmarks of importance, yet seemingly neglected and unwanted.

These are listed buildings that would cost more to repurpose for an investor than a gleaming, income-generating student tower further up in town would. No one to my understanding seems willing to take on the massive costs of refurbishment and so these stunning architectural jewels continue to fade and become suffocated by the endless temporary bars and pop-up pizza places they look down upon. You can almost hear them sigh.

They are the ghostly murmur of what's left of the old docks and an echo of the community that still resides in the hidden streets here, many with a family heritage going back to when those run-down buildings were amongst the finest of the city. Banks, counting houses and marine insurers all showing their power and wealth in their architecture. All stating loudly what a significant city Cardiff was, and what a beating heart of that city the docklands were.

At its peak just before the Great War, there were tens of thousands employed in this neighbourhood, hundreds of ships per week pouring sailors into the surrounding alleys and the seemingly endless pubs and bars hosting them. Many of those pubs, now long gone, had names that declared their associations. The Ship and Pilot, The Baltimore, The Wheelhouse. The last pub standing today is The Packet, which looks from the outside much as it would have at the turn of the last century, but inside is all sports screens and fruit ciders. It's closed as I walk past this morning, but the cellar is open, and I can look down to the red-brick walls below and sense over a hundred years of docks life in some small form of continuance at least. There's barely anything else that someone wanting to taste the past can depend on.

Everywhere I look as I walk north towards the centre of the city, I see what was now fighting to breathe in the onslaught of what is.

Despite its fall from being the city's powerhouse and wealth generator, however, the heart of this square mile is still beating. This southern end of the road through the nation remains relevant because, just as over a hundred years ago, it is still where the capital wears its multicultural cape.

Multicultural Cardiff is not found with its full colour palette in the dull homogenous centre, all gourmet burgers and vodka-fuelled karaoke, nor in the leafy suburbs where the world is shut out for fear of change, and certainly not back a quarter of a mile at the bay side. It's found right here in a long-neglected corner of the planner's map.

Cardiff had a choice to make twenty years ago between building a city for all on the foundations of its heritage or settling for something neat and easy. In choosing the latter it distanced itself even further from the district at its southern water's edge, which had never been, nor ever will be, either of those things.

I walk into the Togayo Café on Bute Street, about halfway between the bay and the edge of the city centre. This is right in the heart of Butetown.

Thirty years ago this would have been a tough place to take a leisurely walk. From the start of the docks' decline in the late sixties and early seventies until probably the start of this century this place was the area of Cardiff you were warned about, and yet crime statistics show that other areas of the city such as Ely or Fairwater caused the authorities far more concern. Butetown had this reputation because it remained a melting pot of race, faith and cultures in one of the city's poorer neighbourhoods.

The authorities, the council and the police had a bad name here, exacerbated by some terrible relationship work that created a huge divide between the city and the local community. Wrongful and convenient arrests and lack of investment in community hubs and services drove a wedge between the former dockside neighbourhoods and the rest of the city. The rail bridge that cuts across the north end of Bute Street was the boundary where the conventional and aspirational city started and a forgotten corner of it was held back.

The residents of Butetown could literally see Cardiff growing in wealth, with new offices, roads, a stadium and a gentrification programme all within sight on the other side of the bridge, while they themselves were faced with the same old damp housing, filthy streets and whole stretches of their neighbourhoods being turned into white-collar flats to support the growing commercial district around the waterside.

I hear this lament and more from Burhaan, a bright and energetic Cardiff-born Somali sat next to me in the Togayo Café pushing his way through a full plate of lamb and rice, and glad to share his time while I asked the questions that I hoped would explain how this community feels today.

Burhaan was born only a street or two away and is the same age as me, but we reflect two totally different Cardiff upbringings. While mine was in a suburban neighbourhood where everyone you knew either worked or studied, his was in a house shared by three families and occasional visitors, with all adults either out of work as the docks declined, or in transient employment, here today gone tomorrow.

'People think this is a Black neighbourhood,' he says, wiping his mouth with a serviette, 'but that's just lazy thinking. That's what got passed around for years, but it's stupid.'

He starts listing the people he knows in the neighbourhood.

'Poles, Irish, Pakistani, Indian, Sri Lankan, all sorts of Africans, both east and west, and my neighbours are from Syria. My daughter goes to the university in town [he points over his shoulder to roughly the city centre] and lives in a flat just at the bottom of Bute Street with a Chinese girl and a Greek.'

He makes his point with a broad smile on his face and arms spread wide as though revealing something obvious.

'But if you go to Cyncoed, or Lisvane' – he's namedropping some of Cardiff's more wealthy and well-provided-for neighbourhoods here – 'they tell you the docks is a Black community. Why?'

He shrugs and neatly gathers his cutlery onto his empty plate.

Looking around me, though, it's true that the café, busy as hell by the way, is almost wholly Somali in this late-morning customer base.

H. V. Morton knew the cosmopolitan nature of Cardiff Docks too. In his book *In Search of Wales* he also spots the divide between the city centre and this poorer area: 'There is another Cardiff', he writes after first eulogising on the beautiful Civic Centre and the castle further uptown. When Morton refers to the area that sits around Cardiff Bay, he does so in that pre-war language that sits uncomfortably with us now and depicts the various nationalities and ethnic peoples of the district in ugly archaic fashion.

Of its time perhaps, but nonetheless an observation that this area, battered and beaten, but proudly with head above water, has always been very much removed from the rest of Cardiff. A worthy observation today too. While any modern-day Morton would be more selective in their use of language, the point he makes that this was Cardiff's forgotten corner packed with working classes of multiple origins, faiths and languages is wholly relevant today. Maybe even more so.

In her brilliant book, *Wales: Epic Views of a Small Country*, Jan Morris described the area of Tiger Bay at the turn of the twentieth century quite wonderfully: 'one of the best known and toughest of all the world's sailor towns ... with its prostitutes, its drug pedlars, its gambling dens, its Chinese dosshouses, and multitudinous taverns.' She then goes on to list the nationalities of the 'hundreds of footloose seamen ... Germans, Swedes, Russians, Norwegians, Danes, and Finns' (Jan Morris, *Wales: Epic Views of a Small Country* (Penguin, 2000)).

She doesn't mention, but could have, the many other nations that deposited their transients and sailors here. The Estonians for example, and the Poles, who each had bars and clubs hosting their own for much of the twentieth century: the Estonian Club in the town centre and the Polish Club on Newport Road out to the east.

Burhaan tells me that the Somali community in the docks area is one of the biggest outside Africa. He proudly boasts of how self-dependent they are, and the hard work they've done in the community to improve the quality of the schools, to assist with language skills and in helping people to get into work.

I'm sorry to see him go as he heads out, and I stay a little longer thinking I might try the lamb. I'm sat a table designed for four and the three other empty seats are rapidly becoming a premium. A tall man with a very long grey beard asks if he can join me and I move a few things off the table to make room. My notebooks, my copy of Morton. He has that classic 'hipster' look about him. The woollen hat, the beard knotted at the end with a leather strip and a military shoulder bag with patches sewn on.

'You're reading Morton?' he asks me. Now bear in mind that, apart from a couple of nods and 'likes' on Twitter when I've mentioned it, no one else that I know in my limited circle has heard of him.

It turns out Dan is a writer and host of a podcast about Ireland and the Irish which I decide there and then I'm going to subscribe to for no other reason than he has a glorious Irish lilt I could listen to for hours.

'I talked about Morton's *In Search of Ireland* on my podcast some while ago. Aah, it's OK you know, but very folksy and obvious.'

Dan is also a long-time Cardiffian.

I put him at about thirty. He tells me that he spent some years living with the traveller community further east along the seafront, and then started writing a book which he shelved but at least got him some attention from an agent, and now he offers articles to periodicals of Irish interest.

'All this...' He points around him with a knife as he pushes rice from one side of the plate to the other. 'It's all because of the Irish.'

He talks, similarly to Burhaan, about the cosmopolitan nature of the area, but puts the Irish in a position of some high-ground significance.

It's true of course that without the flood of Irish labour that came into Cardiff in the early to mid-nineteenth century, the docks would never have hit the heights they did. The building of the docks and the neighbourhoods that supported them – Adamsdown, Butetown, Splott and Grangetown – was largely due to the sheer volume of Irish labourers who made their home here and changed Cardiff in many ways. From this immigration came a need for a wider town-planning strategy, working-class communities with the pub and the church at their heart and, essentially, growth.

My own great-grandfather, John Crimmins, came here from Galway as a boy in 1856 and worked the docks until his death in 1900. His son, my grandfather, did the same until the Great War. They were members of a tight family in a tight community of Irish navvies, stevedores and labourers who lived in tenement housing. The housing in that neighbourhood is long gone, replaced with a Volkswagen showroom and a storage facility. And all just a ten-minute walk from where I'm sat now, listening to Dan's evidence that the docks in Cardiff was the most significant Irish community in Britain outside London and Liverpool.

Looking at the UK Census for 1851 and again in 1891 for the streets around the docks that are no longer there, such as Victoria

Street where my family resided, the period saw a huge change in the Irish population. Where there were Jones and Williams and a huge Preece contingent, those forty years saw an explosion of Shanahans, O'Reillys and four separate houses all containing the widespread Clohertys. Census avoidance was a popular pastime amongst the working classes at this time, so the actual population was likely more.

They spread from Cardiff Docks up the Taff Valley to become ironworkers as far as Merthyr, or to work deep in the collieries of the Rhondda. It's no exaggeration to say that the Irish diaspora were as important to the creation of Cardiff and the development of its wealth as was the flow of iron and coal back down the Taff to the city's port for exporting to the industrial world.

It's been over an hour of stories while I've been here in the Togayo. First Burhaan and his pride in the Somali community here and how the docks remain a positive reflection of a multicultural society, and then listening to Dan positioning the Irish as the creators of the town I grew up in.

Stepping back out directly onto the A470 outside the café door, I need to get a different snapshot of Cardiff. I've heard of almost every nation and nationality living in this small corner of the world, but ironically, I'm yet to find its Welshness.

There's been no sign of Wales, or even mention of it, in my conversations so far. I could be anywhere in Britain. If I've started my journey here in the capital of Wales, how far up the A470 do I need to travel before I find it?

The answer to that comes about fifteen minutes' walk later as the road through Wales picks up the moniker of St Mary Street, possibly the most famous street in the city. In my childhood this was the busiest road in the town centre with traffic running two ways between some of the finest Edwardian buildings in the country. Nowadays it's almost wholly pedestrian, and those elegant buildings have been repurposed to reflect the changing behaviours of the twentieth-century consumer. Cardiff's elegant avenue is now a typical British high street. In my own opinion there's a sadness to this but progress has always come with an edge.

Looking up at the high-sided buildings we can still see some of the elaborate and ornate stone carvings sat on what used to be banks, grande-dame department stores and public houses. Hodge House, built in 1915, sits directly opposite the façade of Cardiff's excellent indoor market and could have been lifted stone by stone from the Manhattan of the 1920s. High-sided and flat to the street, it oozes solidity, security and secrecy. Like much of the centre of Cardiff, this is a refurbished and repurposed building. What was a financial and commercial monolith of the age is now a 'residence and workplace fit for the next generation'. While some of the original features remain, such as the cast-iron columns that gave it elegance and grandeur, or the riveted steel framework still performing perfectly after ninety years' use, the current estate agents pushing it back into use declare that it's the 'new finishes' that give it the 'wow factor'. Like a Botox shot on a Hollywood legend, I guess?

The world-famous arcades of Cardiff, those narrow shopping channels which leak off to the sides of the street, are still relatively unchanged and harbour many niche independent shops of character, but back on the main drag it's all fast food and slow movement. This is largely, though, because today is a rugby international day, and about two hundred thousand people are hanging around the same few streets looking for somewhere with at least a degree of breathing space where they can order a beer.

The scene is washed with red. Of the thousands in my eyeline as I walk north up the crowded street, almost all are bedecked in the red of Wales. The majority are wearing the souvenir rugby jersey or, at the very least, the hat and scarf set that sets their affiliation apart from the occasional New Zealander I also see taking in the scene.

Alongside the team colours, there are people in daffodil-shaped hats, dragon transfers on their faces and the occasional proud committee man in his blazer and badge. With puffed-out chest and red of face, he's a picture of pride and he's in his element. Surely if the A470 will reflect Wales and the Welsh at some stage, this is the perfect moment.

Halfway up the street is one of Cardiff's oldest drinking establishments, the Borough Arms, and stood outside amongst friends is a man whose name I asked at least five times but, through the slurring, never really got the hang of it.

Thinking I might have more luck elsewhere, I try to move on, but his hand placed firmly on my shoulder suggests I may need to politely hang around even for just a few minutes. Either Ron or Rob or even Rolf asks me what I'm drinking. It's genuine and he knows nothing about me, but his first communication is to offer me a drink. Ron/Rob/Rolf is a wonderfully ruddy-faced fellow, short and barrel-shaped and constantly smiling. I put him at around sixty, but that's only due to the silver-grey buzzcut and the face and neck that brings to mind the creases of time. Cigarette in one hand and pint of stout in the other, he's a little offended that I don't take him up on his kind offer of a drink, but gracious enough to stay, albeit a little wobbly on his feet, and chat. What follows is a difficult conversation purely because he must be at least six or seven pints in and punctuates every sentence with either a burp, a swallow or, on two occasions, the singing of lines from '*Sosban Fach*', a song his mates have tried to start up three or four times with no great success.

What I do get from him is a strident and clear pride in Wales. But I wanted to know why, just what is it that makes him the proud Welshman that he clearly is. And it all came down to rugby. More accurately, the comradeship he gets from rugby and his friends here sat around him, all down from the upper sides of the Rhondda Valley further up the A470.

'I luvvit, mun,' he says, chuckling away, 'it's when Way-uls is addits best.'

Or something.

I know it's a wonderful day for Rob, or Ron, or was it Bob, even, so I leave him to his wet-eyed singing as his mates strike up the song again, and make way for a group of guys coming out from within the pub to form a ring of drinking on the street. About seven of them, all clad in Welsh rugby jerseys from various ages, looking like it's not the first drink of the afternoon. After a few general-chat introductions, it's suggested I may want to speak with Des, stood slightly outside the group and finishing a cigarette.

It turns out Des isn't his name, but the nickname he's having to bear today as the 'designated driver' of the group's minibus on its journey to Cardiff from Llandovery, a good ninety minutes away, at least, in Carmarthenshire to the west. Des's real name is Trefor and he is a massive bloke. At least six and a half foot and with shoulders that suggest he could have carried his mates here without having to drive.

I told him about my journey and my attempts to understand what Welshness means, and he turned out to have some very clear thoughts, mainly as a benefit of him only being able to drink orange juice.

'It seems Welshness is in us all, but we only get to display it on a few occasions. The rugby is probably the biggest of those, you know, the underdog against the world sort of thing,' he says with a big bright smile on his frankly massive face. I'm barely able to pay attention, he's so imposing.

Trefor's theory is that, as a nation, we've got little by way of things to celebrate, with a history dominated by our national neighbour over the Severn, so we take the few chances we're given to make a noise, and that means sport and, maybe occasionally, culture.

'We don't even have a national holiday on St David's Day,' he says, giving his shoulders a shrug they could probably feel back in Llandovery.

I'm trying to ask another question when a chant erupts around us.

'Way-uls, Way-uls, Way-uls.'

It gets louder as more join in, and within a few moments we have a choir of hundreds yelling out as loud as beer and oxygen allow.

Trefor is right, this is one of the few occasions where Welshness is presented en masse, where the classes and communities combine to register themselves as one people. People who've never met are waving, nodding and smiling at each other, offering drinks and singing songs from the collieries, all from one heart. You don't get this level of national outpouring at any other social gathering, and there's a sense that it does mean something, but it's not something definable or even tangible.

Frankly, it's not even something fundamentally Welsh.

Rugby is played in many countries worldwide. Today's opponents New Zealand are in recent times arguably the most successful, but rugby itself isn't Welsh. The love of it may well be, but it's born of the English public school system and while the Welsh have adopted it and to some extent become identifiable through it, it does seem a little weak to say it's where Welsh national pride has its roots.

I also find it something that, along with many other things, creates a fault-line between the south and the north of the nation. The south is a hotbed of rugby, either in the club system that exists in its most traditional form along the southern M4 corridor, or in the four full-time professional regional teams that were created in 2003 to bring modernity to the game and attract large private investment.

The success or otherwise of this new regional approach to the game's highest level of competition remains a subject of debate amongst the Welsh rugby community. Many long for the days of the old club rivalries, village against village, but in the twenty-first century, money, television audiences and sponsors need what they describe as 'product', and it's difficult to argue that regionalising or modernising rugby in Wales hasn't delivered that at least. One thing the old clubs and the new regions do well together, though, is work hard at propagating this theme that the Welsh are defined by rugby. This theory is of far less worth in the north, where rugby is less imposing on local communities and therefore exists as perhaps it should, a game within which talent and skill matter, but the nation's psyche is less damaged if the national team loses.

In the south it is far easier to see the stereotypes of Wales, stereotypes I should say that here on the streets of the capital are legion. The choirs, the Welsh rugby shirts and the inflatable sheep are in every direction.

To my mind, no other group of people seems to pander to its nation's stereotypes as much as the southern Welsh. For all the times I've been to France, I'm yet to see even one cyclist in a beret with a bagful of onions, and in Australia I don't think I ever witnessed a cork-hat-wearing Aussie boasting about his barbecue set-up. And unmistakeably here, it's not Wales as a nation that is being celebrated, it's the skimpiest *idea* of Wales born out of (in Trefor's words) the sense that, without it, there's not much else. In the north, this would likely be a festival of myriad things we can consider Welsh; here in the south it's a piss-up.

The crowd is almost unmanageable now on St Mary Street and has been enlarged by other groups joining the fray. The group of girls in pink cowboy hats propping up one of their fading number against a wheelie bin are getting a lot of attention, and I finally break the edge of the crowd where the A470 joins Castle Street and face the magnificent edifice that gives the road its name. Not many cities have such a wonderful structure at their heart, and it makes for such a fantastic backdrop to the thousands making their way to the stadium.

'Oh, it's just wonderful,' says Sean, about two hundred pounds of muscle with arms wider than my legs and a Māori tattoo on his neck that yells, 'Don't mess with me, pal'. His kind thoughts on Cardiff are getting approving nods from his very petite wife, Carol. The two New Zealanders stopped to ask me which end of the town they need to head towards to find the stadium gate they are ticketed for.

Somewhat ironically, bearing in mind I need to send them through a morass of alcohol-fuelled celebrants, its location is at the other end of St Mary Street in an area that was once called Temperance Town, a dry district that wore its sobriety as a badge of honour, and now today seems to be swimming in cheap ale and prostrate drinkers for whom the kick-off time was just a little beyond their wakefulness.

It's Sean and Carol's first trip to Wales, and they're loving the town-centre welcome they've had. 'We just love all the flags along the castle, and all the dragons everywhere – it's such a pretty place.'

Only now do I look up around me, and they're right, the castle is bedecked with Welsh flags, and looking back down St Mary Street it's the same all along both sides. I don't know how I missed it. Am I immune to it? Did my time this morning back in Butetown and along the waterside, where there was very little by way of national signalling, dull my senses to the fact that I'm in the capital city of the nation, or am I just oblivious to it after so many years of walking these streets?

This begs the question of when exactly Cardiff became Welsh. In my childhood, the city didn't present itself wrapped in the dragon flag, or even make any notable contribution to a Welsh cultural life. I could argue that if you removed these rugby days from the city, then Cardiff may not have anything at all to advertise its Welshness, and for a capital, that's a heck of an indictment. Even the castle, the grandest of all Cardiff's historic remains, was a Roman and then Norman project.

As I think about whether the mass of red swarming in the opposite direction to me is celebrating Welshness or just looking forward to a game of rugby and a shedful of beers, I head onto the A470 again along the very aptly named North Road, which will take me away from the town centre and out eventually to the leafier suburbs.

H. V. Morton was very taken by this part of Cardiff. Clearly, he fell for the large parkland stretching behind and within Cardiff Castle grounds that acts as the start of the road north and out of the city, but more than that he appreciated the way Cardiff had maintained a beauty divided from the ugly industrialisation of the docklands. And it's still the case almost a century on.

I mentioned earlier the railway bridge that created a cultural border between the narrow dirty streets that run like veins through the bay, and the centre of the city dressed in its retail finery and Edwardian brick. Well here, more than a mile from the bay, is what Cardiffians really mean when they present themselves as coming from a 'beautiful town'. Morton declares Cardiff as 'the only beautiful city that has grown out of the industrial revolution', which may or may not be true (it's not true), but his reasoning is what still lies behind the cultural divide between the city and the bay. 'This is because it grew up round Cardiff Castle,' he writes. A nonsense to people like Burhaan and Dan who are living proof that Cardiff's origins as a commercial city came from the tenements and slums around the dockside, and the passage to the bay of ore from the valley to the north.

The castle he admires would have been on the edge of only a sleepy fortress town like many that dot Wales, if the docks had not erupted with sweat, toil and the despatching of iron and coal. It's worth noting that there was no defined capital city of Wales until 1955, over a hundred years after coal was first removed from the ground to the north of here, and Cardiff's geographic situation was the factor behind its development. Without industry further up the river valley, the town (as it was then) would have been of little import.

Another crucial factor in Cardiff developing at such pace was the saga of two families that over time defined the perimeter of the city, defined where its wealth came from and defined its two principal areas – the industrial and working-class south and the wealthier and genteel north. The Herberts and the Stuarts were the ringmasters in the circus of Cardiff's rise, and from their union came a dynasty that changed Cardiff from a sleepy crossroads of only 1800 people in 1801 to a spread two hundred times that today.

The town gained its first significance in the late sixteenth century when the port was decreed a centre for customs collection. This decision created a sizeable black market in goods further east and west along the coast, and was another reason why places such as Swansea grew quicker. The Stuarts, under their landed title of the Butes, were the ones who launched Cardiff into a faster orbit. Despite living almost all of the time in their Scottish homeland or occasionally in London when business dictated, they were never in doubt as to what their land, acquired with a marital union to the Herberts in South Wales, could generate.

The first Marquis of Bute, John Stuart, was of a more philanthropic bent than Cardiff had seen previously, and it is to him that the city owes the splendour of Cardiff Castle, as it was he who began the first restoration process. It was also he who connected Cardiff to the outside world via land by creating the first London-bound stagecoach service.

His son John Crichton-Stuart, or the second Marquis, was the one who changed everything forever as he was the idealogue who began the industrial-scale exploitation of the coal fields and the expansion of the valley iron foundries in concert with other industrialists and investors.

His son, the third Marquis, also known as John Crichton-Stuart is the one we point to for the development of the parkland and the green space that beautified the city north of the industrial docks. When the Butes finally came to sell the land to the city, it was his intention, written into the sale, that the resultant development had to be in keeping with his architectural and landscape ideals. Beauty over bludgeon. Pleasantry over production. This led to, perhaps, Cardiff's finest period of architectural growth and the rather stunning set of buildings in front of me as I wander across the A470, known here as Kingsway. With the castle and its gorgeous grounds behind me, I face onto a triumphant triumvirate of white stone.

The Civic Centre, comprising the Law Courts, the City Hall and the National Museum Cardiff with university buildings tucked behind, is glorious. And quietly whispers a degree of Welshness too. The stone dragon that sits on top of City Hall is a note that the founding architects of the city had notions of nationhood after all, even if they themselves were basically Scots looking for a pocketful of profit.

Walking in front of the National Museum (the third of the three heroes of Cathays Park, as the civic area is more correctly known), with its sweeping steps up to two glorious large doors that wouldn't look out of place as the entrance to Mordor, I notice an artist, sat and sketching away.

I say sketching, but that's a huge disservice to Cerys who, with a simple watercolour palette, has created a quite brilliant and yet surreal image of the museum cowering under imposing and towering grey monoliths that don't exist but look in the drawing at least as if they're most definitely there. It's so disturbing that I keep looking up at the museum to see if the towers on each side of it are present and the artist is seeing something I have blindly ignored.

Cerys is a medical student at Cardiff University, who draws to dispel the anxiety and stress that working on the wards creates. From Lincoln originally, Cerys lives now in a student house in the gently bohemian and leafy suburb of Penylan, a thirty-minute walk away from the centre and into a white-collar and blue-rinse area where coffee comes in thirteen different types and the word 'artisan' gets applied to anything from bread to barbers.

In fairness, this is how Cerys herself describes it laughingly.

I ask what she can see that led to the drawing.

'Those towers may not be there, but in my picture, they represent what's happening to Cardiff all around us.'

Her disappointment is directed at the city council. I understand her point. Throughout the city, where Wales's biggest homelessness and rough-sleeping problem is situated, the council is throwing up student accommodation towers almost everywhere, and I see it as knocking down history to do so. We now have student accommodation capacity in the city that exceeds student numbers, and yet the towers continue to rise. Some of them have the character of a mid-sixties East German bus station, and that's being kind.

Cerys seems to drift away into her painting in rather morose fashion. She's wearing a home-knitted jumper with sleeves too long and patch-covered jeans with red smears of old paint on them that suggest a real artist, and I'm way out of my depth in discussing her art, even though it's genuinely made me think and feel.

Standing here next to her and looking up at the Civic Centre which I remember from my earliest childhood, I suddenly sense an awkwardness in me being here. Cerys and I must be thirty years apart and clearly me standing here ostensibly 'hanging around her' makes me feel old. I want to say, 'I remember running up and down these museum steps playing tag with my brother.' But I'm afraid she'll hear 'Do you want to hear me, someone you don't know, talking about themselves while you try to draw something meaningful?'

It's not Cerys, though, that makes me feel old. It's the sense that these stunning buildings are unchanged in my lifetime, all gleaming white and proudly solid, while I've moved from playful boy on their steps to complaining fifty-something falling out of love with my home.

I walk back the sixty yards or so to the main road, the artery that will take me out of Cardiff, and turn right heading further into what was the Bute family playground and what is now a row of administrative headquarters for various public bodies. The university, the police, my publisher, more government offices and, eventually on my right, the rather lovely Alexandra Gardens.

This is a lovely garden, with cherry and cypress trees lining the gap between the university and the old Welsh Office. Immaculately lawned and as silent as the A470 alongside allows, this is also perhaps Cardiff's most poignant space, standing as the city's memorial park to the dead of conflicts throughout the twentieth century and from more recent operations in far-flung battle zones.

The centrepiece is the Welsh National War Memorial, a dramatic circular columnated memorial of Portland stone that forms a ring around a central plinth with bronze figures of an airman, soldier and sailor reaching up to the winged figure atop that represents victory. Further, smaller monuments sit dotted around the gardens, to the Spanish Civil War dead for example, or those lost in the Falklands. Wales does this well, and the people who curate and care for these gardens and monuments in Alexandra Gardens do important and quite wonderful work. A respect for those lost from villages and towns throughout the country permeates local life, and never more so than on Remembrance Sunday, when these gardens host hundreds of people, sometimes a thousand or more paying their respects.

In Cardiff's charge to be twenty-first-century relevant, and its uncertainty over its role and significance in wider Welsh culture, despite its rush to erase so much of its heritage, this small space wrapped in the heart of its most beautiful buildings is a thing of immense beauty, poignancy and, dare I say it, pride. Yes, that's it, something of the city of which I can be proud. I was looking for that and I feel the better for it, having witnessed at the start of my journey a neglect of its most historic community, and the almost game-show presentation of its Welshness through a sport we didn't even invent.

It's with a renewed energy that I cross back over the road and re-join the trusty yellow Vespa. Clem, Gwendoline's owner, needed her for an hour or two while I walked through town, and he kindly meets me here with her, offers some smart advice on fuel consumption that I barely understand and watches me set off again, wincing I'm sure as I overdo the throttle. On further up the A470 and to the outer reaches of the city. I go past the rather handsome Royal Welsh College of Music & Drama, with its stunning curves and its two theatres, one named after Richard Burton and the other, quite appropriately for the land it sits on, the Bute Theatre.

From here it's quickly through the student bedsit land of Cathays with its terraced streets and busy food stores, over the flyover – a concrete overpass that dissects the A48 heading east to west across the city – up through the leafy Heath area and on beyond Whitchurch and its famous school just on my left. Here, Cardiff has left its industrial past behind for a slice of semi-detached comfort and we're as far from the docks culturally as we are geographically.

I don't begrudge the city its move away from dirty back-breaking industry towards the cleaner service-driven economy it currently relies upon. After all, who wouldn't want an easier, healthier, longer life. But I do resent that, to me, the city appears to want to forget or ignore where it came from. The desire to create a Disneyfied form of Welshness on match day, or a retail paradise at the weekends is one thing; doing it without retaining the character of a city built with dirty hands is another. One thing that would go a long way to acknowledging that would be a statue or monument in central Cardiff to those lost in the development of industry. We honour well here; we could honour more. And a place to pause and reflect on the lives of those who built the city with their toil, and not just those who funded it, would be something of a generous tribute.

I don't live in Cardiff anymore, having been one of the lucky ones to see that Wales really occupies the spaces outside it. I am often conflicted in my own relationship with the place. I am proud to tell people it is where I am from, and there is a sense of social justice I carry that was born from observing the dichotomy of poverty and wealth in the city as I grew up. But I feel different from friends who remain here. Cardiffians born, who will never leave and for whom it *is* Wales, people who have an idea of Welshness truly in their heart but shaped only by these few square miles. For me, the city itself was never enough, and it's with a sense of relief as much as anything that I head out to see the valley where Cardiff's wealth came from and where the taking of it has left a scarred present emerging from the past.

CHAPTER 3

ANCIENT WATERS

The A470 isn't a lonely road in the south. For much of its course from Cardiff northwards, it has a parallel partner winding alongside and occasionally under it: the River Taff, whose flow is the story of Wales. Born in the hills and mountains, giving of itself in the choking age of industry and being reborn from near-extinction, creating new life in the shallows and the banks that run alongside it.

The A470 itself becomes a choked dual carriageway at this northern edge of Cardiff, but just yards off it is the remainder of the old road, shouldering the river for the next few miles and passing through three old staging villages, Taff's Well, Glan-y-Llyn and Nantgarw.

Each of these faces onto the river, thankful for the flood banks only a stone's throw away, and backs onto the railway that holds tight to the A470 noisily chugging away behind.

Of these three hamlets, Taff's Well is the more interesting to me, with its neat row of houses, its polite bowling club and its village pub that has had a brush with modernity only as far as sport on TV and a barbecue pit.

The Taff flows fast here, clearer now that the collieries further up the valley have closed. Some of the houses here are typical tiny terraces, but some have a grander and stauncher Edwardian air about them, most likely built for the white-collar pit directors and their families. The terraced cottages touch the road in a communal welcome to me and Gwendoline passing through. They're basic and honest, a foreshadowing of what's to come further up the Rhondda, while the bigger semis hide behind giant hedges, keeping themselves to themselves.

The community that exists here now will almost all make their living in or from Cardiff. The leap from the outer edge of the capital to here is done in less than ten minutes, so quick that it makes Taff's Well seem like a suburb within the city's grasp. The locals, though, are under no such illusion and take huge pride in a self-possession and separation.

They would find it easy to feel a little special though. For this village with a population of little more than three thousand has in its cultural armoury two distinct claims. Firstly, that sitting right at the southern end of the Rhondda, it is the 'gateway to the valleys', the doorway so to speak to the working-class heritage and natural finery of South Wales.

Secondly, and more factually, it is the location of one of the United Kingdom's most remarkable little geographic and geological points of fascination. Taff's Well is exactly that, a well, or more accurately a thermal spring, and it sits behind the bowling club, next to the bubbling Taff – the only thermal spring in the whole country of Wales.

The well sits within a small stone outbuilding, one of the older structures in the village, and is so close to the River Taff that you'd easily be forgiven for thinking the water is one and the same, but the bubbling and trickling you can see in the well has come from a different source altogether. From here the waters below will join the Taff next door and ultimately flow out to the Bristol Channel, but they arrive here with no connection to the river at all. The science is relatively simple to understand, but the timeframes involved are bonkers.

Effectively what I can see in the well bubbling up from below is rainwater that fell in South Wales about five thousand years ago. After landing on the soft ground of the high slopes of the valley some twenty-five kilometres to the north of here, the rain began an interminably slow journey through minute cracks in the ground, sometimes travelling only a metre or so in a year, until it reached a point almost half a kilometre below the surface where things are, to say the least, a little warm.

Picking up that warmth, it then began its slow rise to the surface, eventually rising through the spring to bubble here five thousand years later. The spring was active when there was literally nothing here but a fast clear river and miles and miles of low sloping valley floor.

I'm trying to feel profound, but there's something very South Wales about this too. No airs and graces, no 'look what we've got' about it at all. Just a geological miracle in a stone hut next to a bowls club.

The spring is neatly maintained by the local council here, as is the memorial stood next to it to soldiers fallen in the World Wars and other conflicts.

This is something South Wales shows immense pride in. Almost every village has their small memorial stone, often with the names of the fallen engraved on it, and there is always a neatly kept, proudly displayed floral tribute sat alongside. This memorial is three simple upright stones bedecked with poppies and there are benches dedicated to those lost, neatly polished, nearby. Some of the worst-hit villages lost as many as a third of their boys, and almost nowhere of any scale has been fortunate enough to avoid loss. At a time when people complain about the breakdown of social fabric, and about a young generation with little respect or even knowledge of the past, the working-class heritage of the valleys north of Cardiff and the sacrifices here of many in war and industrialisation are rarely forgotten and still carry a significant currency amongst the families who live here.

Turning away from the spring and the memorial I walk a few yards along the grass-covered flood bank that protects the community here from the occasional surges of the River Taff. It's nice to stand here with the village behind me, looking down at the clear waters flowing quickly and whitening as they clash with the larger of the rocks and stones on the riverbed.

Although the Taff flows crystal-clear today, its past holds a far more difficult and painful story. While this part of Wales became the wealthiest due to the exploitation of the minerals that lie under and on top of the Rhondda, and jobs, housing, welfare, schools, community and security came from it, it was certainly not without massive, almost unbearable, cost. The tearing up of the landscape of the Rhondda to supply coal, and the blackening of the skies around Merthyr to supply iron, had consequences felt for over a century. Not just for public health but for the natural world that they usurped.

The Taff – where once flowed crystal waters from the Cambrian Mountains in Mid Wales – was declared dead as recently as the mid-twentieth century. Filled with the black discharge of industry and the filth of tenement living, at one stage it stopped flowing altogether and became a sickened canal filled with whatever toxins progress leaves in its wake.

The return of the Taff to a richly nutrient river abundant with life flowing down through the valleys at speed is thanks to the sense throughout this region that nature had died and needed encouragement to return. While the steep sides of the valley that the A470 carves through are of a green and pleasant nature, the damage that industry did here is never far from view, and although the political decision to end mining in this valley caused an economic plague that many villages have still not recovered from, it is also true that it gave time, space and oxygen for nature to sing again.

I leave Gwendoline here a half mile or so further up the road at the tiny hamlet of Nantgarw and follow the Taff alongside the A470 on foot to take in some of that post-industrial returned nature, just as the light of the day starts to grey at the end of the afternoon. Just off the main road and to the side of the riverbanks the trees grow tall and shake in a light breeze. I'm trying to listen for birds as I walk, but the A470 is so close that any chance of hearing something impressive is drowned out by the cars heading towards my destination for the day, Pontypridd.

Here in the ultra green side of the valleys on the riverside footpath I'm in a no man's land. With Cardiff behind me, I'm acutely aware that I walk in an area that acts as a cultural and economic border between the 'capital' region to the south and 'the valleys' to the north. For here is the unclaimed land within which you are neither of Cardiff, nor of the Rhondda.

Those two places – the one I've left, and the one I'm heading to – are divided geographically by the cut of the M4 motorway that runs west to east across this green space. But they are divided more subtly by the attitudes each has towards the other.

During my years living there, the prevailing attitude towards 'the valleys' from many Cardiffians was that the people there were in no way as enlightened as in the high culture city. That the valleys were poor, grimy, less educated, living in the past and unsophisticated. This ridiculous notion was fed by Cardiff becoming wealthier and wealthier in successive decades due to its commercialisation and its skewed focus within government and investment circles. Many people from Cardiff I have known, grown men in their forties, would still describe anyone from the valleys as 'trogs', a pejorative term derived from 'troglodytes' or cave dwellers. The thinking, sadly very openly, was that the valleys were awash with backward criminal types whose children played in the street in bare feet and were fed a diet only consisting of chips.

It's also true that a similar bitterness exists the reverse way and the relationship between Cardiff and the valleys remains slightly at odds.

This is felt in two specific areas, funding and, yet again, rugby. For the latter, the Pontypridd v Cardiff game is more of a chance to embarrass the capital, and to 'get one over on the arrogants' as the 'poorer neighbour' bloodies the nose of the white-collar toffs. Far more relevant to Wales and its future as one nation is the former. Money inflows to Cardiff, and infrastructure development of the city has been outweighing that outside the city for many years, giving some context to the frustrations the 'rest of Wales' has felt towards the capital.

The Rhondda in particular has suffered a significant economic decline during the same period that Cardiff has boomed. Where once the mineral and labour exploitation in the valley gave work to Rhondda families and wealth to Cardiff, the ending of coal mining in the area caused economic decline locally and had far less impact on the big city to the south, which had already redesigned itself as a commercial, retail and property centre. A couple of statistics make the point on my behalf. In Cardiff the average annual wage is over £30,000 per year, while in the Rhondda it is over £4,000 less; but on top of that, in an area with many fewer jobs than the capital, and worryingly for the immediate economic health of the region, the majority of unemployment claimants in the Rhondda are in that vital 18–24 age group where social exclusion causes such difficult consequences for communities. And even with its comparative wealth, jobs, infrastructure and investment, Cardiff alone cannot do the economic heavy lifting for the whole region.

Here as I walk up through the green belt south of Pontypridd along the river path, there's no dissent from the local wildlife who remain silent or drowned out by the traffic yards to my right.

This walk into Pontypridd is along a path that has the river yards to my left, and the throbbing two-lane A470 to my right. Effectively I'm sandwiched between the valley's origin and its present. It's apposite, then, that as I'm thinking of a divide of the riches, and a divide of the opportunities between Cardiff and the Rhondda, that I come out of this no man's land and enter Pontypridd through an undisputed jewel that shines as bright as anything within the capital.

CHAPTER 4
WORK AND PLAY

Ynysangharad Park is a massive sprawl of curated green space sitting beside the A470 and acts as Pontypridd's lungs. After years of choking in the industrial air, the park and the river that sits alongside it are alive and vibrant and offer a space that many towns can only envy.

For residents of the Rhondda, this is one of Wales's finest civic parks, but what I love about it is that it tells a story of the people of the Rhondda. From its creation to the present day, it has very much been a people's park, a great leveller of the classes and an enabler of a wider noble existence for those who gave their best years in the hardest of livings below ground, and their families who strived for more than just existence.

Situated in a bulge of the map where the Taff and the A470 briefly part, this was once allotment and waste space. Thirty-three acres of the land was bought in 1919 'for the provision of enjoyment and pleasure for the town's inhabitants', but also bearing in mind the awful losses the community suffered here from 1914–18, it was designated as a 'War Memorial Park' when it was formally opened to all in summer 1923.

When it was opened, it was bordered to the east, where now the A470 hurtles through, by the Brown Lenox Chain and Anchor Works, a remarkable ironworks that effectively had the monopoly on supplying the British Navy but whose products also dressed the *Queen Mary* and, alas, the *Titanic*.

The Sainsbury's supermarket that sits on the other side of the A470 celebrates the fact it is located on the old Brown Lenox site with artistic images of chains, anchors and ships, but as no one wants to be on a downer while they fill their trolleys there's no mention of the appalling working conditions and the deaths and injuries that were commonplace in the chain foundry.

Alleviation from that body- and mind-numbing work in the mines and foundries of the Rhondda was the benevolent thought behind the park's creation. But as previously mentioned it was also meant to be a site of remembrance, and here I find – after a walk from the gates at the side of the A470 down a lush green slope beautifully shaped and curated by the horticultural team – the elegant war memorial that gives the park its fuller name: Ynysangharad War Memorial Park.

The memorial is simple in its construction. Two long narrow walls, some thirty yards or so apart, parallel to each other and separated by a symbolic rock on a plinth in the centre of a grassy area, and a tall cross of remembrance at the entrance to the memorial. Similar to the Vietnam memorial in Washington DC, the memorial here is powerful for what it *doesn't* do. There's no glory or dramatically formed sculpture, just a bare wall carrying the names of over thirteen hundred who died in various wars of the last century, over eight hundred of whom perished in the First World War before this public space was dedicated to them.

It's almost impossible to understand or even conceive of the hardships of life for the working man in the Rhondda at this time, many of whom simply moved from the hellish life below ground to an even more hellish one in the fields of Belgium. My wife's great-grandfather was one of those men who, as a miner below ground, had a transferable skill that saw him become a tunneller under the trenches of the German front line. From one life-threatening existence to an even greater one.

That's what a hard working-class life was in Rhondda, and for the families who were dependent on the survival of the breadwinner, Ynysangharad Park gave them a space to live an untroubled existence, even for the briefest of moments. A place of (almost) clean air, somewhere to run and play away from the confines of their tiny, darkened houses, and somewhere where for a short time, the shadow of the mine and the foundry could be obscured by the trees standing around the park like a benevolent cradle.

Today the park is busy. A football game is going on between what looks like a rag-tag outfit and a more organised one. The latter score twice while I walk past, but the laughter is coming from the losing side and suggests it doesn't really matter. Coming towards me are a group of runners pushing buggies. I stand out of the way and five young mums in designer running gear push up the hill giggling about something baby-related.

Heading deep into this glorious green civic patch in the late afternoon I come upon a statue, or rather a pair of statues, that represent two men who will have been celebrated by an 80,000-voice choir back at the rugby international match in Cardiff. As the Welsh team stood in line before the game, the rousing 'Hen Wlad Fy Nhadau' would have rung out an hour or more ago amid tears and hugging in the crowd. Somehow this song, taken for granted now as the Welsh national anthem, creates a tension, an atmosphere and a togetherness amongst the Welsh match-goers, well in excess of any other piece of art or cultural focal point. And here in this Pontypridd park the statues commemorate the writers of this song of the heart, Evan James and his son James. As residents of the town, in 1856 as the collieries and colliers were just beginning their dark toil, the pair wrote the song as a reflective harp-accompanied piece glorying the banks of the River Rhondda.

Over time it has become the de facto chant of the sport-going Welsh, and the moment in which for a few seconds – as the lyrics reach the twice-sung '*Gwlad*' – we all sing as one nation. Not everyone knows the whole song in its native tongue, but everyone knows when exactly to join in on that bellowed couplet, and somehow it works. Grown men and women weep and children scream. If anything draws all the Welsh together it is the singing of those few words. Sung to drown out opposing forces in noise, sung in schools with children sat cross-legged and holding hands, and sung by choirs and glorious drunks across the nation. A unifier in a nation of undecided, unconnected and uninterested, disparate people who, on any given day, speak different languages from each other, come from wildly different social and economic backgrounds and are as unrelatable to each other as their rural or urban backgrounds dictate.

The statue built in 1930 is not of the two men, the writers of this national treasure, but instead in their name stands a figure with a harp and the figure of a poet. It's so typically Welsh in that we revere them as historic bards of this nation of poetry and song, but we don't let them get so big in their boots as to warrant a statue in their own likeness. *Think they're better than us, do they?*

As in any typical Edwardian civic park, there's a bandstand. You'll know the type with its elegant railings forming a ring and a few steps up to the stage area beneath a red conical roof. This one sits in a sunken area and was added to the park in 1926. The post-war years were the most significant period of construction for the park, and its maintenance ever since has been a source of pride for the residents of Pontypridd and the Rhondda.

Today I'm in time to see a quartet practising for a concert to celebrate one hundred years of the opening of the park next year. While they're a few months off, they find the space on the bandstand perfect for getting together to play without going to the expense of hiring a room. I catch the last ten minutes which seemed to be a hard piece as they stopped and started a couple of times, and as I don't know it, I ask them what it was as they pack up. Expecting something classical or baroque, I can't help but smile along as Alun, the skater-boy dressed violinist, says 'Beyoncé' with a big grin.

I notice a young couple hanging around as the quartet leave and I can't help but admire their commitment to a dress code I haven't been made aware of. He in a black suit, neat shiny shoes and a bow tie, perhaps slightly diminished in presence by a patterned shirt. She in a long blue dress that drags on the floor but covered by a thick padded coat perhaps more suited to an arctic winter and not the mild autumnal day we have. They're walking around the now-clear bandstand looking at all possible angles for a photograph, and as the park's own benevolent existence adds a layer to mine, I offer to take it for them.

Siersa (I even asked her to spell it) and Ronan are students at the university here (formally the Polytechnic of Wales) and are wanting to take a photo to celebrate their engagement, an event of which they are yet to inform anyone they know.

'We're going to put it on Instagram without any words,' Ronan shyly explains.

They spend about ten minutes looking for the perfect bandstand spot, and then another ten attempting various poses ranging from 'looking into each other's eyes lovingly' to 'Ronan kneeling while Siersa puts one leg up on his knee'. This latter one baffles me but appears to be the position of choice. It also seems to sum the relationship up pretty well. With the light fading and after about twenty minutes I finally get the shot that Siersa –who appears to be the sole arbiter on this – is OK with and which, at the push of a button, is immediately sent to everyone they know via social media. I swear it's only seconds before Siersa is jumping up and down gleefully as the responses start to come in.

OMG SIERSA!!

YOU DIDN'T?????

And my favourite, one which recognises at last my technical excellence: GREAT PHOTO SIERS!

Ronan seems a little separate from all this, so I take the chance to ask how we got here, but it seems the investment in the occasion is all Siersa's and our chat is constantly interrupted by her screams of delight as the responses flood in from her native Poland.

'Why the bandstand?' I ask him as he rips off his clip-on bow tie with a 'Finally!' sigh. After all, a boy from Dublin and a girl from Krakow wouldn't normally think of an antique bandstand in Pontypridd as the perfect place to announce their intentions. I'm assuming that their meeting in Pontypridd at university gives the town a real sense of importance in their lives, a focal point that will remain with them throughout a remarkable life together elsewhere in the world. And maybe the bandstand represents this park beautifully for them, a place where their student summers have been spent, revising in the sun, picnicking in the shade of the tall chestnuts and oaks.

'It's where we first had sex,' Ronan says as matter-of-factly as though he was telling me where he got his clip-on tie from.

Bidding this romantic couple a cheerio, I continue my path through the park and now really sense the nature of the place. The natural world that exists here alongside the human one.

Ynysangharad Park offers a lot to the residents of Pontypridd and the wider Rhondda. Aside from the huge expanse of green space alongside the swiftly flowing Taff, there is a football-pitch-sized dog walking area, tennis courts, a bowling green, a children's playground clearly designed by someone who invites the idea of injury, and a fabulous cricket pitch and pavilion that has seen action for almost a hundred years. None of that action was by me, however, as my highest score here in many attempts is still rather derisory. Well, twelve, as you're asking. I played for St Peter's Cricket Club from Cardiff and even though we ourselves were a rag-tag outfit of some little talent, rarely troubling the silver polishers, we were still the focus for Rhondda teams to try that little bit harder and play with a tougher edge. For whatever reason, even though we had nothing different about us to the teams we played here, we sparked that extra fire in those teams just because of where we were from.

Summer afternoons, sat at the side of this ground watching a game, with the tall oaks and the river as a backdrop, is a rather lovely way to spend some lazy hours. Alternatively, if you catch the day right, the fabulous, heated lido is probably the jewel of the park. I say catch the day right, but I should say season. Open from spring to late summer, the lido is a huge draw for people throughout the Rhondda and is the only such facility still open in the whole region. While swimming pools across South Wales are closing fast – the Cardiff one I learned to swim in, hugely historic and beautifully tiled is now, yes, you've guessed it, a student tower – the lido here is a glimpse of great summers past and new family experiences to come. This is what I mean by the park being a great leveller of the classes.

Beyond the park is Taff Street, the main drag that doubles back on the park and ultimately parallel to the river that gives this grey shabby street its name.

Leaving the park, I was hoping my walk through Pontypridd was going to highlight its reinvention after years of post-industrial decay. That I'd see a rebirth of optimism in the town after years of being beaten down and taunted by its capital neighbour sixteen or so miles to the south. Before starting my journey, I had read of new investments and the creation of space for jobs that would be cleaner for the soul of a family than the coal-smeared ones of the past.

But Taff Street is still a narrow shabby road lined with many closed shops, vape emporiums and charity stores. Any regeneration must be elsewhere, as all I can see here as the day ends is the creaking remnants of something that has already been struggling for two decades or more. I've got a longing in my heart for Pontypridd to be better, but as I look around, I see only a commitment to the status quo. The busker in the closed-down shop doorway can only be bothered to play a verse or two of each song, as though the effort to finish the job is too draining. Where Taff Street forks off to Market Street on the left (the glorious Victorian indoor markets of South Wales remain a gentle heart beating weakly under the strain of online competition and the slow erasing of its typical customer demographic), a butcher's van stands as a man in a blood-covered apron yells his end-of-day discounts on bags of chops. His microphone discharges feedback as he gets to the end of his sales pitch and he can't be bothered to repeat it.

This is a sad moment for me in a high street in a town with so much promise. Bridgend, to some extent, is the same over to the west of Glamorgan, and Newport is trying hard in the east but also coming up against the brutal disdain of the twenty-first century. It's no wonder then that I can sense a grey and undercharged hint of bitterness in the air. It's either that or the cheap dope being smoked on the short steps that lead from Taff Street to Market Street as a shortcut further up the road. I'm in time, however, just before the shutters come down, to get a moment or two in a South Wales legend and finish the day with a cuppa and a Chelsea bun in The Prince's café. Quite possibly the best café within twenty miles or more, this place is a Pontypridd treasure and remains largely unchanged in the last seventy or more years.

Just stepping inside is a reminder of how busy Pontypridd could be, and what a community still lies under the grey veil that post-industrialisation has placed on it. Almost every table taken, people are swapping conversations across different tables and the waiting team are avoiding each other in the narrow walkways while burdened with sandwiches, cakes and the treasured corned-beef slice with home-made gravy. Talk across the tables is of the match in Cardiff or of the family. Typical fare in South Wales. Rugby and the people in our lives we share with others. *Did you know that Sian is pregnant again? Four now? She'll be on five if she doesn't get herself done.* Spoken by a lady in a camel coat and a headscarf to someone two tables away. It's nobody's business and it's everyone's.

A smiling waitress in Lyons Corner House black and white points me to a couple of spare seats at an already occupied table. Margaret and Jan are smiling as I approach, and kindly wave me to join them, knowing all the other tables are taken.

'Who are you, then?' Margaret asks directly, while Jan taps her arm in faux shame at her questioning me before I've even sat down.

'Let the boy sit, Maggie!' Jan tuts.

In that opening moment as I join them, some rules are very clear. Firstly, Margaret will be Margaret to me, but Maggie to Jan, and secondly, like all men in this part of the world, to a 'Valleys nan' I will be referred to as a 'boy'.

They are one of Wales's finest commodities, the Valleys nan. They hang around in gangs in their long coats, their sensible shoes and their firm opinions uncluttered by either sensitivity or sensibility. Yet they remain the undying embers of the proud and enduring history of the region. Their judgements and proclamations are handed down from generation to generation and even when this valley is devoid of all jobs, when its cultural beacons have faded and when all we have is the traced outlines of the narrow streets, the Valleys nans will still gather in the cafés and on the benches at the edges of the parks and still commentate on the state of the nation and those generations who have followed them.

The Rhondda has a tribe of them and they all seem to know each other, nodding and smiling as tables come and go.

'Hallo Maggie,' says one of the nans struggling between the tables with carrier bags and taking ages to get past us. 'I saw Eileen in the market – Sheez, you should see the size of the ham she bought!'

Margaret and Jan drop their jaws in shock. Eileen's ham is clearly big news.

Margaret is a Pontypridd native and Jan moved here as a young bride when her new husband swapped an underground job in Mardy over in the neighbouring valley, for one above ground at the Lady Windsor Colliery up the road near Abercynon, gone now like them all, but originally sited only a lump of coal's throw from where I turned off the A470.

In total, and it's almost astonishing to believe, the Rhondda valleys (the slightly smaller *Fach* and its larger twin the *Fawr*) were at one time the site of over fifty working collieries. Some of those, such as at Troedyrhiw or Penygraig, were smaller enterprises giving work to around two hundred men and mined just the one seam. Others such as the Hafod or the Merthyr Navigation would have had three thousand men, most of whom were underground digging at five or six different seams. Those seams were not only rich in volume, but the quality was of a rare and exceptional standard, making Rhondda coal amongst the most sought-after in the world.

Families like Margaret's and Jan's spent their life in and around the coal-provided existence, and despite still being only in their forties when the mines eventually closed, they have remained here in the valley watching time take another toll on the young men here. From toil, sickness and the ravages of heavy and dangerous labour, to a generation now affected by unemployment, drugs, alcohol and the paucity of opportunity coming down like a pit-collapse onto aspiration.

I ask if the bright economic future the Welsh government promises has any resonance here and they both look at me as if I'm stupid.

'No bloody good to us, is it?' Margaret says as though I've insulted her. 'And when do these "green jobs" arrive in the valley, then?' she asks as if I can give an answer.

Jan is softer on me. She has bright green eyes alive on her powdered face and a smile that no doubt sits there most of the day.

'They just want jobs here, you know,' she says as though I'm being let into a secret, 'just jobs. Some will stay until they get one, and others will move away and not come back, and others have been brought up to not expect them, and they're the ones sat out there on *spicy smack*,' she says, pointing at the window behind me to emphasise the street outside, while letting a distasteful grimace flit across her face for a moment before the smile is back.

I talk about wind power, wave power, solar power and it's all clearly wasted words. Not because of any impoliteness on their part, but because there's no trust in those glories of science ever amounting to anything that will change these parts for the better, or certainly not for the wealthier.

Margaret talks about the Pontypridd of days before I ever came here.

'We could go out on a Saturday night and have a drink in a different pub every twenty minutes from six in the evening to throwing-out time without stepping into the same place twice. It's all over in less than an hour now.' The two ladies giggle loud enough to attract the attention of the rest of the café.

There's much giggling for the next twenty minutes, some of it well over my head but all reminiscence, until it comes to paying for their teas and then it's an argument between them as to whose turn it is. My offering to resolve it by paying for them with my own heavily buttered Chelsea bun and cuppa is met with a look of horror from Margaret and a slow shake of the head from Jan.

'As if the like of it…' Jan sighs and pats my hand with a very short 'Thanks anyway.'

Leaving The Princes café is an exercise in patience and chatter. The tribe of nans all want a moment with Margaret and Jan and there's a clashing hum of kerfuffle, giggles and sighs as myriad greetings, goodbyes and smiles are passed around the tables before the two ladies exit.

The Prince's is a fixture. People once upon a time would have come here for afternoon tea (you still can) in a Saturday best frock. The upstairs seating still has the original art-deco look to it, and the windows and cabinets are dressed by people who care about the food they sell. Still owned by the same original family, the staff here smile and laugh as they go about their work. A real team, and by god do they work. There's barely an empty table all day, and never a rush to get you out of their hair. If you didn't know there was a grey unloved street outside, you'd think you were in one of Wales's busiest market towns.

It is with some sadness that I go back out into the late afternoon as the day has darkened, and head to Gwendoline who has been parked up since I left Nantgarw. The walk back will be a tired one, but thankfully the visit to Pontypridd ends on a note of optimism.

Heading out and towards the Taff bridge, with its lovely stone arch looking like something from a train set, I see a hint that new Pontypridd has a chance. Significant money spent on new offices for government departments suggests some new jobs and some new blood will come to the town, and alongside these a fabulous new library, all glass and contemporary, sits alongside a new walkway across the Taff and back into the wonderful Ynysangharad Park.

On this walkway you can look down into the clear waters of the river, and north beyond the town to the green valley that loudly suggests my direction of travel. There's some hope here at this spot that the town planners and investors have a plan at least. That Pontypridd will be given another chance. It's perhaps thirty years too late for many, but a heart still beats here and, with the right treatment, three generations from now the valleys may represent more in this town than reflections of its past. The park, the river, the skills are all here, and the pride in hard work is unchanged, it just needs a prolonged period of investment and not just brief injections of capital in order for students like Siersa and Ronan, and workers and families, to commit their futures here and not to have to wait for something to happen or to simply give up and leave.

CHAPTER 5
HOW GREEN IS THE VALLEY?

The next morning is brighter and colder, and Gwendoline has opinions on the next stage of the journey, north of Pontypridd and deeper into the Rhondda.

Just like ourselves as we enter the later stages of life, scooters take on different characteristics such as, in Gwendoline's case, failure and inertia. Today she at least started, although the high-pitched whistling noise – a new one on me – which sounds like someone very slowly letting air out of a balloon, is concerning, especially on the steep rise of the A470 as we leave Pontypridd and head up through the villages alongside the Taff that were once steeped in blood and coal.

H. V. Morton called this 'Heartbreak Valley' in his work *In Search of Wales* that sits in my shoulder bag as I twist more noise out of Gwendoline. He describes the sides of the sloping valley here as a 'high place of moor and mist'.

Morton spent time in this valley amongst the miners and the steel forgers and has a beautiful way of describing it in the industrial 1930s that still rings loud today: 'Beneath these towns,' he says, describing the myriad mining communities that line the river and road, 'is the beauty of pride and endurance'.

There is something so deeply resonant in these words that to ignore their relevance would be to shut out over a hundred years of history that still play out in this valley today. Pride and endurance in these communities are what fill the soul here where unemployment and investor neglect do not. Pride and endurance are what hold families and lifelong friendships together here where chapel and government do not. And pride and endurance are what the schools and community clubs of the region continue to foster when the economic structures of the commercial and technological futurescapes do not.

The future for this region is in 'green jobs' we are told. That with the end of mining and steel fabrication comes the age of environmental opportunity. Ironically, that's probably what the first colliery owners called it too, but in this new context we're meant to be talking about the thousands of jobs that will come into Wales from green energy systems, renewables, and a combination of solar and wind power. That's not to exclude the gains made from harnessing wave power at the coast also.

Whether the jobs that slowly migrated away from the valleys from the 1980s onwards can ever be wholly replaced may be difficult to answer, but in the meantime, while we wait, and wait, and wait, the many small communities that still sit in the crease of the valley remain proud and continue to endure the longest possible shadow that the death of industry could leave.

Attempts to alleviate the problems caused by generational unemployment have been one thing, successful or otherwise, but the problem of recovering the landscape after decades of mineral exploitation is equally complicated. The Welsh government is aware of the issues, human and environmental, that persist in the post-industrial south-east of the country and hardly an initiative can be commenced without reference to the regenerative impact it may have.

One of the key initiatives in the government's regreening of the valley is in tree planting. Once, these hillsides that Gwendoline and I are scootering through today were crowded with the trees of undisturbed ancient woodlands, until pitheads and terraces demanded their space. Now that the mines are silent, steps are being taken to restore the natural woodland to at least a little of its former dramatic sweep but, to give some idea of the scale of the coal industry impact here, it could take another hundred years before the scars are fully removed.

The nature of the slopes that fold down upon the A470 is one that was impacted through time, not just by heavy and dirty industry, but also in the centuries prior, by agriculture and principally shepherding.

Paintings in the excellent museum back in Pontypridd depict the slopes here, long before the road jagged through it, as a continuation of green alongside the river, and dotted with sheep as far as the eye can see. But to create the pastures for shepherding, the slopes had to be cleared first, and what was cleared gives us a picture of these slopes long before humans took to farming, and long before the earth here gave up its mineral secrets that would eventually bring riches to some and work to many.

Almost the whole valley in its pre-mediaeval time was covered in a dense forest. From the southern entrance to the slopes just north of what is now Cardiff all the way up to the source of the Taff would have been a thick covering of trees that now only remains in patches occasionally darkening the valley sides.

Of course, ultimately the clearing was to aid the extraction of the minerals under the surface, but in the couple of centuries prior to that, this was livestock land and was sparsely populated. To give some idea as to how industrialisation impacted upon the region, we can look at population figures.

Prior to coal and steel, the population of what was then Glamorgan (if we think of that as Cardiff, Pontypridd, Barry, Bridgend and as far north as Merthyr) was around fifty thousand. At this time (the 1700s) most of the regions of Wales had similar-sized settlements all based around either fishing or agriculture – even slate mining in the north was a slow burn until this time. Then when the mining explosion happened in the Rhondda it was a magnet to the working man, not just from elsewhere in Wales but from Cornwall and Ireland. By 1861, the population of the same area was over three hundred thousand, and it soared to over a million by the time of the First World War.

The Rhondda region alone, taking in the two valleys of the Rhondda Fach and the Rhondda Fawr, had a population of around four thousand in its pre-industrial form, growing to twelve thousand at the outset of mining, and in only thirty years to 1891 reached around one hundred and thirty thousand.

This huge growth meant that the human needs of the community had changed drastically from small hamlets to large villages and towns, and the slopes of the valley became filled with tiny, terraced cottages, schools, chapels, pubs and of course the deep mines. The forest floor lost its tall trees and saw them replaced by tall winching wheels, and the many shades of green rapidly became the shadowy blacks and greys.

Many of the villages in the Rhondda still give away their heritage and the wooded landscape from which they were shaped. Places with *coed* in the name, such as Coedpenmaen, refer to the *woodland*, and *gelli* harks back to the *groves* or smaller wooded areas.

The Welsh government's tree-planting initiative I referred to earlier is a creative approach to regreening the landscape. The premise is this: every single household in the country from 2022 is offered a tree, at no cost to them, in order for them to plant and add to our nation's defence against climate change. Local hubs have been created at which you can stroll up, select your sapling and wander off to plant, in your garden or elsewhere if you have the permission. So that should result in around a million and more trees taking root around the nation.

Aside from tree saplings for individuals, the Welsh government also recognises the need for landowners to be involved in wider environmental action with its clever Woodland Creation Grant, offering financial support for farmers and estate owners to plant trees and install environmentally sustainable fencing and gates. We could possibly be starting a new relationship between the Welsh and the land we live on, far removed from the one that dictated the economy and society in this area a century and more ago.

I don't for one minute doubt the desire and commitment to adapt Wales for the future climate and environmental changes which will undoubtedly be dramatic and life-changing for many, but like all governments, in Wales the *message* that they understand the problem and are committed to doing something about it is louder than the sound of them doing something we can witness.

Involving us in tree planting is a loud advertorial, but it's not the sweeping strategy that's required, and all the noise around creating green jobs is not getting the red-carpet welcome in the former mining communities alongside the A470 that was hoped. These villages have seen enough stop-start initiatives and slogans in the forty years since the mines closed and now actually just want to see the promised jobs.

The commitment to net zero (the buzzword of fashion in carbon-neutral circles) by 2050 means little here, which is a frustration for the Welsh government, which, in fairness, talks about it a lot more than the locals do. That may be something to do with the lack of jobs, opportunity and income directed to the region, whereas Cardiff in the south continues to grow and chug carbon into the skies without losing a dime. One local resident of the capital said to me it's a simple equation: 'Cardiff is a construction paradise. Construction, by necessity, throws out crap into the air and takes up green space. The city grows and grows but no new transport infrastructure is created alongside it. Cardiff is clearly an exception to the Welsh government's green initiatives, whereas it actually needs to be the cast-iron, first-up role model and priority for "greening."'

The age demographic along the Rhondda is a dramatic indicator of what each post-industrial generation thinks of these initiatives.

By 2021 the population of Cardiff had increased by almost 5 per cent in the preceding decade, whereas Rhondda Cynon Taff (the local authority's name for the region) grew by just 1.5 per cent.

Population dynamics and the numbers behind them are way beyond my own comprehension but even I can see that the age demographic would be concerning. In 2019, over 45 per cent of the Rhondda municipal area was over forty-five years old and less than 30 per cent were younger than twenty-four. That shift is only getting more concerning.

Statisticians will refer to the 'Old Age' index as a measure of the age structure of an area. This is effectively an indicator number resultant from dividing the over-sixty-five population by the under-fourteen-year-olds (pensioners divided by children) and multiplying by one hundred. The Rhondda comes in at 110 on the index, uncomfortably shifting to an older demographic than the UK average.

This matters because alongside wealth and health, we can use this data to forecast the living standards for a region in times to come. It won't be a surprise, then, to note that the Rhondda, and Wales more generally, has some headaches on the horizon. It's worst in the UK for pensioners at risk of poverty in later life, low down on social connections, low down on educational attainment of older people and low down on later-years employment.

Swansea University has produced an excellent and often deeply concerning report called *Benchmarking the situation of older people in Wales* utilising the UK Ageing Index, and it examines the concerns of having any region in the UK with a rapidly ageing demographic. In the Rhondda, it is no surprise then that Welsh government 'green' initiatives provoke less immediate enthusiasm than those that impact on health and social care, long-term income security and community safety.

The first village north of Pontypridd as we head out up the screaming raceway that the A470 appears to be here is Cilfynydd. Effectively, like many villages built to support colliery activity, it's just a series of terraces along a main road stretching for a mile or so with a few narrow arteries for smaller cottages off to each side. There's room for a few warehouses or commercial buildings at the rear of the housing, a rugby ground of course and the well-maintained war memorial.

The big employer here, and the reason for the village's existence, was the Albion Colliery. First sunk to the seam in the late 1880s, this was soon providing work for over fifteen hundred men and boys but holds its place in South Wales social history due to the terrible tragedy there in 1894.

On a summer Saturday in June that year, a fatal combination of a gas explosion then igniting coal dust caused an explosion of such atrocious scale that 290 men were killed, many unidentifiable, and almost the entire mine stock of over 100 horses was also lost.

The community was ravaged by the tragedy. Barely a family was unaffected by the death of one of their number, and stories are that one household on Howell Street lost as many as eleven, including a father and four sons, alongside their lodgers.

Despite the tragedy, the Albion itself kept working until 1966 when it was finally closed, but until then, and still now, it is the tragedy of 1894 that remains the principal historic and indeed contemporary significance of Cilfynydd. But it is by no means the only tragedy that has fallen on the community.

The war memorial at the northern end of the village carries the names of over 90 men from this tiny community who lost their lives in the two World Wars. By 1918, almost 20 per cent of the menfolk of the village had been lost to either mining accidents or war.

The stripped pit is now the site of the Pontypridd High School, a reminder that education has always been a guiding principle in the Rhondda. Despite the often-meagre beginnings children have faced growing up in the valley, there has never been a neglect of the worth of an education. Often this is seen as the one crucial factor in raising someone away from the narrow and harsh existence provided by dark industrialisation. Science, humanities and arts have had equal standing here and this tiny village alone, Cilfynydd, has produced two world-famous opera singers and a home secretary.

After a night's sleep at a friend's house – 'I won't be there, but the key is on a string behind the letter box. You can help yourself to anything but the fridge is empty and I sold the TV' – and a morning giving Gwendoline a damp rag and a pat, I ride just three miles further on, to Abercynon, where I'm able to get a clearer picture of today's valley's life with a couple of local stalwarts of the Rhondda, Peter and Philip, who work the Fives Café on Margaret Street, located just around the corner from the clock tower war memorial outside the library.

Memorials and libraries, two pillars of valley life.

The breakfast here, a classic fry-up, fills a big plate and comes with a mug of tea the size of a bucket, for less than a fiver.

'People can't afford more here,' says Peter with a gentle smile of understanding on his face. 'We haven't put our prices up since Covid because you must look after people *as well as* make a living. No point doing one without the other, is there?' he asks me rhetorically.

A look at the menu makes no further explanation necessary. Hot children's meals for just around two pounds, and a whole family can eat for a tenner. On the walls are copies of cheques raised for various local charities. An attempt to start a pictorial tea-towel theme was arrested at just two or three stapled to the walls, Paignton the most recent (possibly ten years ago by the look of it), but the atmosphere is created by the two men themselves, not the walls.

I find it hard to write about some of these establishments that characterise life in a South Wales village. Particularly in the post-industrial valleys. The veneer is sometimes shabby, tired perhaps, not always spotlessly clean, with businesses, including cafés and restaurants, stripped to the barest basics. Underinvested where capital is a rare commodity and underappreciated in an age where food has become a field of expertise for all with a television.

But the truth is, while the Fives Café *is* tired, and does need some attention around the walls, it needs absolutely nothing in honesty, kindness, care for its customers and value for money.

There is a heart here that beats for the poor who live in the village and a decency to acknowledge the stranger who walks through the door. Today, Peter is taking care of front of house which means serving four of the nine tables, occupied in turn by a rucksack-burdened hiker, an old and tired gent struggling to convey toast to his mouth with any urgency, a young mum with a buggy, and myself.

Peter's charm is in making each of us feel welcome as though we were in his own home. A joke here, a quick clear-up and tidy there, and always a self-deprecating smile.

'Perfect!' I say to him as he delivers a basin of tea to my table.

'Am I?' he says with mock pleasure. 'You hear that, Philip?' he shouts to the open kitchen at the back of the shop, 'Perfect I am!'

He tries to bring other customers along with the chatter. Looking and smiling at each as he celebrates my thanks. The young mum smiles, the walker too… but the old gent still wavers his toast in front of his wide-open mouth, oblivious to the fun that Peter appears to be starting.

Philip, clad in apron and a baseball cap, looks from the kitchen area with a theatrical eyeroll, and a smile. This is a happy place. He's juggling three or four orders with great skill. Beans are heating, sausages are frying, eggs in various forms are sizzling and toast is popping. Nobody is kept waiting and the food when it arrives with Peter's theatrical delivery is wonderful.

When I'm the last customer in the café, Peter and Philip join me and we talk about how it's such an important fixture in community life here.

Most valley villages have two or three of these places and Abercynon is no different. Many were started by immigrants in the early twentieth century and the 'Italian café' is a feature in many parts of the Rhondda. Over time they have become a stereotype reflected in television and theatre such as Bella's Café in the children's television show *Fireman Sam*.

In this programme, the titular firefighter works in the animated village of Pontypandy that to all intents could be any South Wales village in its sketched form. Albeit an incredibly dangerous one as, aside from the fire station, there's both a mountain rescue team *and* an ocean rescue station. More typically, however, aside from the Italian café, there's the farm, the mountain, the church, the garage and the police station. In short, it's Abercynon, although for bizarre broadcasting purposes, after the first couple of valleys-based series they decided for future generations of watchers to move the whole village to the side of the ocean, hence the dramatic doubling of rescue infrastructure.

It may be a village in post-industrial decline, but Abercynon has also earned the respect of the railway lovers of the world, being the site of the end of the line of the first steam railway journey, made by Richard Trevithick between the ironworks at Merthyr and the canal basin here.

That importance as a transport hub led to Abercynon being the smallest place in Wales to have two railway stations, one offering a stop on the Cardiff to Aberdare line, and one in the neighbouring valley on the Cardiff to Merthyr line, the location being a natural fork in the valleys where the rivers Taff and Cynon meet.

'The railway was very important here,' says Philip, 'and it still is for people who want somewhere affordable to live while also being able to work away. Cardiff is where the jobs are, but Abercynon is where young people can afford to buy a house. 'If they have a job that is,' he adds looking over his glasses as if bringing me into his suspicions.

A quick look at an estate agent's website suggests a starter home here, about twenty miles north of Cardiff, would be around £100,000, which is half the price of the same in the capital. So, is this the future of Abercynon now? A bedsit town for Cardiff?

'It already is,' says Peter.

Since the closure of mining in this area, Cardiff's boom has been a lifeline for valleys life, and with commitment to public sector jobs in Pontypridd and further north in Merthyr there is at least a simmering of evidence to suggest that Abercynon *may* be a beneficiary in the next generation or so. But the atmosphere in the village doesn't suggest that optimism is rife.

The local charity shop is called Valleys of Hope and the library has that shine of the almost new, but the streets remain deathly quiet, and the damp air creates a grey mood.

It's difficult, then, in these narrow grey streets built to accommodate hundreds of families dependent on what could be dug from the ground, to imagine anything immediately transformative to people's lives. I can't echo the importance of a green agenda in local economic policy enough, but the ambition to build a green economy here won't be enough on its own without further investment into all aspects of the regional economy. There surely has to be a parallel plan to enrich people's public service provision and at the same time introduce more sustainable practices that will become a legacy through future generations.

The Welsh government may well set that green agenda and the framework of laws and guidelines that will encapsulate it, but it will hang as successful or not on the levels of investment that are directed by the private sector. A sector not currently falling over itself to make commitments to the Rhondda, it must be said.

No matter how much the Welsh government embraces and demonstrates the principles that defend against climate change, or provide sustainable economic futures, the well-paid jobs in South East Wales will remain principally in Cardiff, with a respectable level of public-sector jobs in hospitals, government agencies and local authorities only dotted up the valleys. It seems to this untrained eye somewhat unlikely that the Rhondda and the Cynon will see a transformative green industrial revolution that benefits the majority, and school-leavers in particular, in my lifetime.

That pessimism paints the streets of Abercynon, and even with their jaunty and friendly personas, it is clear that Peter and Philip back in the Fives Café see it, too.

'You'd only buy a house here and live here now in order to have a decent level of disposable income from a job you have in Pontypridd or Cardiff. Most likely Cardiff,' Philip says with open hands as if revealing something we all know anyway.

That war memorial built into a clock tower tells the same story as the one in Cilfynydd. People from hard-working communities worked the hardest of jobs to provide for families, and gave their lives for an ideal beyond the fair demand of the working man. But in doing so, the community remained, and whilst there was work, even of the most demoralising and back-breaking kind, for the next generation there was hope.

A community remains here, filled with good and decent people, but hope and optimism seem to have largely moved somewhere else.

It's only a short ride north to the next ex-mining village of Treharris. The characteristics of the last thirty or forty years are the same here as in many other villages in the surrounding area. The pit has gone and been built on, in this case with a sports field.

The mine here, the Deep Navigation Colliery, was a tough one to mine. The seam was so deep that shafts of up to two thousand feet and more were dug into the earth, making this the deepest in the South Wales coal fields. The coal was particularly high quality from this seam and at one time exclusive supplies were swallowed up by the Cunard shipping line. In fact, the coal here powered transatlantic crossings throughout the early part of the twentieth century.

North again and away from the road we come to the three villages that effectively act as the door to Merthyr Tydfil, the last of the urban and industrial South Wales towns.

Troedyrhiw and Pentrebach sit north of Aberfan. Even if you've never been to this valley or wound your way through the terraced-cottage-lined main road that links these villages, you will know of Aberfan.

Probably the most tragic of all the terrible events that have plagued this valley since industrialisation, the collapse of a colliery spoil tip that engulfed Pantglas Junior School and nearby cottages cost the village and its neighbours the lives of 116 children and 28 adults. This simple travelogue through the roads around here is not the place to inform or educate about the awful events of that October day in 1966, but I can't help but acknowledge the strength and the dignity that this community has shown in the years since.

There is a resolute nature to these villages of the Rhondda that almost defies belief. The ways in which they pick themselves up from the absolute pits of despair, after continuously being beaten by the worst vagaries of fate, and yet continue to simply be.

The Aberfan Disaster Cemetery here on the western slope above the village stands as one of the most emotionally resonant monuments to lives lost that I have seen anywhere in the world. Each monument to a fallen child stands as a simple, pure white arch and casts a bright reflection of the late morning sunlight over the houses below.

I don't want to add anything more, feeling somewhat incapable of addressing the magnitude of this disaster and the impact that losing a whole generation of children from these villages would have on the northern Rhondda for all the years that have come since.

To find out more and to really understand what the people of Aberfan went through that October day, and the dignity and grace with which the community and survivors tried to recover, I can recommend Gaynor Madgwick's incredible book *Aberfan: A Story of Survival, Love and Community in One of Britain's Worst Disasters*.

So, it's in a quiet mood that I head out of Aberfan and into one of Wales's most surprising towns, Merthyr Tydfil.

CHAPTER 6

REBELS AND MARTYRS

The town of Merthyr – and how it gets its name – sits on the site of the killing of the martyr, Tydfil, daughter of an ancient king, and victim of a band of murderous pagans. It's no surprise, then, that the town born out of drama is still a soap opera 1,600 years later.

In fact, the word 'surprise' wildly understates what Merthyr presents to a traveller riding through on a journey out of the industrial past. It is a town of historically important social and political influence, of violence, of some of the south's most wonderful architecture and of faith and faithlessness.

To stand in Penderyn Square – we'll come to Dic Penderyn (who gives it its name) a little later – and look at the glorious red-brick-fronted Old Town Hall is to twin the town in your imagination with Glasgow and Manchester, and the Carnegie Library next door stands as a monument to the benefactors of the town who saw education and social advancement for all as a legacy in their gift.

These two buildings, both renovated in the early years of this century, represent an ethos that echoes throughout not just the Rhondda but all the south-eastern valleys: that toil, family and education create societies of value. It's not a coincidence that the Old Town Hall is now an arts centre; it's a continuation of principles that, while dented and buffeted by harsh economics in more recent times, can still be found thriving in pockets of this noble place.

It's difficult to believe as I walk alongside these two glorious buildings that, at the beginning of the industrial revolution, this was Wales's biggest and most important town. Merthyr was the home of the iron that built the nation and for many years, in the first part of the eighteenth century, the forges here and in nearby Dowlais brought jobs to the masses and wealth to the few who then in turn created the town and the community around them.

I was talking about surprises. How about the fact that this was the site of the first ever steam railway journey. Before 1804 the iron bars and slabs forged at sites such as the Penydarren Ironworks would have been towed to the canal for transportation down to Cardiff, but foundry owner Samuel Homfray and famous engineer Richard Trevithick contrived to create together a steam-driven locomotive running on rails for nine miles, that took the loads of the horses and multiplied the carriage capability thirtyfold.

Trevithick didn't make a commercial success of the 'iron horse' but at least lit the fuse on the idea, which then exploded into a phenomenon in the ideas and vision of other engineering notables of the time such as George Stephenson. But the birth of the railways – yes, took place in Merthyr.

To understand Merthyr, we really need to understand iron. It's impossible to gauge the shape of the town, the investments that built it and the wealthy landed families that forged it – pun intended – in their image without understanding first how they came to be there.

People had actually forged iron here since the mid-sixteenth century, in small and almost cottage-industry form. But on a more detailed survey of the land as the industrial revolution sparked, deposits of all the essentials in one place – iron ore, coal, timber, water and limestone – meant that, logistically (and therefore cheaply), a better place to build large-scale foundries could quite simply not be found.

Huge ironworks sprung up here: the Dowlais, the Plymouth, the Penydarren (of railway fame) and the Cyfarthfa. Each of these was owned by industrial dynasties, and the Cyfarthfa by the dynasty whose name has lasted the longest here in Merthyr, the Crawshays.

When we think of the great industrialists, the families who lived in the big house outside town and lorded it over the working families below, the Crawshays were they.

If you've read Ken Follett's book *Fall of Giants*, you will have gained a flavour of the relationship between the landowning family and the industry they owned in the village on the edge of their estate. In that book, the fictional Fitzherberts are the family of immense fortune, and the Williamses are the representation of the working family who owe their livelihood to them. I have no idea if Follett, a Cardiff-born writer of terrific talent, had the Crawshays in mind when he wrote the book but, my goodness, it's a close fit.

The story of the Crawshays and Merthyr is a perfect framing for much of what you see in Welsh political history: 'those that have' shaping the nation within which 'those who need' toil.

Richard Crawshay was one of those who had a lot. In fact, at the turn of the nineteenth century he was one of Great Britain's tiny handful of millionaires. Some years earlier he had jumped on the Empire's military aspirations and become a supplier of cannon from the Cyfarthfa Ironworks he had partnered in. By 1810 he had assumed sole ownership of the venture and expanded it massively. Two blast furnaces, a rolling mill and countless methods of converting pig iron into bars.

In short, he turned Cyfarthfa into one of the world's most productive and important ironworks, Merthyr into one of Britain's most important towns and the people of Merthyr into dependants.

Seen as bit of a tyrant, this single-minded industrialist left Cyfarthfa to his son William who had more interest in living the life of a man about town in London, and so it is to *his* son, William the Second, that we turn for the most significant impact on Merthyr and its place in history.

For *that* William built Wales's most glorious family home Cyfarthfa Castle, which looks down on the town still today from its height on the slopes of the Taff Valley, and was one of the focal points of protest for the Merthyr Uprising of 1831. This is both remembered *and* celebrated around the town today, and forever linked his name to that of Dic Penderyn.

It's only a ten-minute ride out to Cyfarthfa Castle and my goodness it's worth it. The castle was built as a family home, but unlike mine, a simple, square, detached place with a modest garden, this is a family home that has fifteen castellated towers, over seventy separate rooms and a less modest garden of almost 160 acres. But more than its imposing scale and representation of the power that wealth brings, its location was fundamental to stamping the Crawshay name on the town, for it looked directly down on the ironworks that working men laboured in for the barest living.

This was what we call today 'statement wealth'. At the end of a full shift in the blasting and lethal heat of the furnaces and in amongst the crashing and clashing iron rolling out from the mills, the working man would walk home under the shadow of this enormous castle, only dreaming of the life within.

When it was built in the mid-1820s it became a high-society location as well as a family seat. Lords, ministers, members of parliament all took rest and relaxation here, industrial policy was formed here, and the younger William Crawshay never fell short of influencing those who formed the laws.

Many will say that he wasn't by any stretch the tyrant that his grandfather was, and there is evidence that he learned from a very young age as an ironmaster that you get what you pay for, but he took advantage of the huge migration to Merthyr of workers from around Britain in search of employment, to maintain control of wages.

Literally thousands of people worked the forges around Merthyr, man and child alike, and it is impossible to think of the working conditions as anything but desperate and dangerous. In Joe England's book *Merthyr: the Crucible of Modern Wales*, the author talks of the children working, sometimes as young as six, and getting life-destroying burns, and even of an eight-year-old boy with rickets working from 'light to light' holding a set-hammer for straightening hot iron bars.

So, walking around Cyfarthfa Castle today, now a municipal building housing art galleries, social events, weddings and conferences, it does gnaw a little how enormous the divide between the Crawshays and the working families who toiled for them was. The point is the wealth was never hidden. It was stark and thrust in the face of the locals.

At some stage, something was going to give.

In May 1831, something did. Crawshay, taking advantage of the defeat of the Reform Act in the House of Lords that would have compelled him to negotiate wage settlements, decided to drop the wages of the workers at Cyfarthfa.

This prompted mass protests in the town, and the destruction of shops and money institutions was signalled by the waving of a flag dipped in cow's blood to be seen as bright red by the rioters. This is the first use of the red flag to represent the power of the worker.

Taking this rebellious action further, in June, the mob (as it was branded) marched all over the town and surrounding neighbourhoods to stop production at the nearby mines and forges, and created a huge crowd of protesters who then entered the town to be confronted by a brigade of the 93rd Highlanders, armed with bayonets.

Fearing that the crowd was both too large and too angered, the army fell back to protect the Castle Inn public house where local industrial magnates were holding a meeting.

Crawshay, one of those at the meeting, took, in hindsight, perhaps the wrong option to lean out of the upper window and tell the crowd that they were an insurrectionist mob and that if he found any of his workers were protesting, they would lose their jobs and their homes.

What followed was a chaotic clash of workers versus the army on the streets of Merthyr, with guns being fired and protesters killed. This was the Merthyr Uprising.

The workers held the town for three whole days until the Cavalry were called in – literally – and the soldiers in greater numbers were able to retake Merthyr and reimpose order. But order wasn't enough and a show trial of over twenty protesters condemned many to prison, some to Australia and two to death.

One was Lewis Lewis for robbery – a sentence which ignored witnesses who claimed that Lewis saved the life of a soldier in the chaos – and one was Dic Penderyn (I said we'd get to him) who was accused of stabbing a soldier in the leg. Thousands more took to the streets again to petition against Penderyn's sentence, claiming it was a lie and that his death was merely a message from the government to quell disorder. They were right. Earl Grey, the prime minister, ignored the petition and Penderyn was hanged in Cardiff in August of that same year.

Any optimism the government or Crawshay and his ilk might have had that this would be the end of social rebellion amongst the working class of Wales was way off the mark, for here in the Merthyr Uprising it began in earnest.

It is something of splendour, that in this town I'm standing in Penderyn Square, with the Dic Penderyn public house behind me. Perennial monuments to a man hanged as an enemy of the state.

Socialism, or even in its more contemporary form, the Labour movement, is the predominant political movement in South East Wales by an enormous margin. The massive populations of working men and women who built families and lives in the bleakest of conditions and often extreme poverty were never going to leave a legacy of capitalism and the free markets after all. They believed in community, the sharing of wealth for the benefit of all and in institutions that protected and served the communities they lived in.

That sense of a power and influence in the hands of workers is still the dominant social attitude in these parts today, almost two hundred years later. In fact, the Labour movement, and its link to working families through trade unionism, has proved to be a consistent shaper of communities here in the south-east valleys both pre- and post-industrial.

Whereas trade union membership over the border in England runs at about 20 per cent of the workforce, in Wales it is much higher at 35 per cent. In fact, that figure has been dented substantially since the 1980s, not by a perceived lack of progress in trade unionism, but more by the impact of job losses throughout the area.

An example would be the Hoover Electronics plant that built washing machines here from the aftermath of the World War Two through to its demise and sale to an Italian company in the mid-1990s, who eventually moved their production from Merthyr to East Asia. At its height, as many as five thousand people were employed here, as much as 12 per cent of the entire working population of the town. With the rest of the Rhondda also facing its post-industrial economic collapse at that time, Merthyr then entered a spiral of low investment, low opportunity and unemployment.

It is easy to see, given its history, that the relationship between worker and political conservatism was never an easy one here. Given the amount of rebellion throughout South and Mid Wales and of course throughout the wider United Kingdom in response to poor working conditions, poor pay and, most importantly, democratic representation, it is something of a surprise that it wasn't until 1918, after the losses of millions of working men in the Great War, that the Representation of the People Act gave all men over the age of twenty-one a ballot vote, and extended that to all women who controlled property.

Merthyr was largely a Liberal seat in parliament throughout the nineteenth century prior to the forming of the Labour Party in 1900, but since the extension of the franchise after the First World War it has been regarded as a safe Labour seat. My father would often only half-joke that if you dressed a sheep in a red rosette in Merthyr it would win an election.

The far-from-sheepish Keir Hardie himself, the father of the contemporary British Labour movement, sat as an MP here in the early years of the twentieth century, when its population and economic value returned it two MPs to Westminster. More contemporarily, in the latter half of the twentieth century and up to the present day, this has been a Labour stronghold.

On average in the elections since 1983, when the constituency was reshaped as Merthyr Tydfil and Rhymney, Labour has won 70 per cent of the vote whilst the Conservatives, in national power for twenty-seven of those forty years, can muster only about 9 per cent. To say the people of Merthyr are a tough audience for capitalists to crack is a glaring understatement. In fact, the Conservatives have pretty much stopped trying.

It was that anti-establishment rebellious streak here that enabled the Brexit vote in Merthyr to exceed that of the national vote to leave the EU. Over 56 per cent of voters staged their protest over our links with Europe despite millions and millions of pounds being granted here by the EU to create better roads, and to renovate the beautiful town hall from its run-down, neglected, former nightclub self into a community arts hub of real worth.

This area of the town, named after the hanged Dic Penderyn, has that old town square feel to it, a place where contrary opinion can be shouted under flaming torches, but it's neatness and its adjacency to the Town Hall and the Carnegie Library suggest a real public space of importance far more real than the cartoon image of the 'pitchfork mob'. When I ask people around here which way they voted in the Brexit referendum, the majority tell me they voted to stay, suggesting many have belatedly but without admission changed their mind. Perhaps they feel with some regret or realisation that the garden has not turned out to be greener, in fact it's turned out to be very dusty and in need of immediate re-seeding.

Either way, the majority vote was for a change of position, very much unlike the General Election vote to return the local MP which always transpires to be a vote for the same again. Effectively both are a shout into the darkness, a rage against the machine, if you like, a chance to punch upwards if we are feeling free and easy with our metaphors.

It's also the case that the people of Merthyr feel more Welsh than British, and so any chance to impose a Welsh belligerence against authority is one too tempting to refuse. Over 70 per cent of Merthyr Tydfil residents identify as 'Welsh and no other identity' whereas only 10 per cent say they are 'British only'. But despite these allegiances, I never read the Brexit vote here as anti-foreigner or anti-immigrant. It was more, reflecting the Uprising of 1831, a statement that they would not be ignored.

The Taff and Rhymney valleys have long been a place of welcome to people trying to start a new life here. The Italian cafés found in most of the villages and towns here are far from the only sign of this. While the foundries and mines in the Rhondda were at their peak, many Poles, Lithuanians, Czechs and Slovaks lived and worked here, only to leave for more stable economic activity as the rolling mills and pits ceased.

The allied commerce that supported this town as it grew in its industrial importance drew in workers from India, Bangladesh,

China and other countries, who set up businesses providing food, household services and more.

But work was handed down from generation to generation here. Grandfather would be replaced at the foundry by grandson and so Merthyr was always a 'locals' town and never a widely cosmopolitan one. Until the end of industry and Brexit, anyway, it had always had its place as a town that took in outsiders, but at nowhere near the scale of Cardiff or Barry which benefitted from being port cities.

One group of people who did come and made a significant impact on the town were the Jews, whose community has its origins in Merthyr as far back as ten years or more prior to the 1831 Uprising. Stalls were set up in the square and Jewish families sold cheap clothes and second-hand kitchenware to the working families of the town. Small credit lines were set up and families could come to the square to settle debts that kept food on the table until payday.

It's said, albeit in legend, that the Jews took to Merthyr due to its pious nature. That the chapels were full, and people read the Bible, so then it would be sensible to settle amongst God-fearing and worshipful folk.

And settle they did, erecting a synagogue in 1855 which was replaced by a larger one in 1877 as the number of Jewish families increased significantly. Standing in front of that later building now, I'm first struck by the sheer bloody-minded ambition of it. Narrow-fronted but four storeys tall, it has the appearance of a castle keep about it, steeply stepped to the front door and with only narrow windows that help to exaggerate its height.

Over a century and a half after its building, it is Wales's oldest built-for-purpose synagogue that still stands, and after falling into several different hands as the Jewish community diminished here on the death of industry, it is now fittingly back within the Hebrew fold and will re-open as a Jewish heritage centre. Whether that attracts the community to attempt to prosper here again as it did in the era of the foundries is uncertain.

At the last census in 2021, no Jewish families were recorded and, for the first time, 'No Religion' was the dominant declaration. A far cry from the days of pious worship and Bibles in hand.

As I walk away from the old synagogue, the light is starting to fade and I decide it's time to find the people of Merthyr to see if they carry the town's rebellious, anti-establishment blood in their veins. What could be a better place than the Dic Penderyn pub back a couple of hundred yards in the heart of the town?

At around six in the evening, the pub is already full or well on the way to it. It fronts on to Penderyn Square, so it is well within the shadow of the town hall and library, but undoubtedly gets more traffic than either of those terrific buildings.

There's no clear seat but I ask an old fellow if I can take one of the empty seats in the corner he's watching the world from. Just a nod comes from him under a cloth cap, and he slumps somewhat sunken into an oversized parka coat.

I offer my thanks and he blinks it away not impolitely, but without any suggestion that a conversation might follow.

This is a Wetherspoons pub, and without making any snide comments as to the quality of that, you know what you're getting. The beer is cheap, although a couple of local craft ales sit on the long wooden bar also, and the menu is copied and pasted from every other chain pub you've ever been in. Fish and chips, chicken tikka, burger and all points breaded.

It's a good atmosphere here on a Thursday night and within twenty minutes of my arrival it's standing room only, mainly due to the hen party that just poured in like lava from a volcano.

The bride-to-be is joyous, accepting offers of drinks from all and creating a space around her that is part throne room, part dancefloor and part stage. Clearly already a few in, she and about eight friends are starting the night with gusto. What I love about it is the sheer camaraderie of the bunch, which ranges from late teens through to probably a nana and her similarly aged friend. An hour later and they're gone.

I look to the fellow alongside me, who's still nursing the same pint he had when I came in, and suggest I top it up for him, and he raises what's left of his beer in some sort of thanks. By the time I get back to the table, the last two seats are taken by Dak and Wobble. I'll let you take that in again: Dak and Wobble.

They're arguing about whose round it is and, receiving a silent nod as I gift the old fella his pint, I settle in to watch the bout.

After around thirty 'fucking hell's and countless 'wanker's, Dak gets up and takes on the duty. It's now that Wobble introduces his and his mate's names to us.

That embarrassing moment when you can't ask someone to repeat their name more than twice after they continue to put guttural noises together instead of actual syllables suggests he could be Robert or Bobby but I sure as hell take it as Wobble.

'All right Jim! Ready for a big Thursday night?' Wobble asks the old fella and gets a raise of the eyebrows in return. 'Nice one!' Wobble responds, as though subliminal thoughts have transferred between them without my knowledge. Perhaps it's a Merthyr thing.

Dak comes back with four pints of something purple and I worry for a second that he thinks I'm in a round with him, but it's two each for him and Wobble, and Wobble's first is gone in what seems like seconds.

'Who the fukk are yoo, then?' Dak asks. 'Biker, is it?' noticing my crash helmet alongside me.

I seem to gain some kudos when I explain that, far from being a biker, I'm accompanied on a ride by a yellow scooter of low competency.

'He's a fuckin' Mod!' Wobble says. 'WEARETHEMODS WEARE-THEMODS,' he yells out in football-style song, and the old fella winces at the gale force.

'Right!' Dak announces. 'You good at quizzes?'

There's no pub quiz at the Dic Penderyn, but one of Dak's mates is doing a pub quiz in Cardiff and clearly texting the questions back and forth sporadically.

Wobble and Dak both have remarkably similar features. Both polo-shirted, Wobble's a plain blue and Dak's carrying the Ryder Cup golf logo.

'You a golfer?' I ask Dak as he punches erratically at his phone.

'Fuck. Who played Captain Mainwaring?' he says out loud ignoring my question. 'You'll know that, Jim.'

The old fella just tuts and ignores Dak, sups slowly at his beer and sinks further into his parka coat. I know the answer, Arthur Lowe, but this is the wrong time to act like a know-all, even if it is only about an old TV show. Dak continues to bang on his phone and Wobble seems bored, so I start a chat with him instead. It turns out that Wobble and Dak are partners of two of the girls who zoomed in and out of my life about thirty minutes earlier in tiaras and sashes.

Right – we can get this,' Dak announces, looking at me in expectation.

'What underwear do you get if you mix bromine and arsenic?'

I'm dumbfounded. I literally have no idea what the hell the question would be talking about.

'Bras,' says Wobble. I issue a polite chuckle at Wobble's childish joke, only to receive a sideways glance as reply.

'Bromine and arsenic,' says Wobble. 'Bras. Table of elements. Br is bromine, and As is arsenic'. Satisfied at the ludicrous ease of his answer, he then heads back into his bright purple beer.

'Nice,' says Dak, nodding his approval.

Wobble throws in more over the next ten minutes.

The Volga.

Latin.

Edward Scissorhands.

Damascus.

Robert Kennedy in Los Angeles.

I'm out of my depth. Wobble seems to have any answers to questions on tap, and Dak nods and taps away happily at questions he doesn't need to raise.

I feel a bit of a louse. Beer lads plus Valleys pub is a trope bounced around the white-collar warriors of Cardiff's glass and steel finance offices. The truth is that when Dak and Wobble sat at the table with me and the old fella, I feared that my hopes of a nice evening watching Merthyr at play would turn into a sad macho night of swearing, spitting and pissing, but it was a stupid assumption.

Once the quizzing is over, I'm able to chat and be noticed at the same time, which is nice.

Dak works for the Welsh government at their Merthyr 'outpost' as he calls it. 'Demographics,' he says with no small degree of pride.

'Policy can't get announced until we understand the demographics of the people who it'll affect, so my team do all the study and stat bouncing.' It sounds throwaway, but it could be one of the most important jobs I've ever heard of. Far more important than my old-nonsense insurance job in Cardiff Bay that seemed to be more about how to make money from things other people do.

There follows a really good conversation about Welsh government, and Dak has real insight into the difficulties involved in spreading wealth and opportunity beyond South East Wales. The lack of infra-structure, the lack of academic establishments, the lack of affordable housing and the general apathy towards the plight of the rest of Wales from the almost untouchable capital, twenty-odd miles south.

Wobble throws in the odd comment in support and can back it up as an administrator at South Wales Police. Between gulps of a beer that I topped up for him, he has equally pointed comments about how the poorer parts of the country are blighted by crime.

'Watch how the statistics always show places like Merthyr and Ebbw Vale as hotbeds of criminality, because they're measured per one thousand people,' he offers, and I notice that the more they drink, the more sober Wobble and Dak get, and the clearer they speak.

'The actual truth is that the worst crimes are happening in Cardiff and Swansea. Drugs are rife on Cardiff streets, you can get them anywhere; at least you've got to turn over stones to find them here in Merthyr!'

At last, at this we get a sound from the old fella as he laughs enough to have to cough in consequence for about five minutes.

Wobble's point is that while money is spent to clean up Cardiff streets and put labour in the capital, no great investment is made by Welsh government to improve the quality of life in places like Merthyr, and so lesser crimes because of poorer circumstances just continue to increase.

'That's not fair,' says Dak. 'We had investment for fuckin' years up here from the EU and yet, when it came to it, we told them to fuck off. That money ain't there if we rely only on Welsh government, so it is what it is.'

I try to steer the conversation towards Welshness, but the purple pints are empty and they're moving on. Night has fallen and my Airbnb has texted to wonder where I am, so the evening has come to an end. I'm sad at this as I think Merthyr has shaken my thinking about the shape of Wales and how we seem to consider the past the past where I come from, while the past is alive and well in our small towns still, all jostling for attention.

The Uprising is reflected in the names and shape of the town here, the plight of working families (still sometimes unfairly balanced between scarce jobs and unemployment) and the social and political environment is still informed largely by attitudes to social justice and the perception of the behaviours of an uninterested elite. Merthyr is stubborn and steadfast in equal measure.

'Nice couple of lads,' I say to the old fella as I get up to go, and he finally speaks.

'Aye... not bad... good Merthyr lads. Smart. Clever.'

It's with this reference that I leave him to the end of only his second pint in about three hours and head out.

Tomorrow morning I'll be leaving South Wales behind, but more importantly I'll be leaving its commercial and industrial heartland in my mirrors. The part of it that works and in large part maintains the Welsh economy today, and the part of it that created the wealth in the first place before losing it down the railways and canals to the south.

I feel I haven't spent enough time in Merthyr as I weave away the next morning after another ride around the town that once was Wales's most important and now could just be Wales's most interesting. Radical, rebellious and proud of its past, you can still sense it today if you look and listen carefully enough.

Part Two
THE GREEN MIDDLE

CHAPTER 7
THROUGH THE WARDROBE

The stretch of the A470 onwards from Merthyr takes us at last into open country and the opening sweep of the Brecon Beacons. It's not an easy stretch for Gwendoline and we argue fiercely, me deriding her performance and she sighing and phutting at every attempt I make to edge her on.

We're only a few miles north of Merthyr and already the terrace-dotted valley sides and the mix of grey urbanity and historic red brick are behind us and will remain so for some while. Now we're on a straight stretch of the road, with steep green slopes rising to the right and shady glens and groves to our left. The wind is more striking here than it was coming up the southern Rhondda, and it seems to career around me in a whirl as I push Gwendoline on almost like a jockey on the last furlong.

It's a nice sensation, though, as the sky is clear and the possibility of rain seems a long way off, and only as I get the usual beeps from the cars waiting to pass me, and the polite waves from motorcyclists as they overtake, do I concentrate on more than the glorious scenery opening in front of me.

Something rather wonderful has happened in the last ten minutes. It's the sensation of leaving something familiar and routine behind, and riding into something completely different. It's as though I've crossed through the wardrobe full of grey and beige clothes and entered a whole new world through the back of it, not to a land of centaurs, talking lions and snow queens, but one of breeze, buzzards and beauty. And water. Lots of it.

Water, water everywhere, and not a drop to… actually, there's a hell of a lot to drink, and flush and bathe in, as on my left as I pull past the tall ferns and dotted farmhouses that site themselves here, are the massive reservoirs that constitute one of Wales's most valuable resources. When we talk about the environmental future of the nation, and wind and wave will be a crucial part of that, we cannot help but contemplate just what a significant resource we already have, sat here on the winding way up to the Brecon Beacons.

Like everything though in Wales, water is of course a cause of huge political and social controversy. It's also a political football that has its reach into such resonant topics here as independence, our relationship with the United Kingdom as a whole and, more contentiously, our position as a resource to be drawn on over the border in England's hugely populated Midlands.

The reservoirs are in the perfect location for a regular top-up. The annual rainfall here is substantial by UK standards, and the geography in this area in particular – all tall hills and mountains – and its sparse population, make for a perfect place for nature to go to work. This is the opposite of the English Midlands, where the opportunity to collect water from deep valleys and voluminous rivers is almost impossible, let alone trying to collect it from a flat, over-industrialised landscape.

So, at the time of the industrial revolution, Wales became a provider, whether it wanted to or not. Little consideration was given at that time to Wales's economic development and needs of its own, and engineers went hell for leather on manipulating the landscape, and creating systems and flows that took the water miles beyond its natural setting.

To give you an idea of the scale of the three reservoirs here in the Beacons, we are talking about a regular volume in the billions of gallons and the one I have pulled over to the side of, the Llwyn-On Reservoir, spreads itself over 150 acres. Ignoring a lay-by just another hundred yards on, I settle for leaning Gwendoline against a low brick wall which itself lies about thirty yards from the water's edge. I can see the level is low, and in fact only six months earlier there were real concerns that it would run dry as the record heat of the 2022 summer caused the greatest evaporation since the mid-1970s.

The Llwyn-On is the most southerly of the Beacons' reservoirs and therefore attracts lots of people up from the valleys to the south to fish, picnic and generally laze, even today on a crisp autumn day. It's in order to chat to one of those that I've pulled over.

Glyn from Merthyr has been fishing here for over 'fuckin' too many years'.

'Best brown trout in the whole of South Wales,' he says as though it's common knowledge and I'd be an idiot for not having that as well settled in my brain as the difference between left and right.

Every sentence rises triumphantly to its end, and he widens his eyes as though he's shocked that he even has to tell me.

'You can't keep 'em though; you gotta throw 'em back, haven't you!'

I feel like it's a question but somehow, it's also a rather aggressive form of tuition.

Glyn doesn't look like a stereotypical fisherman. There's no tweed hat bedecked with colourful fly-baits, or green quilted gilet. I've clearly been watching too much *Countryfile*, as the typical fisherman from Merthyr, spending a breezy autumn day at the Llwyn-On Reservoir, dresses in ankle-high wellies, skin-tight brand-free athletic shorts and a grey (once white) T-shirt that suggests he might have been on Midge's stag night in Bristol. I watch for about five minutes as he casts, tuts, tuts louder and then throws a few crumbs of something over the surface of the water.

'Water level going up and down pisses 'em off,' he mutters.

I'm not going to get much from Glyn beyond different frequencies of tuts and sighs, so I wander up to the lay-by where I see a couple in folding deckchairs sat with their backs to their mobile home, with many years of Caravan Club stickers on the windows. One of these certifies them as 'twentieth anniversary members' and I'm envious as they pour a cuppa from a flask and lay their cups on a folding table between them.

'You've got a great view here,' I say, but nothing comes back. 'Beautiful, isn't it?' I venture.

The two completely ignore me, or at least I think so; there's a slow nod from the elderly lady which may have been an acknowledgement or might just have been the beginning of a nap.

Her husband is a rather ruddy-faced gent, all cracked capillaries and bright pink cheeks. I notice his face matches the rinse in his wife's hair, and together on their pink deckchairs they look like some sort of dessert.

I try to crack them with a fascinating fact.

'Did you know over two hundred billion litres of water go from Wales to England every year?'

The man shakes his head but pushes his bottom lip out in an 'I couldn't give a shit' gesture and, suddenly, I hate the Caravan Club. Looking at the nearest window of their van inappropriately stickered with the word 'elite' in large blue cursive, there is another sticker suggesting that 'what goes on in Caravan Club stays in Caravan Club', but clearly whatever goes on it isn't a demonstration of generous spirit.

Last try.

'I hear there's a fabulous van a few miles up towards Brecon that sells great food and tea, but you look pretty set yourselves?'

'It's not for us.' The Arthur Lowe lookalike has a voice after all (that's him not her) and there's such a finality to his words that I find myself stuck in a precarious moment of manners. Do I just walk away and feel I've dealt a card of some rudeness, or do I give some sort of response that prolongs the discomfort of being around these two.

'No. I'm pretty sure it's not,' I say, hold my ground for a second or two then give them a smiling but faked 'Cheerio' and turn back to Glyn and Gwendoline.

It's a stereotype that the typical mobile homeowners are retired, antisocial, dismissive of company and aching to be left to decay slowly by the side of some glorious vista that they can look up at, between mouthfuls of Yorkshire Tea and reading the letters page of the *Mail on Sunday*. These two did nothing to dispel that stereotype.

But looking at it from their perspective, was I in fact just being a pain in the arse and interrupting a rather blissful moment of serenity between a couple still in love after a lifetime of work, and finally getting some respite from a world with too many demands?

I pause for a moment to give it some thought. No, they were twats.

The Llwyn-On Reservoir takes some viewing as I prepare to ride on.

Glyn is still angrily fishing, wishing he wasn't but drawn to it just the same. Like the golfer who can't break into a single-figure handicap, he hates and loves what he does with equal measure but can't step away.

I'm feeling the same about this journey. There's so much to see further up the road, but the camaraderie is only fleeting and it's becoming a lonely exercise. I want to crack on, but there's an equal urge demanding to know 'What's the point?' It's a low moment brought on by the couple from the Caravan Club and watching Glyn enduring and not enjoying something he's done all his adult life.

Travelling has been the same for me. I've always done it, from pathetic attempts to run away from home as a child to more dramatic journeys like crossing the US by hitching or venturing into the darker parts of central China – or they once *were* dark but are now lit up like the backdrop to *Blade Runner* – but often the joy of it is tempered by the whole sheer emotional exhaustion of it. This trip up through Wales was meant to be the counterpoint to those more distant and perhaps more exotic trips.

Maybe this sudden glumness isn't down to the radical right wing of the Caravan Club at all, but it's me facing up to a lonely journey made in discomfort, when I could have done it in comfort with my wonderful wife instead. She's at home with Dusty the ever-bonkers golden retriever, and Bluebelle the ever-asleep show cat. It's a picture in my mind, suddenly, of domestic wonder.

I've felt this before when travelling. I've spent time travelling with people who have destroyed potentially glorious trips. The couple that hate each other and spill their venom outward to others instead of just facing the inevitability of their future state sat outside a mobile home in silence. The bloke who could start a fight in a foreign bar just by walking in, and the casually xenophobic colleague who would much rather have stayed home viewing the world solely through the prism of football. All of these gave me grounds for going home, but this today is something else. I'm not thousands of miles from home, but only thirty or so. I could easily just say forget it – Wales is a fragmented jigsaw of beauty, ugliness, pride and shame – and call it a day. But it's Glyn who changes my mind as he packs up alongside where I'm getting ready to ride.

'Giving up I am, mun. The trout are playin' funny buggers today.'

'Time to call it a day, then?' I say, perhaps more to myself than to him.

'Aye… for today. Back next Sunday. Gotta keep tryin', 'aven't you?'

It's not exactly ground zero in philosophical thought, but it has a ring of optimistic nihilism about it that resonates with me, and even if only 20 per cent of my brain was ,egging me on to turn back, the other 80 per cent has just woken from its dull slumber and I'm ready to ride on.

As I roar (sorry, whine) past the Caravan Club morticians, I have a sudden urge to yell something about the joy to be found in the temporary companionship of a fellow tourist, but it's pointless. I don't see them anyway as they're hidden by their van, which I laughingly notice has a sticker on the roadside window suggesting 'Caravanners do it better'.

*

The Taff Fawr is the waterway that flows through the reservoirs here, and after Llwyn-On Reservoir comes the Cantref Reservoir. And beyond that, the Beacons Reservoir.

The three of them are vital to the supply of water throughout the country and mark yet another South Wales engineering marvel to rival that of the collieries, the canals and the railways that were positioned so impossibly brilliantly throughout the harsh landscape here.

Considering the wonderful scenery around me, I'm longing to get a longer break from dull whining Gwendoline, and I get the perfect opportunity at the lay-by at the foot of Pen-y-Fan, the glorious sky-reaching mountain that beckons hikers and walkers from across the nation.

With the mountain sweeping up to my right as I idle to a stop, I'm drawn to a gathering of about a hundred people on the opposite side of the road, stood in a rigid but beautifully observed respectful silence.

I disrobe myself of helmet and gloves as quietly as I can and watch the scene.

Clearly this is a gathering of runners, mostly stripped to their vests and shorts, some shivering in the wind that is forced through the V-shaped valley from the south, buffeting us and heading on to the Cambrian Mountains an hour or so further north.

They're all stood in a line, heads down, until a man in a more robust outfit of snow jacket and bobble hat blows hard on a whistle, and everyone claps and starts to run on their spots.

I'm looking to ask another spectator what it is I'm witnessing, when a further loud whistle sounds and the runners form into a packed group ready for a third and final blast which sends them running, some at a sprint, others at a gentle jog, up the steep scree slope ahead.

This is the annual Fan Fawr Fell Race, and I've arrived right at the start, after a minute's silence for previous runners no longer with us.

Peter Ryder has been stewarding and organising this race for many years and is that exact 'man without whom' character who organises the runners, helps set out the course flags and basically creates the environment for runners to exhaust themselves in the pursuit of fun. Or, for some of the more serious runners I see leading the pack up the thickly grassy and stone slopes, in the pursuit of victory. For this is a serious event, too.

For thirty-four years on the first weekend in October, club runners and international athletes alike, chase each other up and down the one-thousand-foot elevation of Fan Fawr, covering a slog of two miles across rough terrain and slippery slopes in high winds, to be the first back at the bottom and back to the warm clothes and hot drink waiting for them.

Graham Patten holds the men's record: back in 1991 he made it up Fan Fawr and back in only a second or two over sixteen minutes. Jill Teague on the same day (weather conditions must have been superior to today), was the fastest woman ever at seventeen minutes plus.

It's unlikely the records will be beaten today, as the wind pushes the runners hard at their faces as they hurtle downhill and Steve, a runner with a sprained ankle so not running today, reflects relaxedly that the record isn't the point.

'Fell running itself is the challenge, the actual up and down, not the runners around you.' He points a crutch at the crest from which the first returning runners come back into view.

'Just like with golf, you're up against the course, so get your own best time and you've won, you've beaten the course.'

Steve last ran the Fan Fawr in a little over seventeen minutes himself so is no casual jogger, and he breaks off from our conversation to shout up, completely smothered by the wind, and unheard by the leader.

Sporting a dulled white vest with two black hoops, Wyndham Turner seems to be breaking the laws of physics by coming down the steep, irregular, deathly slope as smoothly and efficiently as if he is on a gentle ramp, but the nearest challenger is not yet in view and so we feel we have this year's champion in sight.

It seems appropriate that the lead runner is from the Mynydd Du running club. Based locally, these runners spend all their practice and competitive time running over the Beacons and the Black Mountains, a short buzzard flight across the range towards Abergavenny, so it's almost their course and, whether local knowledge is a factor or not, Wyndham presses home and passes the finish in a very respectable time of a few seconds below nineteen minutes.

His legs look as though he's waded the entire race in sewage and I'd not be wearing those running shoes again, but his smile, interspersed with panting, suggests that sartorial elegance isn't on his mind right now.

The smiles around him as he shakes many hands and gets a warm embrace from Peter are a sign of a community and of being a part of something rather lovely, welcoming and inspiring. I see Steve sharing a couple of laughs with the winner and there's more celebration as the second runner comes through to the finish just about half a minute later.

The sides of the mountains here form a very sharp valley and so some of the sides are incredibly steep. The old red sandstones have pushed themselves upwards from the earth over millions of years, creating in some cases almost vertical slopes. Pen-y-Fan itself has a long, easy slope and a flattened top, providing for a rather pleasant ramble, but others here such as Cribyn, a lower mountain at two and a half thousand feet, can be a tough ascent and so my admiration for the fell runners, all of them, junior, club or elite, is immense.

Fan Fawr, the scene of today's exertion, is the sort of walk I would do on a mild sunny day, with all the time in the world to take in the surroundings. Running up and down it in less than twenty minutes seems like idiocy, but the scenes of comradeship and mutual enjoyment around me as the drinks start to be passed around suggest it's me who's missing out.

I wave my thanks to Peter, who shepherded this event, but he's busy watching the other runners coming down the slope and so I stride manfully down the bottom of the course, slipping on loose stones and tripping over a rock embedded in the track. Blushing, I look back in the hope that my few steps on the bottom of Fan Fawr weren't noticed by the athletes who ran up and down its sides without incident.

Walking back to the side of the A470 where Gwendoline is parked opposite the Storey Arms Outdoor Centre, the home of Beacons exploration, I feel a twinge of further embarrassment. There, parked either side of her, creating a Vespa sandwich, so to speak, are two of the biggest motorcycles I've ever seen. Gwendoline looks like a trout swimming between two sharks. Even with their riders nowhere in sight, they fully diminish her in the shadow of their machine power.

I start to feel resentful, and then plain worried. Bloody hell, I could knock one of those beasts over as I clatter around to get Gwendoline back on the road. Imagine the chaos and the embarrassment as the massed runners and their supporters, only fifty yards away, hear the smash and scrape as a fat metal machine tips onto the road, cars swerving and beeping, and I'm just stood there, the only suspect on the scene, holding with white knuckles and wet cheeks onto a tiny yellow scooter.

The prophecy builds an acute anxiousness in my stomach and I'm so stressed at the potential for disaster that I miss the first call-out from the other side of the road.

'Sorry... wait up, let me come and move that.'

Two men walk across the road towards me in full sci-fi motorcyclist garb. Black all over, padded to the point of enormity and with helmets so enclosing of their faces that they look like the National Guard from some riot-torn neighbourhood.

They turn out to be two incredibly nice fellows from Belgium on a motorcycle-riding holiday across southern England and into Wales. The whole point of their vacation being the ride through the Brecon Beacons and on to Snowdonia.

This stretch of the A470 we're meeting on, as the guys free Gwendoline from the trap they set earlier, is beautiful enough to have merited a mention in *Het Nieuwsblad* some years ago, and they've kept the article for the day they can follow the road.

They're not the only motorcyclists rushing past on this day. In fact, this part of the road from north of Merthyr and on to Brecon, passing under the slopes of Pen-y-Fan, is seen by riders as a 'freedom trail', a stretch of road usually quiet on a weekday, with fast straights and wide-reaching bends that allow for the most sensuous riding experience, cutting through some of the country's finest and most glorious scenery.

The two Belgians have stopped here looking for a coffee on their way through this stretch of the road, known commonly and familiarly as Storey Arms after the outward-bound centre at the side of the road, in a hamlet that sits in shifts along the route and offers up occasional houses and picnic spots.

As we talk, the conversation is drowned out by a group of six riders on supercharged machines shooting past in perfectly spaced rhythm. RARR... RARR... RARR... RARR... RARR and finally a screaming YEEEARRRRRRRRR as the last one came a little closer to us than was comfortable.

These bikes were different to the ones belonging to my two Belgian friends. The roar just now was of low-slung bikes with riders atop in racing pose whereas Luc and Luc (purely coincidence, they assure me) own what look to me like three-piece suites on fat wheels. Massive bikes that seat two in such comfort that I'm surprised they don't come with a side table and a lamp.

We talk about their trip and how until now they've been bored by the roads through England and how much this next day's ride is something to look forward to.

Asking me where they can pick up a coffee, I reassure them that only a half mile or so on from here is the most stunning roadside refreshment van in the whole UK, and as I'm heading there too, I cheekily ask if I can show them and at the same time get a lift on the back of one of the monster bikes.

Luc 1 gets on first, kicks a stand away from under the bike and then nods for me to get on the passenger seat behind him. It's already far more comfortable than Gwendoline, and the footrest is wide enough for me to stand on if I had the urge. I feel wrapped around too, with panniers, and a seat-back that gives me a sense of enclosure that I could never get on a Vespa. Here, I'm feeling as safe as if I was in a car and, as the engine starts, I can feel the whole 1200cc surge under me, giving me the sense of being sat on a rocket prior to launch.

As we pull out, something else strikes me. Far from watching the road in front of me as I crawl over the yards, keeping myself as far from traffic as I can, on Luc's bike I can at last feel the air while watching the great green slopes interlocking around me and get a real understanding of the steep-sided valley as we move from a slow cruise to a deep throaty roar at speed.

I can remember a friend of mine, Steve, giving me lifts home on the back of his motorcycle thirty years ago after a day selling carpets in my first Saturday job. I hated the prospect every time, but never said no for fear of seeming weedy (they were different times), and so spent half an hour every week with eyes streaming, clinging onto him as though we were in a tandem parachute as he weaved like a madman in a Bond movie between cars and trucks that sounded their horns and swore violently at us as we passed.

This ride with Luc was completely different. I was effectively sat in an armchair, on a bike so wide that cars held back and handed us the freedom of the road, and though the lift to the lay-by housing the burger van was only about five minutes, it was sheer bliss.

As we cruised around the wide right-leaning bend that led to our stop, I had a stunning view of the valley to the north of Pen-y-Fan just as rays from the sun pierced the clouds and lit up the pastures at the foot of the slopes. Ancient stone walls forming loose, shaken grids along the valley floor as far as the eye can see, and the myriad sheep dotting the scene and getting buzzed occasionally by sparrowhawks attempting the grace of the kites but somehow failing.

We pulled into the lay-by which has effectively become a motor-cycle park, and joined the queue of twenty or so riders at the van selling all the calories one would need for a long ride up to Mid Wales and beyond.

I suppose 'burger van' is a bit of a misnomer. It's one of those throw-away phrases that tells you what something is without doing any justice to the infinite nuances and details that make up that thing. A bit like the phrase 'engagement ring' tells you what the jewellery is but tells you nothing of the bond and the promise it represents between two specific people and the love they share now, and for the unending future. So, on that basis, this isn't just a burger van, it does bacon sandwiches too.

In fact, it does the all-day breakfast roll which constitutes a huge bap (as they are called in this corner of the country), filled with… Are you ready? Two slices of bacon, two sausages, an egg, mushrooms, black pudding and onions. The nearest defibrillator is back at the outward-bound centre at the foot of Pen-y-Fan.

At six pounds it represents super value, and my god it's great. Watching the guy in the cabin work is like watching a supercomputer blinking away: you know it's doing something, but it's lost in its own calculations and moving too fast to be sure what. One second, he's at coffee, the next he seems to have four arms and he's flipping stuff and holding stuff out at the same time. He's the Herbert von Karajan of the outdoor catering world.

He can take three orders at once, serve three he's already finished and top up the ketchup bottle at the same time. And he has to, because the queue of bikers and motorists is stretching out and as I'm halfway through the mountain of food in my hands, I count twenty-three people wanting his attention.

No chance of engaging him in conversation but he seems to have the same conversation repeatedly.

'Well, you must just about have the best office in the world mate,' a crash-helmet-wearing biker will muffle from beneath his lid.

'Yep, don't want to be anywhere else,' he replies, while cracking two eggs, slicing black pudding and dropping a teabag into a cup, seemingly all with the lower of his eight hands.

It begs one question for me though: why in heaven, with the most astonishing view up the valley to the north, with the sun cracking through the clouds in bright rods of gold, does he park the van with his back to it all? The smart answer is he needs to have an eye on the road and where the customers are coming from, but the romantic in me suggests if it was my business I'd face the beauty and not the tarmac. His business would clearly last longer than mine. From where he is, he can still look out over the hotplates to the steep grey and green slope in front of him, circled by hungry red kites, but effectively he's looking at it over the bonnets of cars and across the road traffic that skirts his lay-by.

I look one way, his view, and then the other way, behind his van and into the astonishing valley, lined with stone-wall capillaries and the fast-flowing artery of the Nant Ddu, which will head south through the reservoirs we passed earlier. I'm looking north onto the next leg of my journey, and already I am refilled with energy. After getting a morale-punching low on my rather depressing introduction to Mid Wales at the reservoir guarded by the Caravan Club ghosts of holidays past, the sun shining through the clouds and gloriously embracing the interlocking hillsides of the Beacons has given me an injection of desire to see more.

There are multiple times on the A470 that you get lost in the beauty of Wales, but this view is one of the absolute gems. Luc and Luc feel that their ride is only just beginning and after they consume the fattest hotdogs of their lives, they run me back the half mile to Storey Arms and Gwendoline, who seems somehow smaller and tinnier after my experience on the motorcycle equivalent of the Space Shuttle.

I make some pointless and shameful excuse to not start riding again yet, not wanting the two Lucs to witness me starting Gwendoline up. There's nothing worse than watching couples fight on holiday, after all. We say our goodbyes, and as they ride off to the north again, I feel a moment of gratitude that I get to ride that wide bend at the valley's edge once more. I even toy with the idea of another bacon sandwich.

CHAPTER 8

SOLDIERS, SCOUTS AND SAXOPHONISTS

Fifteen minutes later, I'm heading to the town of Brecon along a glorious stretch of the A470 and towards the village of Libanus. We're in the county of Powys now, where the space is wide, the air seems fresher than I've ever noticed in the industrial south, and the breeze makes your eyes water as you come down the long hill into the village, which in no small measure punches above its weight as a tourist attraction.

The pub here, the Tai'r Bull Inn, seems busy and a load of walkers and backpackers are either just arriving or just setting off, but it's the Brecon Beacons Mountain Centre that makes them gather here. A walker's paradise. The centre acts as the starting point for many hikes, and the shop is neatly stacked with maps, walking equipment and gives terrific advice on where and when to step out.

You can get a guided walk here, too, although today the staff's attention is taken up almost wholly by the three army trucks parked outside and the eighteen or so soldiers who are currently laughing and joking together, but clearly within seconds would have enough firepower at their disposal to subdue any radical member of the Ramblers' Association who felt like taking them on.

Looking out from the centre, you can see the highest peaks of the Beacons, across to Pen-y-Fan, sharp-edged like a giant piece of flint, and Corn Du, crowned by a flattened Bronze Age mound. As I do so, I hear the loud call of a soldier with a clipboard and the military gathering is suddenly split with beautiful choreography into two squads. There's a quick discussion between Sgt Clipboard and the heads of both squads and then each soldier checks the backpack of a partner, gets a quick pat down and a nod.

On another shout the two squads head off in different directions and so a painful trek for 22 miles (as a backpacker nearby suggests) begins in aggressive earnest. They're off at a hell of a pace and I feel a little, well, frankly diminished watching them file quickly into the distance.

Only a minute or two later and the three trucks pull out and away, too.

The army often take centre stage in the Brecon Beacons. Why wouldn't they? After all, as an outdoor training location it probably can't be bettered in the UK. Ideal for representing some of the global locations the soldiers will face under far more threatening and dangerous circumstances.

The soldiers I saw head off would be from the British army's Infantry Battle School here in the Beacons. A look at their website gives you a list of the skills they are trained in and it's not for the faint-hearted. Live fire tactical training, close quarter battle, dismounted battle and urban tactical battle training suggest a harsher world out there than I'm experiencing here in beautiful Powys.

The barracks, five miles on in Brecon itself, is the army's main headquarters in Wales and throughout the year it despatches recruits and senior officers alike into the wilds of the Beacons to be tested, tested and tested again.

It reminds me of one of the great legends of my youth, told to me at a summer Scout camp only a mile or so from here, back in the hot summer of 1976. You know the sort of thing, sat in a ring around the open fire as night fell, miles from the nearest locals, with a backdrop of thick woodland, and older boys outdoing each other by scaring the living daylights out of the younger boys, such as me.

'Pooley' is the sort of bloke who was shaving at eleven and worked on building sites for spare cash at fourteen, started the tale. 'The army have a special exercise here where they send you out on your own with a three-hour start and then they come to get you. Nobody has ever lasted for more than half a day, but there was one soldier who they never ever found. They found discarded food he'd eaten so they knew he was there, but they never even came close to seeing him. Then, one by one as they looked for him, soldiers started disappearing. He was setting traps and taking them out one by one. Squad after squad was sent out to bring him in, but they just kept losing men. He once killed two at the same time with a huge carved stick and stuck them onto a tree like a kebab. Then he takes their stuff and just becomes stronger.'

Then Pooley, to a ring of eleven-year-olds already missing home, delivered the story's *coup de grâce*, '... And he's STILL out here. Waiting for anyone in uniform to come onto his patch. No one knows where he is, but he lives off the wild, stealing from farms, and he'll never ever be caught. But don't ever go into the hills here wearing a uniform or you'll never come back.'

The next day we all had to put on our own uniforms to go for a hike.

It is true that the army do indeed carry out extensive exercises all over these hills, and it's also true, I'm sure, that they test individuals' commitment and skills by having them spend time here isolated and searched for. But while that whole day was spent looking with some degree of fear for clues to a wild-man-cum-kebab-killer, I was fairly sure it was just Pooley humouring himself by trying to terrify a group of kids who, at that age, would believe anything an older boy told them.

Pooley went into the army himself later and I wonder if he was thinking of that story himself as he padded carefully between the trees. In fact we do know that some young soldiers have suffered terrible fates whilst training in this area, even fatalities. A point worth remembering that, while some will face horrors on service abroad, there are dangers within the Beacons during their preparations which should definitely not be underestimated.

Nearly all the slopes in the Beacons would have been covered in trees once, ancient forests that have been tamed and cleared for pasture as we moved from hunter to farmer in ages past, but as I move beyond Libanus to my port of call for the night it's just occasional farms and a few lonely pairs of cottages until we reach the outskirts of town.

Brecon actually has three names. Powys's well-positioned market town at the conjunction of two rivers, including the Usk which flows down through industrial Gwent to the south-east, is also Aberhonddu (or 'mouth of the Honddu', the other river) and archaically it is Brecknock.

It's always been a military town, with the modern British army being current residents of a line that stretches back to the Romans, who had a garrison here in the first few hundred years of the Christian era.

Entering the town, you are in no doubt as to that military presence. The barracks which I park in front of is a massive gated and stone-walled building and keep that dominates the main street. It has been a military building since 1805 and as Victorian Britain became more embroiled in military campaigns throughout the nineteenth century, it enlarged to become barracks to some of Britain's most elite fighting men.

The 24th Regiment, later renamed the South Wales Borderers, famed for their role in the Anglo-Zulu wars, came from here, and a museum dedicated to them was opened in Brecon just before World War Two. Currently, the residents are the 160th (Wales) Brigade whose colours list Gallipoli, Gaza, Normandy, the Bulge and the Reichswald amongst their honours. It's a proud history, and the town of Brecon is clearly proud of them, and the wider military also.

Leaving a hot, tired and complaining Gwendoline to cool, I walk into town to check into my hotel for the evening. Keeping up the military history of the town, it's the Wellington Hotel, which looks down onto the main square and a statue of the man himself.

The hotel turns out to be wonderful, a real Georgian treat in the middle of this market town, and the smiling staff seem as delighted to see me as I am to kick back and do nothing for an hour. My room is great. Bright, airy, and through the window I can pick up the gentle buzz of the town going about its way.

A ten-minute scooter-ridding shower and I'm fresh and ready to get a beer and catch up on a little local history from the busy team working here. It turns out the Wellington Hotel is one of the oldest commercial buildings in Brecon and is regarded locally as a bit of a treasure and, combined with the statue of the duke positioned a few yards from the hotel's door, suggests a very close relationship between the town and the 'hero of Waterloo'.

Unfortunately, there's no relationship at all, and there's no record of the man himself being a regular visitor to the town. I don't blame him though, as the carriage ride from his palatial home at Apsley House at Hyde Park, across England and up and down the slopes of South Wales into Brecon, would have been a nightmare, and he wouldn't even have had the opportunity to stop for an all-day breakfast bap. The A470 then would have been a maze of two-lane tracks giving no real sense of direction and he would have given up long before Merthyr. He may well have been a Knight Grand Cross of the Royal Guelphic Order, but would he have braved Dowlais Top in winter? History doesn't say but I have my doubts, hero or no.

No, Arthur Wellesley, first Duke of Wellington, KG, GCB, GCH, PC, FRS, twice Prime Minister of Great Britain and defeater of Bonaparte, doesn't have Brecon on his CV, but is honoured here purely out of distant respect for his military heroism.

The statue was put up in 1856, just four years after the duke's death, after being donated to the town by its sculptor John Evan Thomas, who was born here. It's a grand monument for sure, showing the duke not in military action, nor astride his mount Copenhagen, but standing tall, scroll in one hand and the other stilled but prepared to reach for his sword. It's a symbol of proud defence rather than aggression and I have a sense that this also represents Brecon's relationship with the military.

Having the barracks here in stone grandeur in the heart of town reflects protection and safeguarding, not necessarily a demonstration of might.

There are more signs of soldiering dotted around the town. Not least in its many pubs and restaurants.

Aside from the Wellington, there's the Rorke's Drift pub, the Gurkha Corner restaurant and the Khukuri, by name a Nepalese military blade, by design a rather excellent South Asian diner with a menu that looks worth presenting arms for.

There's also, less militarily, the Sarah Siddons pub. Now a decent enough place to get a quick pint and mix with the many locals who clearly see this as Brecon's number-one hostelry, but in 1755, when known as the Shoulder of Mutton, it was the birthplace of Sarah Kemble, later Sarah Siddons, the leading female actor of her age. Born to a family of touring players, she later married an actor and found fame on the stages of London.

Think of her as the Dame Judi Dench of her day, tragic parts a speciality. Lady Macbeth was her signature role and she had enormous success, and eventually wealth. Mixing with monarchs, painted by Joshua Reynolds, and commemorated now with a sculpture in Westminster Abbey, she could lay claim to be Wales's finest ever treader of the boards and her house in Brecon pays grand tribute to her in its new role as hub of the community.

Thinking of her as Welsh gives me a start. Because just as I've seen throughout my journey so far, there's little to support the notion of Welsh statehood here. If anything, the presence of the army makes this perhaps Wales's most British town. There's the odd flag, some rather niche shops which of course sell Welsh souvenirs, but in essence this is a typically British market town with a strong character of its own, but not demonstrably a Welsh one.

Finishing a pint I'd been nursing for over half an hour while reading some more from Morton, who didn't seem to give Brecon much more than a few cursory comments on the weather here in the Beacons, I step out to wander.

In a few minutes I'm at the town's cathedral and it's an impressive sight. Rather lovely, it is surrounded by tended lawns, and there's a beautiful, large, stained-glass window dominating one of the walls which seems to be the church's main attraction. I can't go in right now, not because I might turn to ash as a non-believer, but simply because there's a wide ladder in front of the door and two men are seeming to discuss the merits of its stability. Preferring to wander around, I can take in the full splendour of that stained glass. Even if, as I suppose, God doesn't exist, the idea of him or her is still pretty inspiring sometimes, isn't it?

The cathedral, like most in Britain, has been through a whole drama in its period of existence. Probably beginning in the aftermath of the Norman conquest, it's supposed that a church first appeared on this site in the twelfth century, which in turn would have inspired the beginnings of trade and the distribution of agriculture in the neighbourhood. That means the good people who lived around it would have seen the rise and fall of Catholic Britain, the birth of the Church of England, the rise of the Puritans and the Restoration. Now the cathedral sits as a busy reflection of Christian life in a largely secular town. But this house of God is also involved in the town's love affair with the military, and the regimental honours of the South Wales Borderers (24th Regiment), they of the Anglo-Zulu wars, are held on display here. The triangle of God, military might and Breconshire market town meet neatly here. And there's a tea room and gift shop to waver over, too.

Being proud of its institutions is clearly a Brecon thing. There are signs you can find as you walk around that the town has been touched by royalty, with one near the market celebrating Queen Elizabeth II's visit in the summer of 1955. There are some great images of this visit in occasional shop windows still, such as her bouquet being nibbled at by a horse uninterested in the presence of a monarch at the Brecknock Agricultural Show. Sixteen thousand people turned up to see her that day, as she moved from animal pen to animal pen, handing out rosettes and being, in fairness, genuinely interested in the livestock and produce of the Powys farming community.

Wales has this relationship with the monarchy. Even in the cynical twenty-first century when coolness dictates that we aren't impressed by or committed to anything beyond our fashionable selves anymore, the presence of a queen or princess still brings out the crowds, from the most working-class deprived areas of the nation to the well-heeled. And while this is an excuse also to wipe the dust off the Welsh flag, it is seen more often than not on these occasions with the Union Flag of the United Kingdom. The pollsters Omnisis have recently suggested that 57 per cent of people in Wales are in support of the monarchy.

I decide to end my day back at Sarah Siddons's house for a nightcap and enjoy a little of the local banter that seems to be based on a poor fellow failing his driving test for the eighth time. He doesn't seem in the least embarrassed but that's more likely down to the empty glasses lined up in front of him, the sign of someone drinking away the sorrows brought about by a badly executed three-point turn.

After a rather excellent night's sleep and a breakfast kinder on the heart than that at the roadside cabin the day before, I'm looking forward to wandering around Brecon again before heading out by lunchtime, and so walk along one of Wales's other historic transport arteries.

Like many of the market towns dotted around rural Wales, Brecon has developed through time as a major destination for the neighbouring farms to sell their produce. Cartloads of fruit, vegetables, livestock and timber have made their way to the town across narrow paths and bumpy tracks for centuries, and when the loads were heavier the way to go was on the Monmouthshire and Brecon Canal, which basins here in the town after lining the way north-east from Pontypool.

No longer a busy waterway for horse-pulled barges, it's now more commonly a place for day trippers to mess about on the very still water or for canoeists to paddle between pubs on a warm summer's day between Brecon and Crickhowell, a rather pretty village very much in Brecon's own image, a few miles to the east.

A canal has been here since 1800, originally linking Brecon to the Monmouthshire town of Abergavenny and later linking up further into industrial Gwent to form the 'Mon and Brec' which I'm stood by this morning while joggers and goose feeders go about their day. Some of the older parts of the canal run under the road near here but where it is clear it does still have that 'old world' image that attracts a certain type of person to a slow week or so's holiday away from the crowded coastal resorts around the nation.

I had a canal-boat holiday once with my two young daughters and my mother. It was as close to a vision of a slow death as I have ever come to. I remember phut-phutting along past some parked-up barges and being yelled at for going too fast by someone probably related to the Caravan Clubbers back near Pen-y-Fan. I would have taken their complaints seriously if it wasn't for the chap overtaking me on the towpath whilst walking his dog. A very slow dog.

Strolling back into town I see in the window of a vintage goods store a very shiny golden saxophone in a black case that's lined with red velvet. The case looks old, battered even, but the sax looks perfect, and reminds me of another of Brecon's main attractions. Jazz.

The Brecon Jazz Festival is one of Wales's summer festival highlights, alongside the Green Man Festival only a few miles from here. In fact, throughout August, you can spend a month in a thirty-mile radius of here and move from one arts festival to another without having a spare day. And the jazz festival isn't just a local blower and his mates; it's the real thing, with some of the most globally celebrated musicians of the genre arriving at the Beacons for some all-day and all-night swing. Alongside it is the Brecon Fringe which wonderfully supplies free events hosted by many of the pubs, cafés, galleries and restaurants in the town.

But for the real Brecon experience during the jazz festival, you want to try and catch a gig at the marvellous old Guildhall. It's said that there has been a civic building of sorts on this site for as many as seven hundred years, and in fact it was a centrepiece of the town when Mary I was on the throne in England and awarded Brecon a Royal Charter. There's no photographic evidence of her in the town of course as there is with the namesake of her Tudor nemesis. Brecon may have some pretty heavyweight royal connections, albeit at distance, but in this busy market town in the Powys hills it's the soldiers, merchants and musicians who hold court.

At that moment looking at the saxophone in the window, I realise my own musical limitations and decide to head out and walk back to the waiting Gwendoline.

There's something odd about her. Something that doesn't seem quite right although I can't put my finger on it. She does her usual trick of failing to start without the benefit of my anger and abuse first, and after a gentle pull on the throttle we're away to a clatter and a scrape and it's then I realise what the difference is. It's the carefully placed beer cans, tied around her rear light in a chain, that make me sound like the world's worst steel band as I move. Clearly a couple of squaddies on return to the nearby barracks felt I wasn't making my presence known well enough. They're probably looking out from a high window now, patting each other on the back, so I dismount and strut coolly around Gwendoline to nonchalantly remove the cans and make it clear I'm bigger than that. And then Gwendoline falls over because I didn't put her stand up.

CHAPTER 9

COW TOWN

Leaving Brecon to the north, the country really opens up ahead. The A470 becomes a little more winding and undulating so the journey gets a bit wearing, but I'm trying to put some distance into the day so that I can get a feel for the more rural Wales that the geographic centre of the country offers.

It's after I push on through the hamlet of Felinfach that I come to one of the A470's more eccentric points. A result of the bureaucratic joining of roads across a civil servant's desk more than any geographic common sense.

Here, with the Black Mountains of Monmouthshire lying moodily away to my right the A470 does something bonkers. It takes a ninety-degree left turn at a junction, while the road I have been on since Brecon carries on without interruption under a new guise as the A438. It's stupid. I've literally left the A470, and within a second or two as I turn to the left, I am actually back on the A470. Now, in reading this I understand you are both confused and not entertained; however, I cannot adequately explain how maddening this is.

If the A470 is really, as the Welsh government likes to say, the only road that links Wales from south to north, and from coast to coast, why does it take such stupid, erratic directional changes? The answer lies of course in the fact that it is only a single road in concept and hundreds of different ones in reality.

As we ride towards Llyswen, only a few miles on, the road takes another sharp turn. This one, however, is necessary to remain in Wales, for here we meet the River Wye, and to follow it east will take you into border country and over to England, while the road north-west is our route into Mid Wales.

Meeting the River Wye here is a very satisfactory thing for me. Just as I have favourite bands, favourite cricketers, favourite chocolates, all forged in my long distant youth and still held as such today, I also have a favourite river.

The Wye in parts is surely one of the United Kingdom's most glorious waterways, from its birth much further on from here to its winding way acting as the natural border between Wales and England. It becomes tear-inducingly breathtaking at the Forest of Dean and flows into the Severn as the lesser of two massive river partners, out into the Bristol Channel.

I have camped at its side, canoed on it, paddled my daughters in it, and slept alongside it under the stars. And now it's a rather lovely thing to be chugging alongside it as I follow it backwards in its time. It's only a teenager in river years at Llyswen, and I'm heading back into its infancy. The Afon Gwy, to give it its birth name, flows pretty fast here at the village of Boughrood and under Lady Milford's Bridge which spans the river at Llanstephan, but I'm heading on to Erwood which is one of those marvellous little places that seems to exist purely for the sake of art.

Erwood is a tiny bohemian dropout in Powys's agricultural back-drop. If Brecon is where tweed meets khakis, Erwood is where smocks and Birkenstocks meet to swap arts and crafts talk in a rather beautiful setting, situated right at the spot where the blue Wye picks up its pace. It hurtles through here, careering off the rocks and boulders lining the bed of the river. The path alongside it makes for a lovely walk and I've never known the air so fresh.

While Erwood itself is nothing more than a hamlet, it does have an excessive ratio of arts to population, and the centrepiece of this is the Erwood Station Gallery, which is a restyled railway station transformed into a crafts centre that displays and sells original works by local and national artists, and also provides a café on the old platform that could be one of the best-situated in the whole country. A couple of old carriages act as stationary restaurant cars, too, giving the atmosphere of being placed in a different time as you sip at an Earl Grey and rip open a scone.

Walking through the village, many of the houses have signs outside suggesting craft and art for sale within, and there's a sense that the local community is no doubt inspired simply looking around them.

Much of the art here is nature-themed, and at the old station there are some wonderful life-size animal sculptures made from local wood that I'd be delighted to have in my own garden back home. I've taken a real shine to a deer that looks rather monarchical with its head held high and its pose one of regal confidence. Then I look at the price and decide I could replace Gwendoline with a newer model for the same money. I say this quietly, though.

Throughout this gallery, and in the windows of some of the houses in the village, almost all the arts and crafts for sale take their inspiration from the local natural world with the occasional tiger or bird of paradise thrown in. It helps me understand why some of the greatest artists of the industrial valleys that we passed through earlier, like Nan Youngman or Ernest Zobole, become so dedicated to capturing the grey and the grit of the Rhondda's working life. If it's in you, you put it out there on the canvas.

Similarly, here then, artists with a real belonging to Mid Wales and its Powys hills represent it in its full glory. In one cottage window as I leave Erwood and continue my journey is a painting of Erwood Station in its earlier guise as a halt for the diesel locomotives that chugged around here in their prime. I can see from this that the gallery conversion is very true to the station's original form, and the backdrop of the hills behind.

Then, incongruously, next to that is a painting of a field gun. And next to that, yet another painting of a field gun. And this painting has a name: 'The Gun That Points at Erwood'. Popping back to the gallery to see if this means anything, I'm considered a bit of an ignoramus for not knowing the story, but very politely pointed to how I can get to it because, yes, there actually is a large military field gun, a German howitzer no less, pointing at this inoffensive artist community in sleepy Mid Wales.

It's a short but steep walk up the grassy slopes of Twyn y Garth hill and I'm not exactly wearing the right footwear because the sodden ground is seeping through to my feet, but I'm assured it's worth it. Panting rather faster than I prefer, I get to the crown of the hill, and yes, there in front of me is a huge howitzer.

The story I'm told is that the gun was trophy spoils from the Great War, purchased by a local woman, Nessa Williams-Vaughan, in honour and memory of her brother John, who lost his life with many other local men at the Somme in 1916.

John Williams-Vaughan was a South Wales Borderer. As I run my hands over the barrel of the massive gun, I think back to the regimental colours stood against the wall of the cathedral back at Brecon and the relationship between the military and the people of the area becomes clearer, and the placing of the gun in these surroundings becomes less incongruous and instead wholly appropriate.

The gun does indeed point at Erwood, and while I'm no artillery man and any velocity calculation would be beyond me, peering through one eye from behind it, I can guess it would be aimed roughly at the Wheelwright Arms pub in the village. At least the gallery would be spared.

After that war, the British government sold off many of its captured spoils to replenish the Treasury's vastly depleted coffers, with the then War Office taking out notices in the press as though they were a wholesaler advertising a closing-down sale. I guess that's exactly what they were.

When Nessa purchased this, she would have had no thought that it would become such a marker for national remembrance, but Cadw, Wales's national monument trust, has now taken it into their ownership and care, and it stands as another of the nation's many memorials to the fallen.

Leaving Erwood and continuing north, we ride through some more of the tiny hamlets that line the road, such as Abernant and Alltmawr.

Alltmawr on the A470 is no more than a few dotted outhouses and the edge of a nearby farm, but also has a tiny treasure of its own in St Mauritius Church, possibly the smallest church in Wales. I say only possibly because if there is one smaller it's probably been lost with someone's car keys.

Pacing out alongside it, I reckon it's about ten metres or so long, so maybe rather than hold a congregation, the local priest shouted his sermon from within and everyone waited outside in polite and solemn earnest.

Alltmawr translates as 'big hill'. And in fairness it does lie at the foot of one. But there are many names for hill in Welsh. Likewise stream, and road, and field, and forest. A *bryn* is a hill also. So, Brynmawr (in Gwent and also Pennsylvania in the United States) is also 'big hill'.

Both these villages, Abernant and Alltmawr, would have been simply a small grouping of farms and smallholdings when the church was active, probably only servicing a local landowner's family and a few others. But everyone here would have made their living, subsistence or otherwise, from the land. Those with a little more land would have been able to graze more sheep and perhaps would have benefitted from the nearby markets of Brecon, a few miles back, and the busy little town at Builth Wells which we ride into now. A town built on farming and still, in the twenty-first century, perhaps Wales's most notable agricultural centre.

As with Brecon, almost twenty miles to the south, Builth Wells arose from being at the confluence of two rivers, the Irfon, which trudges in slowly from the west, and the Wye, which we know is the speedster of the two and takes the waters onward.

You're in no doubt you are in farming country here and I park Gwendoline at the rugby club, known by all as the Bulls. Their badge is a rampant bull in readiness to catch a high ball under the posts. Even the name Builth itself is argued by some to be of farming heritage, derived from the ancient Welsh *Buallt* or 'Ox pasture'. Not being an expert, I'll trust the source, but the addition of 'Wells' is one we can pin down. It was in the mid-nineteenth century that tourism in the Victorian age became a pastime for those with a little money and the aspiration to travel and embrace the natural world.

A similar vogue was erupting in France at this time, giving birth to the impressionists and the *plein-air* artists and, not wanting to be dismissed as nothing more than a farming outpost, the good burghers of Builth added the name Wells to market their home as a spa town to the well-heeled. Both saline and sulphur springs were found just west of here in the 1830s and a whole new image was created. Where once the streets were filled with livestock moving from pasture to auction, there were now the beginnings of shops and cafés catering to a different class. When the railway arrived in 1864, so did the visitors, and Builth Wells changed from a cow town to a resort of note.

A century and more later, it's still a busy little town and a place for tourists to stop off on their way north to Snowdonia or west to Cardigan Bay, but its heady days as a spa town are long past and farming takes centre stage once more. Especially each July when, just over the wonderful historic stone bridge across the Wye in the next-door-neighbour village of Llanelwedd, the annual Royal Welsh Show transforms the area from a population of around four thousand to one of a breathtaking two hundred thousand, the largest agricultural show in Europe.

Much like Brigadoon, then, Builth comes to life and presents itself to the world for only a few days each year. When the show is not in town, like on this autumn day, it's very much just getting by, although with more cafés and souvenir shops than most of its kind, likely propped up by the boom generated in a sunny July that must last for most of the year.

Sat in one of these now, The Cwtch, I look through a mountain of tourist leaflets trying to find the essence of Builth. I'm struck by how much of what is recommended isn't in the town itself but outside and beyond. It's as though the advert would be 'Builth Wells... come here to find out what's going on somewhere else', and I'm sad that it doesn't shout a little louder about its history. After all, this would have been the Welsh 'Bath Spa' once.

It's busy here so I offer to share my table with the lady stood looking lost in the middle of the café after placing her order. Amanda turns out to be, coincidentally, from Cardiff and is now living a few miles from here in another spa town at Llandrindod, away a little to the north-east, but tragically for me not near the A470. I say tragically because Amanda is a zealot for Llandrindod and once I've presented myself as disappointed in Builth's ability to sell itself, she starts selling the glories of her adopted town instead.

It transpires there's something of a rivalry between the two towns, with Builth somewhat bitter at its neighbour's good fortune at being the county's centre of administration and therefore a better location for jobs and opportunity. According to Amanda, it did not go down well here that in 2017 Llandrindod was voted the 'happiest town in Wales'. She chuckles as she says it, but adds that it's all a nothing really, although she wouldn't want to live in Builth as there's not much to do here. A little twist of the knife as she pulls it out.

I mention the huge agricultural show, and wouldn't that be an event to enjoy, but she seems nonplussed.

'A good time to go on holiday somewhere else,' she says, adding that 'the crowds are ridiculous and the place just becomes bedlam's car park.' Nice line that, I'll tuck it away I think, as she goes on, 'Although the Llandrindod hotels do very well out of it.'

Moments later a toasted sandwich I ordered a while ago arrives in front of me from the smiling waitress, and I start to dig in. The 'local' cheese and ham toastie is excellent, and with the bread made on the premises the waitress boasts that every ingredient comes from within four miles of the café. Looking around the walls as I eat, I see a hand-chalked menu board that offers similar reassurances if eating local is an important factor for the customer.

The chutney is home-made, as is the red cabbage and indeed all the pickles. The sausages come from a farm back towards Alltmawr and the cakes are all made by a cake maker working from her home just along Castle Street.

'Looks nice,' Amanda says, 'although there's a fabulous place that does a better one in Llandod,' she adds, shortening the name of the town into its locally spoken version.

It's a chance for me to ask a Mid Wales local about the relationship here with Cardiff. Especially as Amanda is from there originally. In fact, coincidentally we went to the same school, although I'd like to think (and of course not say) that Amanda was there a few years before me.

'I'm pretty much done with it,' she says. 'I still have family there, but it doesn't mean anything to me as a place anymore. It's just a smaller Bristol now.'

I ask the question I've been wanting to ask: whether she feels more Welsh here.

'Not really,' she says looking upwards in clear-thinking mode. 'That's a good question I suppose... but Cardiff isn't very Welsh anyway, and you're a little more exposed to what the Wales of the guidebooks looks like here so perhaps you do, yes.'

It's all rather non-committal but I translate it as the Wales we try to present to the world is clearly visible here in these environs, even if the soul itself doesn't ring loud with the sound of male voice choirs and the fiery roar of the dragon.

The point Amanda makes about jobs and how the local authority presence in Llandrindod makes for an easier employment climate than elsewhere in the region is fundamental. Walking back up Castle Street and looking in the newsagent's window a few doors down from the café is quite revealing about the local economy outside of farming.

The overriding notice of available work, or work wanted, is in the domestic cleaning profession. All the following have cards in the window pinned to an A3 cork board, alongside the notice of a forthcoming 'Gentleman's Evening' at the rugby club and a motorcycle for sale.

Bonita's Cleaning Services
Bee's Knees Cleaning Specialists
Jodie's Supreme Cleans
Hammond Cleaners

As I ponder just how many cleaning services companies a small town of, say, three thousand people or so actually needs, I notice another similar board at the other end of the window, this time advertising a series of holiday lets.

Putting two and two together, and thinking that in a town with little employment the ageing demographic shifts a few years older, there may be many pensioners looking for help, and so cleaning becomes a rather sensible business model to operate, especially with the added customer base that holiday-let properties can offer.

With Brexit now kicking in also, and many Europeans in domestic services heading back home to a place they might actually feel welcome in, cleaning, gardening, white-van removals and day labouring suddenly become the way for locals to earn money and be able to remain in a town they call home.

That trend can't sustain a town on its own though, and so farming and the allied trades such as engineers, mechanics, feed suppliers and animal husbandry remain crucial and in some demand. A demand that's not met with any great interest from local school-leavers, who instead prefer to depart the region for college if they have the qualifications, and to try Swansea or Cardiff for work if they don't.

A column in that day's *County Times*, the local journal, alongside 'Powys man poured lager over wife in row' and 'Plea from Powys football club for lost balls', suggests that the cost of employing farm labour has escalated to the point that some local farms have become unmanageable. A local farmer states that before Brexit he could manage with four skilled labourers on fifteen pounds an hour each, but now he's struggling to find more than two and the going rate is twenty pounds.

I'm not au fait with agricultural economics but clearly the anecdotal evidence is the supply of skilled labourers is down, and the cost of hiring them is up. Yay! Another win for the Brexiteer.

In July 2022 the Welsh Parliament published a research briefing entitled 'The Farming Sector in Wales' which revealed some startling statistics about an industry which is so important to Mid Wales, Powys and Builth Wells in particular.

Talking about the sector as a prospective employer, it states that agriculture, fishing and forestry accounts for less than 2 per cent of total employment in Wales, and has been in decline since 2015, the last year before the Brexit vote for those of you who haven't been hammered enough by my point yet.

In fact, Wales has suffered the most in employment decline of all four home nations. In that period of decline, the agriculture labour force in Wales has fallen by almost 14 per cent. No other home nation's decrease is in double figures, and England and Scotland have both only fallen by less than 4 per cent.

The ratio between land use and income is becoming dangerously skewed. Almost 90 per cent of Wales's total land area is used for agriculture and yet the total profitable income is the lowest of all four UK countries, including Northern Ireland. In fact, the average farm income in Wales in 2020–21 was £34,300, only a few points above the UK mean average wage across all industries. And when you consider what it takes to run a farm, which in many cases is also a family home, that income, for the work it represents, is incredibly low. Over half of Wales's farms are considered 'small' but that still represents up to twenty hectares, something you'd find hard to manage on your own. Add into the mix the fact that well over half of that income is from subsidy and you have an industry, an employment structure and a government agriculture policy on the brink.

Some would say Wales doesn't have a chance, with almost 80 per cent of the nation's land area being classified as a 'Less Favoured Area' (LFA), an EU designation basically saying, 'you can't grow much here'. In fact, over half of the land is classified as 'Severely Disadvantaged' or, in other words, 'you can't grow *anything* here'. This gives some explanation for the sheer volume of livestock we have in the country, with sheep free to graze on the wild and sloping lands that simply won't accept planting.

From the moment Gwendoline and I left Merthyr behind and entered the heart of the country's mountain landscape, we have seen sheep the entire way. Sometimes in large groups close to the road, but nearly always spread like dots across the steep hillsides. Cattle and sheep farming on LFA space is the most common farm type in the country.

The astonishing statistic, and bear in mind that Wales is not a tiny island, is that 86 per cent of all Welsh agricultural land is used for grazing.

Farming, then, might not make Builth Wells rich, but of course it's a fundamental block of our society. Not only is it the industry that sustains us, it is the core economy of the region providing employment despite the fractures in the model, providing crucial land management of one of our most environmentally rich landscapes, and providing a cultural focal point for most of the inhabitants of Mid Wales. From my research, barely any government operating in a free-market economy anywhere in the world has the answer to a non-subsidised economic model for agriculture, and more than a little respect should be afforded to those who continue to work in it on our behalf.

That lack of industrial diversity in these parts, though, gives a little more context to the shops I find as I continue to walk around the heart of Builth. A cross between places to buy food, charity shops and places to buy something that says you passed through here. I don't want in any way to sound dismissive of the town's character. In fact, there's a liveliness to it and it's certainly a friendly welcome I get in every place I stop, and when I say I'm writing a book on the journey through Wales I get lots of snippets of information that I should add. Not all of it makes it into my notebook, but I nod happily and gratefully even so.

Eventually, after asking in several places, I finally find someone who will put me in touch with a local young farmer, a café owner's nephew, and even though he doesn't have time to meet, Will is kind enough to take my call and give me a few moments of his precious time before 'cracking back on with the cows'.

Will has farmed since he was a boy. His father still farms up west towards Llanwrtyd Wells, and Will spends a few days a week there while studying over in Aberystwyth. I tell him I'm not looking for a great exposé on the sector, or even any information on how to run a farm, but I'm simply looking to hear some first-hand reports about how tough it is. I'll be disappointed by Will, as it transpires. Will loves it.

'I'm not sure it's what you need,' he says in a beautifully clipped fashion as though he's whistling, 'but I love the community aspect of it, you know,' that last word sung far higher than any other in his sentence.

'Almost all my friends grew up on farms and to us it's just what we do,' again that last word probably heard by dogs in Carmarthenshire.

I'm not getting much of what I was wanting to hear, and I can sense that Will doesn't know what I'm looking for, so I try the Welsh angle. Does farming inform his Welshness? Does growing up in generation after generation of farmers, *Welsh* farmers that is, matter perhaps differently compared to me, who grew up in an anglicised city with not a grazing sheep for miles?

There's a silence at the other end.

'Will?' I ask.

'Oh yes... I'm here. It's just I've never thought about it like that. Aberystwyth is *very* Welsh, especially for a university town, but around Llanwrtyd it's just... I don't know... just what you're used to, I think.'

I ask him about the relationship between Mid Wales and Cardiff, the capital.

'I love Cardiff,' he says, 'love it. We have some great days there, what's the pub with the goat on the picture?' he asks.

'That was the Goat Major,' I say. 'It's got a different name now.'

'Oh, that's a shame.' Will sighs and it sounds like he means it, too.

I try to get more of a flavour of the hardships in the life of a young farmer, but he is far too satisfied with his lot to give me anything of note.

In short, I've got nothing from Will. No drama about the state of Welsh farming, no trauma about his economic opportunity, and no real sense that he's anything other than lucky in the life he's got. So is that the actual story here, that farming is simply something that will always be? In fact, it is rather heartening to know that, while the world tumbles through change, this most essential of industries is in the safe hands of people like Will, and the generations born to the land who will come after him.

And towns like Builth Wells that are symbiotically linked to the industry will also simply carry on. Unlikely to see any great change, unlikely to develop further beyond its market-town character, and unlikely to reap the reward of significant investment from outside the industry either.

Castle Street will continue to be a hustling narrow street where you can get a great locally made lunch, the rugby club will continue to be a hub for the town, successful in its own right, and it will always be that pretty place where the River Wye turns blue and where the biggest agricultural show in Europe takes place.

But actually, that last bit is a lie. Yes, the show is massive, yes, it brings almost a quarter of a million people here each year – god knows how the town copes, frankly, but I bet the accommodation is spotless – but the place the show happens in, despite all the marketing to the contrary, is *not* Builth Wells.

Rather it is just a short drover's walk over the wonderful stone Wye Bridge that is one of the wonders found on the A470, in the riverside hamlet of Llanelwedd. You can throw a fresh farm-hen's egg from Llanelwedd to Builth, and probably further, it's that close, but to be pedantically accurate it's there and not in Builth Wells that the big show takes place.

It's difficult to put over what a unique place Llanelwedd is. Running only the Wye's width from Builth Wells, in the same manner of the slightly grander Buda and Pest, it is difficult to see how this tiny place could have any significance. There's a petrol station, a school, the site of a now-unused railway, a hotel that houses a Thai restaurant, a couple of farms within sight, and frankly not much else. Oh yes, sorry, there's also the massive Royal Welsh Showground. One hundred and fifty acres of land set aside for the enormous event in July and a few others of lesser scale throughout the year.

The July one is a beast.

When almost a quarter of a million people gather over a four-day period in a tiny rural corner of the country, you get something beyond understanding. A bigger crowd than the Glastonbury Festival in a pocket of land a quarter of its size. They have Beyoncé and the Rolling Stones; Llanelwedd has Massey Ferguson and the best Jersey cow in Europe.

And don't think I'm being flippant, far from it. The event requires as much planning if not more, and is four days of equal celebration. Farming, food, nature conservation, community, rural life, arts and crafts, military displays, horse-riding competitions, the ever-popular sheepdog trials, and of course the judging of some of the most pampered and beautified animals in the country.

It's also at the same time becoming a food festival of some prestige, and indeed worth, which is no surprise when you see stalls offering a Scotch egg for six pounds.

It also benefits massively from the 'Royal' prefix. King Charles the Third is a regular visitor, or at least he was in his princely guise, seeing the show as very much aligned with his own concepts of celebrating rural life, nature conservation and heritage.

On four hot July days it's the centrepiece of the British agricultural and rural calendar, but as Gwendoline and I skirt the site on this late autumn day, it's simply a massive expanse of land beautifully maintained and readying itself for the winter. I see a sign suggesting it's also a perfect location to host your family wedding, but I'd imagine that's at a different time to the show. Although actually, bride, groom, mothers and a Hereford bull would make for a terrific photo.

I'm in two minds leaving Builth Wells. I don't see the town in anything other than a stasis. It's pretty enough for sure, quirky definitely, with some of the weirdest vintage and second-hand shops I've ever been in, but it seems somewhat resigned to being on the edge of a bigger world and not within it. Literally on the edge, in the case of the Royal Welsh Show. This begs the question of development and economic planning, of course.

I don't expect any Mid Wales market town to reach for exponential growth, but there must be some plan to create jobs and an economic foundation for families to stay and contribute. Otherwise, like many other towns, they just become visited and not lived in. They become a bolthole for those with extra cash for a holiday home, or a population of retirees who prop up the town for eleven months of the year by drinking tea and eating locally made cakes and hiring cleaners from a newsagent's window.

I look up Airbnb on my phone and check accommodation for next July and see that I can hire a two-bedroom terraced house for 'show week' for over £2,000. I imagine the owners of the house jumping in a cab and driving past the crowds at the show and heading out to St Lucia for the week, and suddenly feel a little less concerned about the place, but I also have a sense, as Gwendoline and I ride on, that if I come back in five years the picture will be the same.

CHAPTER 10
THE DEVIL AND THE KITE

I want to make a couple more stops before I stay over for the night further up the A470, and I'm ready for a beer. The perfect stop for that would be Newbridge-on-Wye, which is only six miles away but allows for some beautiful scenery as the Wye temporarily drifts away from the road to the west and allows for a serene plain to emerge.

The Cors y Llyn National Nature Reserve sits alongside the road here, and harbours some of the nation's most treasured wild-flower meadows. The wild flowers have such wonderful names. The fen violet, the greater water parsnip and, my favourite, the common enchanter's nightshade.

Wales's national flower is the daffodil and, without getting all Alan Titchmarsh about it, a high spot of the year in the garden back home is when the golden trumpets emerge each year from the cold, stored bulbs under the soil, triggered by the slightest lift in the warmth of the air.

My wife is a superb gardener and in late February or early March each year – it does seem to be getting earlier – when the yellow brightens up the borders at the bottom of the garden, it's a little bit of spring joy at the end of the winter and a little bit of Welshness in perfect timing for St David's Day. Our kitchen, like many in Wales, is filled with vases of daffs, as my mum calls them, at this time of year.

St David's Day (1 March) was a big day when I was a boy. We would have the school eisteddfod and all dress up in something typically Welsh. Boys would inevitably and unimaginatively arrive in rugby kit (easy), or perhaps as a miner (less easy and requiring smart torch work), but the girls would look fabulous in a shawl, lace pinny and stovepipe hat. The classic 'Welsh lady' look.

I'm sure my nan was never seen in this national dress. She wore a pink nylon housecoat that would have gone up like a Roman candle if she'd strayed too close to the coal fire as she was tending it, and I'm sure she never had a stovepipe hat.

Wales doesn't seem to me to have a national costume in the same way that the Scots display their tartan in kilts and sashes, although, bizarrely, there is something called a Welsh kilt, which seems to make an appearance only at weddings and end-of-season rugby-club brawls.

But yes, it's true that you can see in some old sepia photographs older Welsh ladies in shawl wraps, draped with lacework and occasionally in a tall black hat. Some.

It probably gained more resonance with people in Wales as a part of our heritage after the English painter Sydney Curnow Vosper displayed his work 'Salem' in 1908. If you look that up, you'll see in the foreground the old lady clasping her Bible to her heart as she stands in the Capel Salem Baptist Chapel in Gwynedd, North Wales.

The painting is very sombre and the other characters in it are a few men either bored or praying (or both) and a couple more ladies in that distinctive costume. The character also said to be in the painting, that's *said to be* and not explicitly represented, is the devil.

Now, I've stared and stared at this painting, and I can't make out a thing, but many will say Vosper has put the devil into the left side of the shawl that the lady of the main image is wearing. The folds in her shawl at the arm are eyes and nose, the fringe of the shawl is a beard and the creases above, near her shoulder, are the horns. It is seen as a contentious warning from the artist that sin is always with us, even in the holy and even in God's house. This debate took place when Vosper was still with us, and he denied it vehemently.

Me, I just see an old lady holding to her faith in amongst a bored congregation of a tiny Welsh chapel. She's steadfast in belief, firm in her manner and bearing, dignified amongst those who are there only for show. In short, she's everyone's Welsh nan.

I see a couple of them now at the side of the road with no stovepipe hats, but tartan shopping trolleys in hand, chatting away as I ride into Newbridge-on-Wye. The devil certainly doesn't appear to be here. In fact it's a very serene little place where the Wye has come back to join the A470 after disappearing away to do its own thing for the last few miles.

Its history is in being a stop-off point for drovers as they moved their stocks from market town to market town. Placed between Rhayader and Builth Wells, the few buildings and public houses here would have been a perfect spot to rest cattle and take in a lunch to break the journey. In fact, the drover is celebrated here in a statue on the village green, cradling one of his flock of geese, which must have been a nightmare to control from one point to another.

For such a small place, Newbridge-on-Wye is certainly well equipped for pubs. The New Inn, the Golden Lion and the Crown Hotel. The latter is the most interesting due mainly to its wrought-iron porch, which displays its name on one side and 'Temperance Hotel' on the other, indicating that the devil may well be in an old churchgoer's shawl, but he definitely isn't found drinking here. The days of it being truly a temperance house are of course long gone, and it stands now as one of the several places in Newbridge you can get a beer and a ploughman's lunch. Or in this case, most appropriately, a 'drover's lunch'. Which appears to be a ploughman's after all.

A couple sit in the other available window seat next to me and poke rather suspiciously at their food. He's definitely not happy and she's clearly grumbling away at him to say something. He puts his cutlery down and stares at his dish, which holds some sort of pie, and looks every now and then at the barman as though the mere thought transference will suffice. Picking up his cutlery he moves things around his plate to make it look like he's had a good go, and his wife is getting more agitated by the minute. Finally, uninvited, the barman pops over to them, a rather skinny late teen in a black shirt too big for him but an enthusiastic skip in his step.

'Is everything OK?' he asks. 'How's the pie? I had one earlier and it was superb.'

The man says, 'Yes, it's fine, thanks,' and as the barman walks off, the man's wife rolls her eyes.

My lunch is fine. I don't know if there is a standard line-up for a ploughman's (drover's) lunch, but I would always argue for a hunk of cheese, bread, an apple, some sort of salad thing which must contain onion but must *never*, and I can't say this firmly enough, *never* contain tomato.

As the non-complaining but still dissatisfied couple on my right sit in a silence of shame-meets-embarrassment, I look at my watch and realise I need to rush.

Hurrying to the bar and tapping away at the countertop loud enough to be heard by the lone teen somewhere hidden from view, I'm beginning to stress and fluster for the first time on the journey. Finally, he sees me and after a delayed transaction ('Sorry about this… the signal is terrible around here') I leap onto Gwendoline like a Duke of Hazzard. She must sense the drama as, thanks be to the Vespa gods, she fires up first time.

*

I need to be at my next stop at a fixed time for something I've been wanting to see for many years, and it's onwards towards the important crossroads town of Rhayader.

I get the first glimpses of what I'm looking for directly above my head as I leave Newbridge-on-Wye and head out into green space. Two red kites are holding their position above a field off to my right. It's a challenge to ride looking at the road ahead with its occasional wind and still keep my attention on the glorious russet-coloured birds above.

The red kite is reverentially admired here in Wales and is even given the status of Welsh national bird. From a dismal population of only a few pairs less than forty years ago, we now have skies seemingly full of them, flashing red-brown across the sky or hovering on the breeze, wings outstretched with characteristic forked tail acting as rudder. The shift in numbers, and the respect the nation now has for this most elegant of predators, is in no small way down to the Powells of Gigrin Farm.

I pull into the farm just a mile or so shy of Rhayader and wind up the path to a welcoming centre, gift shop and café. No ordinary farm, this. Taking my ticket, I chug up to a spot to leave Gwendoline and walk down a narrow track to what will be, very shortly, a scene of beauty and carnage. A one-act play devised by the Powells and performed by almost one hundred and fifty balletic kites, with rooks and crows as extras at stage left.

This is one of Wales's most notable tourist attractions: the feeding of the red kites at Gigrin Farm.

The field at the bottom of the lane is host to a series of wooden shacks or 'hides' set in a horseshoe around the bottom edge of the slope which is then, at the upper edges, surrounded by tall trees. In front of the hides a few crows patter around, and a rook sits watching blankly from a broken fence. Off to the north, something is clearly about to happen as the sky which held a few kites ranging in a circle a few moments ago is now becoming more full of the birds. The numbers are swelling as I watch, with more drifting in from over the hill to my left and from behind the tall trees to my right.

The hide is open from waist height in front of me with a handy ledge to lean on as the irritable caw of the crows is replaced by the low rumble of a tractor engine, which seems to be the signal for the forty or so kites above to be joined by many, many more over the field right in front of me.

The tractor pulls to a halt and a robust fellow jumps out and starts digging at the contents of his trailer and scattering it around the ground. Offcuts of beef. The grassy ground is soon very much littered with grey and pink shreds and lumps of meat. You can smell it as he scatters it in a widespread arc towards the hide. It's that old meat smell that puts you off eating but it signals to the now hundred or more kites circling ever lower that dinner is served.

It starts with the crows taking a peck or two, acting as food tasters for the kites. Clever birds, kites. They'll let a crow take the hit if the meat is bad, but these crows seem happy enough and so the kites start their attack.

It's astonishing in its violence but also its grace.

The shrills become louder and fill the air, and the dives are direct and fleeting. It's a superb display of air skills and at no stage do any of them touch the ground. It's a steep dive, a flattened approach and a skim of the grass only. The birds pick up in a blink and then soar skywards to feed in a perfect parabola. At any one time, a dozen or more dive at the meat and depart the scene in a chaotic yet clear choreography. The crows still pad around, but they know to get well out of the way as dive after dive is launched by these stunning creatures.

As the carnage continues and the sky fills with more and more of the birds, I notice another bigger bird watching from the trees to the side of the field. A buzzard, completely nonplussed, sat patiently observing the riot below. Does he want to avoid the crowds or is he simply bored by the spectacle that has become a daily one now here at Gigrin Farm?

It's never-ending. The tractor has left now after leaving a spread of the meat laid out close to each of the five hides.

My hide is enclosed but one of them is more open and accommodates some serious photographers and some lenses beyond a length that I've ever seen before. This is a wildlife photographer's heaven.

It's easy to conclude why the Welsh want this bird to represent them as a national symbol. It's quite beautiful, born of the mountains and free. If we want to characterise ourselves as a nation, we couldn't better that. And national symbols matter.

They're something to rally around, to claim as our own. We want them to represent who we are, and that's why so many nations have lions or eagles at the heart of their national symbolism. Strong. Proud. Fearless. Don't mess with us.

Wales, of course, has the dragon on its flag. The dragon flag is one of the oldest in the world, with sources saying it was a representation of Welsh peoples as far back as the seventh century. Stories are that it became red to differentiate it from the white dragon of the Saxons, and that led to marvellous myths and legends I can remember from my youth, of the red dragon overpowering the white one and still lying beneath the mountains of Gwynedd, ready to rise again to send the English invaders back whence they came. This legend, also known as the tale of Vortigern and the dragons, was a wonderful story often read by the kindly Mrs Owen at the end of my primary-school day, and memories of that I still hold close.

It is very much an exciting bedtime story for a young Welsh boy or girl discovering where they're from. Perhaps they could read it at their next school eisteddfod as I did, dressed as Gareth Edwards.

It's a nice tale. In fact, many nations the world over have similar stories of a guardian of the land waiting in the wilds to be recalled to defend its peoples when in need. Creature symbols therefore have a power. The Russian Bear, the Indian Tiger, the Canadian Moose. All tell us something of the people and what they want to represent. The Bear is power. The Tiger is strength and beauty, the moose is… well, a moose.

But the dragon is something else because it is by its very nature mythological. So likewise, the notion of a free Wales in a United Kingdom has also become almost mythological. The Welsh flag doesn't appear on the Union flag at all. Not a hint. The cross of St Andrew of Scotland is there, as is the cross of St Patrick and the Cross of St George. But St David, and the mighty dragon, are nowhere. Is it any wonder we sometimes feel unnoticed in a nation of unequals?

In fact, in a rather gobsmacking display of neglect, the Welsh flag wasn't even recognised as our national flag until 1959.

It was Henry the Seventh who created the first images of the flag that we know today. A Welshman by birth, from Pembrokeshire, he added the green field and virtuous white as a backdrop to the blood-red dragon on his standard at the Battle of Bosworth, and it is a modification of that iteration that we still see flying in various parts of the country today, and of course en masse at sporting events.

As I'm watching the kites circling like demons above and hurtling like screeching dive bombers in front of me, they do indeed seem worthy of national symbolism. There's a wildness to them but it's communal, almost orderly, as they take turns to make their flight down to the bloodied field. On their own they are of a silent beauty, but in this host of hundreds they conjure up a menace and a power that seemingly nothing could possibly obstruct. They're also an admirable social bird, mixing amiably in this chaotic cloud of red, and mating for life.

How Gigrin got to these enormous numbers of birds feeding each day is a story that starts with just one pair that were roosting on the farm in 1993. The Powells took to feeding them, or at least making sure there *was* food for them. The RSPB, recognising that this would be a way to keep such a rare bird in observation (at the time there were supposedly fewer than four pairs across Mid Wales), encouraged the farmer and by the end of the first winter the farm had six kites. Now, careering around the skies above the farm for around twenty thousand visitors a year, forty years later, there are up to three hundred kites.

Fascinatingly, a recent DNA test revealed that all these local birds can trace their lineage to a single female that flew overhead here forty years ago. It's a real conservation story with a beating Welsh heart.

On the flight away from feeding, some meat gets dropped close to the hide, and I'm focusing on that in the hope that one or two of the kites will see that as the target. I'm not disappointed as, within a few moments, one glorious, huge bird swoops towards me, spreads its wings out wide to brake in the air, and I get to see its full magnificent glory.

The wings are heavy and full, and spread out almost two metres wide with feathers at the end like goalkeepers' gloves. There's a flash of red, grey and brown yards from my eyes and a high-pitched but muted scream and whistle as it flies in to do a full turn away from me and sweeps off into the crowd.

Its call changes now it has its feed in its claws. From the whistle and scream as it arrived it now changes to a dalek call, all deep and snarling. As though the one call was 'Stay clear, I'm coming in' and then changed to 'This is mine, stay away' as it leaves.

In flight, the bird's wings brush high and deep, like an owl, less a glide now, and more a drive for power, and it's gone. The sound of those wings will stay with me. Beating only yards away like a sail in the wind with a whoosh and a thud. It's breathtaking.

At this point, incongruously, I notice, away to my right, the farm cat sat watching the whole display, moving only when a crow gets a little too close. The kites don't care, they strafe and swoop without any care, knowing they could handle a farm cat with ease if they needed to. The cat likewise has no fear and, with better things to do than birdwatch, starts to wash. The cat must have seen this a thousand times, but still comes for the show. I guess mog feels that the birds are too much to make an effort for, and too big a challenge. Instead, after a brief scrub behind the ears, the cat takes to sniffing around the bushes for mice and voles. A quicker win.

After half an hour the numbers have dwindled but still some come. Perhaps the ones who drew the short straw, so to speak, and have to mingle with the crows and rooks who potter amongst the relics of the feed like looters at the end of a battle.

It's been a magnificent spectacle. The kites range around the skies above, many sated, some still feeding in the high trees or on the wing.

The noise and the colour and the power will stay with me for a long time as I wander back up the track towards the welcoming centre, but I still look back over my shoulder every few yards as if drawn to return in case there's more of the violent but beautiful tumult to witness.

I'm of course as proud as anyone of our flag, born as it was, not out of conquest but out of simple representation of who we are, and the fiery red dragon is indeed an excellent, if mythical, symbol to cast fear at those who wish us diminished.

I like the white sky of purity and the green field of the natural world, simple ideals in a changed world though they are. But if Wales had its own paper currency, I would put a graceful, powerful, gliding kite on there for sure.

I'm sorry to leave Gigrin Farm and take a last look around before I ride on. A tortoiseshell cat is sat on Gwendoline and six or seven others are lying nearby. A gentle push from me is not welcomed and an attempted scram followed by a complaining yelp is my reward for disturbing the mog's relaxation.

A wave to the smiling fellow at the ticket booth on my way out is reciprocated with more grace than the tortoiseshell cat ever tried, and at the bottom of the lane I re-join the A470 to head into Rhayader, a genuine crossroads town if ever there was one.

CHAPTER 11

RECIPES, ROADS
AND REBECCA

In all the times I've travelled up this road into or through this little town, there have been roadworks. Constantly. It's as though the whole road maintenance world comes here to practise, and yet again temporary traffic lights hold me back from entering the town, and yet again there's no one here doing any work.

Roadworks are a blight throughout Wales, and yet the Welsh government says they are committed to the 'free uninterrupted movement of traffic' throughout the nation. That would be difficult to sell to those traversing Mid Wales from east to west or through the always-blocked M4 tunnels near Newport that create such misery. Winner by a country mile, though, would be the A55 – hilariously called the North Wales Expressway – which on any given day is the world's narrowest but longest car park.

Finally, the lights turn green and I can push into Rhayader, with the small town opening in front of me at a crossroads. I've arrived on the A470 at a strip that is called South Street. To my right, East Street, which will take you towards England. To my left, West Street, heading out to the Elan Valley and the path through the looming Cambrian Mountains, and ahead of me, yes, well done, North Street, which will be my A470 out in the morning.

In his book *In Search of Wales*, H. V. Morton describes Rhayader as a 'prim little town with a faraway look about it' and I understand him perfectly. It's the slightly more contemporary cousin of the Transylvanian village from *Dracula*.

As you can imagine, any town that grows around a crossroads, particularly a four-point one, has been a welcoming place for travellers, and so before checking my notes again for the address of tonight's accommodation, I park up on West Street and find that welcome in the form of a smile and a cup of tea in the Old Swan Tea Rooms.

We're at the edge of the Cambrian Mountains here and the landscape takes on a rugged and raw edge compared to the more rolling green of the Beacons. These mountains are where the huge dams and reservoirs of the Elan and the Claerwen Valleys, off to the west, perform the same crucial role in Welsh natural resources as those we rode by between Merthyr and Brecon. Huge expanses of water, filled regularly by the high precipitation of the area.

It's not raining today though, although it is a very cold autumn day. No surprise, then, that Rhayader holds the record for being Wales's coldest place, hitting a body-quaking minus twenty-three degrees in 1940.

I'm able to watch the crossroads from the window as my tea comes to the table in an elegant china pot. The traffic seems to always come to some sort of tangle here. There's no 'one in one out' agreement and there's quite a bit of 'Sod it, I'm going' as a minibus comes from north to south and a truck pulling a farm trailer tries to cut across from west to east.

Looking down on all this, and just a few yards across where East Street joins the junction, is the historic clock tower which marks, so those without surveying equipment would say, the border between North and South Wales.

The clock tower is the memorial to the fallen of the Great War and World War Two, and stands proud as the traffic creeps around it. It's then I notice that the selfishness of the drivers isn't the issue; it's the clock tower itself causing the problems. It takes up so much of the road that any attempt to get around it is bound to lead to a snail crawl in front of vehicles coming from one of the other entrances to the junction.

Each road that arrives at this crossroads is narrow, with no possibility of widening them as some of the properties that line them are listed as of seriously historic interest. That includes the café I'm currently sitting in, which may date back to the mid-seventeenth century, when the widest vehicle passing through would have been a cart loaded with hay.

I'm looking at the menu while listening to the aggressive beeping outside and see with delight that I can order cawl. A favourite of mine throughout my life, and a dish I associate warmly with my mother, who made a wonderful version of her own. A simple soup you might think, but no dish of Welsh heritage is more discussed or subject to such heated debate.

I see the lady on the table next to me has finished hers and I ask if it was good.

'Nice… but not,' she pauses and looks to see if any of the staff are listening, 'not what I would call cawl.'

Here we go again.

The same discussion I've heard my nan, my mother and my stepdaughter (who must be on some mind-altering drug as she thinks you add barley to it) have, every time I raise the subject.

I remember a few warm summers back, when I was completing a portfolio of travel writing, that I tried to nail this argument once and for all and met a lady called Alice in Fishguard, Pembrokeshire. Despite the sun shining brightly, and a warm breeze brushing us kindly that day, Alice was building up to a rage as she passed me a Welsh cake on a wafer-thin china dish.

It was my own fault. I'd ordered a pot of tea for us both, introduced the subject I wanted to talk about, which was the various methods of making cawl, and then suggested there could be different ways to make it. The look that appeared on her face was as though I had slapped her in the face and crumbled a Welsh cake over her head.

'*Different ways! Different ways!*' she was screeching, so hard the couple on the next table thought we were fighting.

Three weeks earlier, a colleague had put me in touch with Alice. I had mentioned that I would be in Pembrokeshire and wanted to find a way to write about this classic and ancient dish, and she had told me of a friend of hers who made it every week and who had an 'original' recipe handed down to her from six or seven generations.

Alice answered the phone when I rang with a beautiful, singing, Pembrokeshire lilt and, although I had been told she was in her eighties, she sounded as sharp and as precise as anyone I knew.

But a week or so later, sat opposite her at the quayside in the historic town, I felt more than a little intimidated. Think a combination of Miss Marple and a wartime sergeant major barracking his conscripts. She was a heady mix of twinset and derision.

'There's no *different* ways to make cawl,' she said, letting the word 'different' fall from her lips with distaste.

Alice's view, exclusively and uncontradictably, was that cawl was beautiful in its simplicity and any playing with it was a heresy.

She can't remember when she first made it but was clear that the recipe she has was her great-grandmother's, and that it had passed through many hands before that.

She had it written down once but thinks it may have been posted in a Christmas card to a cousin in Canada by mistake. There then followed a series of Alice's thoughts on Canada, which I confess I lost the thread of, so cutting in perhaps a little abruptly, I asked her to tell me what exactly is the classic recipe she holds so dear?

'No need to write this,' she said impatiently, nodding at the pen I had just picked up, 'you can add it to memory. Lamb. Water. Potatoes. Carrots.' She started tapping a sleek finger into the palm of her hand with each ingredient.

'Swede. Leeks. Salt and pepper.'

I looked at her, waiting for more.

'That's it. That's all. But you *must*,' pointing at me angrily now, '*must* have everything cut to the same size.'

The rest of our sunny cup of tea together was nice enough, and Alice did give me her method too, but I was still wary from the anger she had expressed earlier – any contemporary view I may hold on Welsh cuisine was best held back.

Cawl is a simple recipe indeed, and one that filled shepherds' bellies after a long day on the cold mountains of Mid and North Wales. Like many of the world's great cuisines, it's born of peasant food, the things that would grow easily in tough soil, and the available protein, in this case the lambs that almost overpopulated the grassy hillsides.

I follow that recipe now when I make it, but also fry an onion and garlic with the lamb first (which I then discard) and put a cup of white wine into the water. There's no way I would tell Alice that.

My reflecting self is brought back to the present by the waitress here in the Old Swan café in Rhayader and she asks if I want to order any food, so I take a deep breath, think of Alice, forget my recent ploughman's (drover's) lunch, and ask about the cawl.

'Traditional,' the waitress tells me, or in her words, 'straight up and simple.'

When it comes it does indeed look like a perfectly straightforward cawl. Clear broth, well stocked with lamb, potatoes, leeks and carrots. At this point Alice would almost give a nod of appreciation. Ten minutes later and I'm looking down at an empty bowl and call the waitress over to ask how it's made.

She nods at each of the ingredients I list and when I run out, she says, 'Well, you've missed out two. Those two are egg white to clarify the broth, and sadly, a secret one.'

That last element makes me smile. A recipe hundreds of years old and still a closely guarded secret.

Feeling a full satisfaction after eating, I head out for a stroll around Rhayader, the travellers' crossroads.

*

Many have stopped on their journeys and refreshed themselves here over the years. The Romans, seemingly everywhere throughout Wales at one time, had camps to the west in the Elan Valley, and the 'way', which is an old, discarded nickname given to the east–west road, would have seen monks walking between abbeys.

Then of course there was our old friend the drover, who would have stopped here after, perhaps, pushing his flock from Aberystwyth to as far as Gloucestershire and even London. This would have been a crossroads of much activity, centuries and more ago.

That activity, the movement of farm goods and livestock, was proving to be an expensive business in the mid-nineteenth century and the tollgates, of which there were six around Rhayader, were rapidly becoming the source of much frustration for the drovers and farmers of the neighbourhood.

From 1839 to 1844 the town, and its tollgates, became a centre for civil disobedience and rioting that reflected the tensions arising from increased costs to farmers amid a context of low revenue from poor harvests.

The then British prime minister didn't exactly alleviate the situation by relaxing duties on foreign meats and foodstuffs entering the country and, in Mid Wales in particular, the locals considered enough was enough. The tolls had become what was considered an unfair tax and farmers, shepherds and drovers took aim at them as a symbol of authority that must be struck down.

So was born the 'Daughters of Rebecca'. Groups of men dressed as women, in the guise of the Bible's Rebecca, tore at the tolls in a riotous act of disobedience that spread for three or four years across the region. 'And they blessed Rebecca, and said unto her thou art our sister: be thou the mother of millions, *and let thy seed possess the gate of those which hate them*.'

The tollbooths were a perfect 'gate' to be possessed, and even destroyed.

Rhayader saw many such riots, which only ended when it became clear that criminals with other aims were taking the Rebecca guise and using an until-then widely supported political act of protest to cover more nefarious aims.

Other locations in Wales continued the rebellions against unfair tolls and taxations at a time of agricultural depression and rural poverty, with significant riots in Pontarddulais, Llanelli and Aberystwyth that led to ringleaders being tried and sentenced to transportation on convict vessels sent to Australia.

I recommend the Alexander Cordell novel *Hosts of Rebecca* for more of the background. It's a fictional account, not a historical record, but Cordell writes with such skill about the livelihoods of the rural community in Wales that the backdrop he creates gives real context to the poverty and political negligence that existed in that period.

Some say that Rhayader or Rhaeadr Gwy (the waterfall on the Wye) is the oldest town in Mid Wales, some archaeological digs suggest it possibly existed as far back as the fifth century, and it's certainly the first town that the Wye comes to on its flow from its source at Plynlimon, high in the Cambrian Mountains that edge here.

Like many Welsh towns, it housed a castle, originally built to hold back any Normans who ranged this far, and after swapping hands many times between Welsh landlords and English overlord forces, it was finally destroyed by fire in the thirteenth century, by soldiers coming down from North Wales. There's nothing here now where it stood but a ditch that runs alongside a field just outside the centre of town. I don't know why I thought I'd find an actual castle here, but I made my way to the site expecting much more than a field and a ditch.

The castle, like the dragon, is one of those enduring images of Wales. There are well over four hundred of them in some guise or other, from the dramatic and imposing such as at Caerphilly or Caernarfon, through to the bare remnants such as the wall and turrets overlooking the River Usk at Newport. I'm not sure if the ditch I'm standing next to at Rhayader appears on the list, but I'd feel short-changed as a castle-spotter if it did.

I think my Airbnb is outside Rhayader to the west so it's a short ride off the A470 for a mile or two, as if I had Aberystwyth and the Welsh coast as my goal, but I'm riding for what seems like far too long. I double back the way I came, checking the directions on my phone and end up in Rhayader again.

So that's twice now along this road and I've seen nothing that could claim to be my accommodation for the night, and I don't want it to be so far out of town that I miss out on a quick crawl around the historic pubs that sit on the crossroads.

I must have crossed the Wye Bridge that sits just outside the west edge of the town three or four times and still don't have any understanding of where my hosts are. The skies are getting heavier and darker as I sit at the side of the road just after the bridge, alternately staring at my phone and then up again down the road, completely helpless.

A car that passed into town a few minutes earlier is coming back my way, pulls over and the driver rolls down his window to call to me.

'Are you looking for us?' a kindly looking chap with John Lennon glasses asks.

Thank goodness he stopped. He is indeed my host for the night and was expecting me an hour ago.

'You're heading the wrong way!' he says cheerfully, as if it's the funniest thing he's seen in Rhayader for a while.

I follow him back into town on a road I have become very attuned to over the last hour, until we get to the crossroads and turn north back on the A470. He slows down and puts his hazards on to indicate we've arrived about two or three hundred yards outside the centre of the town. I walked past here two or three times earlier in the day.

'Our fault!' he says, laughing again. 'We got you mixed up with a couple staying at our place on the Elan Road. I've been motoring around looking for a lost man on a scooter!' This followed by more chuckles.

It turns out the fellow and his wife were waiting for me so that they could then head off back to Warwickshire where they live, after having a few days in one of their boltholes in the Welsh countryside.

Once they've left, it takes less than a minute to look around. Bare kitchen, Ikea build-it-yourself furnishings dotted everywhere, and the narrow stairs lead up to a single bedroom at the back, a double at the front and a tiny toilet and shower space I could use if I was a contortionist.

Clearly, the single room at the back is for me, as the double, which I assume the owners have been using, is cleared of all bedsheets. The house has the air of 'do as little as you can to make it homely, and charge eighty quid a night'. It also, if my study of the estate agent's window in town is anything to go by, is currently for sale and overpriced.

I struggle with this whole Airbnb thing. As a complete hypocrite, I occasionally use it, especially in locations where hotels or B&Bs are not common, but it is a sour taste in the mouth when a couple from Warwickshire can buy local properties to use in the holiday market when locals find it impossible to earn enough in their own communities to afford to buy somewhere that then allows them to *stay* in their own communities.

This is a massive problem in Wales in particular, but also to a large extent in other tourist jewels of the United Kingdom such as Cornwall or the Lakes.

It's a far more complex situation than I can find any solutions for but, having spent a few days in these rural communities, it's clear that places like Brecon, and the market towns that line the stunning rivers and valleys of the country, are unaffordable for people starting out on their journey of finding work or starting a family.

An example, from here in Rhayader.

The average price of a property in 2022 was £240,167, which suggests a farm labourer or rural worker in the neighbourhood would need a deposit of around £25,000 to buy a house. The average wage for that same worker would be typically £23,000 per year. Even if they had saved a deposit, the monthly repayment would be crippling, especially in the high-interest-rate climate at the time of writing.

Some parts of Wales have reached such astonishing levels of house-price inflation that even those with better-paid jobs are having to move away from home to find somewhere they can afford to live. The 'second home' purchaser has had the effect of driving up prices, breaking up communities and rendering some of the most beautiful villages and towns of Wales almost bereft of locals. Outside of the 'vacation months' of the year, many of these places are barely occupied at all.

It has become a blight on Welsh communities, in the towns and villages of some of the most stunning countryside in the UK, such as here in Mid Wales, up into Snowdonia and across the Llŷn

Peninsula, where some places such as Porthmadog or Criccieth become ghost towns in the autumn and winter.

I'm pondering this over a pint of some indescribably gassy beer at the Castle Hotel, next to the traffic-troubling clock back in town.

Next to me are two likely survey candidates in Gemma and Ross, who have been arguing for the last five minutes about something to do with *Game of Thrones*. Ross seems rather laissez-faire about the whole property thing as he already rents a flat back down South Street just outside town, but Gemma still lives at home and seems to have an anger about the subject.

'Don't ask!' she says when I broach the topic of how a young couple might get a start here.

'It's pointless to even think about,' she says. 'My mum and dad have a neighbour who seems to have spent the last year doing his place up, and only stays there weekends. We reckon that'll be a holiday place soon. He only ever knocked on the door once and that was to borrow a ladder.'

'Move to Cardiff, I said,' announces Ross, much to Gemma's irritation.

It's clearly an answer as far as work and opportunity goes, but it won't resolve the property problem, with Cardiff becoming one of the fastest-rising property-price locations in the whole of the UK since 2010. I also feel the need to give Ross a heads-up on the actual shade of green that the grass of Cardiff currently represents, but I stop short of wanting to dent his aspirations, if that is what they truly are, as he seems to find the discussion rather dull anyway.

Ross is an electrician so reckons he can find work anywhere, but Gemma wants to stay and find something here, close to her friends who, timing being everything, all seem to arrive at the same time and, rather than be the old bloke stuck in the middle of a Tik Tok and vodka Red Bull night, I down what's left of my beery fizz and nod my cheerios.

On my way back to my Ikea show home for the night, I feel a bit of a louse. Nothing I can do will ever solve the problem of diminished communities and the departure of a youthful generation from the towns and villages they grew up in, but I do feel as though I'm part of the problem.

It's hardly a martyrdom of note, but as I'm walking back along South Street, I cancel the following night's Airbnb and vow to try for the good old bed and breakfast at the next day's end instead. The whole act of cancelling an Airbnb in the worst possible Wi-Fi becomes a very stressful experience and, as I put my phone down, I don't know whether I've cancelled it, booked a second night or sent a picture of myself to the owner.

I also end up having a crap night's sleep as the place is freezing cold and I couldn't be bothered to make a warming hot drink and use the Warwickshire couple's Ikea mug. I also feel bad that I'm starting to have such negative feelings for a couple who are just exercising a perfectly legitimate right to buy a retirement-supporting property and, after all, came looking for me when I was lost earlier.

CHAPTER 12

HIPPIES, GANGSTERS AND TEXTILE MILLIONAIRES

The next morning, I leave a thank-you note, a perfectly acceptable reference without gloss on their Airbnb profile and kick Gwendoline into life for us to move on.

She waits for a typical third or fourth start and finally chugs something of a complaint at me as we move off. First though, before I head north, I go back into town to the clock memorial and decide to show it some respect by riding around it as if it was a roundabout. True to form, an oncoming tractor gives me a beep and unnecessarily slams his brakes on, causing a small hatchback coming from West Street to beep at him as I ride away, giving the clock a wink in my mirror and wishing it good luck on its day of traffic hassling.

Gwendoline and I head out past my last night's accommodation and back on the long unwinding road north for the real Mid Wales rural village experience.

The old scooter is not herself this morning, her complaining has changed from a simple ugly whine and a moan, and she's now adding an occasional sarcastic click when I tempt her into a little more speed. As we approach the fork in the road at Llangurig that gives you your heads-or-tails between heading to Aberystwyth or Snowdonia, she suddenly throws all her weight into slowing and it feels like I'm sat on a washing machine, not one of Italy's most elegant gifts to the motor world.

She turns herself off and sulks silently by the side of the road. Ever since I picked her up a few weeks before the journey and gave her a few test runs she's been a difficult charge, but now she seems to have simply downed tools all together.

I'm already about seven miles out from Rhayader and sat on the roadside verge just a mile or so from the village of Llangurig, a tiny place of less than a thousand people and I'm guessing it's unlikely to be home to a Vespa specialist.

My mechanical skills are very limited, but I know a machine that's performing below par when I see one, and Gwendoline is most definitely below par. I don't make the call back home, though, the 'come and rescue me' call to either my wife, who in fairness would be here in a few hours, or to Gwendoline's owner, and instead I sit and thumb through a few pages of Morton while I think about what next. After about a quarter of an hour and sensing the old scooter might have cooled down a little, I try to coax it into one more try.

It's bizarre: with just one twist she hums into life and sounds like she's meant to. No whistle, no whine, just the high buzz of a low-powered motor, almost exactly as she should sound. I have no idea what games she's playing now but, clearly, she's past her sulking and prepared to move on. Not wanting to waste this burst of activity, I twist away carefully at her throttle and we move on through Llangurig, past its pleasant village green, its rather 'Hornby' style fifteenth-century church and on out of the village past the few houses of the hamlet of Cwmbelan, and on towards Llanidloes.

It's as though something that was wrong with Gwendoline before has righted itself. That irritating clicking sound has gone, too, and I'm wondering if the scooter had something rattling around inside that has fallen out. Like that episode of *Star Trek* when Sulu had swallowed something that put him in a coma, but then it came out of his ear, and he was better again. Or something.

Llanidloes has come a little too soon for my liking. Now my ride is back on form, I should be taking full advantage and pressing on, but Llanidloes is an important part of the journey because, as we move away from the young and bubbling Wye here, we have our first meeting with Britain's biggest river, the Severn.

I've got a relationship with the Severn that stretches back throughout my lifetime. The bridge crossing where the river widens out to its estuary and into the Bristol Channel at its most southerly point has figured in my travels since I was a boy.

My wife and I sometimes walk over the Severn Bridge in the fog just to see the towers disappearing into the clouds above, and she can (being a quite brilliant photographer of note) take the most terrific, moody pictures of the structure looming like a monster out of the mist.

Sat high above the treacherous brown waters below that swirl with menace, we would look over the edge of the bridge together, imagining the dive. The threat of the Severn there under that bridge has fascinated me forever.

Here at Llanidloes, the first town the river meets after rising at its source, which, like the Wye, is also at Plynlimon in the nearby Cambrians, the Severn in comparison to its wild and wide old age, is barely a trickle.

What strikes me first about the Severn here is that it's flowing north. Of course, I'm used to it being a river that flows south, out to one of the country's great southern waters, so it does feel a little incongruous for it to be heading in the 'wrong' direction next to this pretty market town. I'm imagining Llanidloes as a malign magnetic force, mischievously dragging the river briefly away from where it should be going.

The mountains around the town appear gentler here, carefully rolling around it, forming something of a cup for the buildings to sit in, and it does give off an air of shelter. As I walk around on a cold autumn day, there's a feeling here that everything is fine and in some undisturbed order. Not in a creepy *Midwich Cuckoos* way, but something more understated and underlying. I get more 'Good morning's here from people walking around town than I have so far on the journey and, unlike Builth and Rhayader, people here seem a little more comfortably off. While we're still clearly in farming country, and still within a low employment demographic compared to elsewhere in the country, the general vibe the town gives off, while short of affluent, is definitely 'we're OK, thanks'.

The town's original wealth came from it being the centre of the weaving industry. While there wasn't a centre of production as we might think of factories today, many of the houses and civic buildings here in the late eighteenth and early nineteenth century would have had weaving machines in their lofts or basements, contributing to the town's wealth as textiles were sent out from here to Shrewsbury, Liverpool and Birmingham.

The decline of that industry came in the mid-nineteenth century, and as Llanidloes was never able to compete with the intense mill towns of the north of England, decline was inevitable and led to another of Mid Wales's rebellious movements. Where Rhayader had the Daughters of Rebecca, Llanidloes became the centre of operations for the Chartists.

The Chartists have their history throughout Wales. They were a movement with demands for greater workers' rights, for more accountable parliamentary representatives and for broader and more transparent democracy. As the textile industry declined here in Llanidloes, so did the workers' income, conditions and opportunities, and radical meetings and agendas sprang up in this weaving town under the noses of the town's burghers, who were powerless to halt proceedings when violent rioters overthrew them in 1839.

In a foreshadow of the terrible events in the Rhondda in 1911, when the 'national hero' Winston Churchill sent troops onto the streets of Tonypandy to brutalise miners striking for a living wage, likewise troops were sent in to regain control of Llanidloes from the Chartists seventy years earlier.

It's a scene witnessed throughout Wales's industrial history. Industry declines, pay and conditions become intolerable, working families are neglected and are forced into radical action to make themselves heard, and the government resorts to brutal tactics to overpower and break the will of a people who then become statistics in an impoverished environment for years to come.

It was seen in the early 1980s in the Rhondda, the early twentieth century in the same places, and back as far as the mid-nineteenth century here in the pretty, timber-framed town of Llanidloes.

Today, Llanidloes seems far from radical and revolutionary. Liberal and bohemian, yes, and more than a few of the locals walking around seem to have that dropped-out and retired-from-the-rat-race look about them.

The most impressive building here is the wonderful, wide town hall. Being from the early twentieth century, it appears different to some of the historic white and black Tudor-style timber buildings such as the Market Hall, which dates back almost four hundred years. I like the town hall more because, built in 1908, it has that pre-Great War optimism about it. Grandeur and solidity as the nation heralded a new century. The old queen and her somewhat narrow views of a class-based society were dead, and the working class had forged a new, dynamic and technically innovative century out of the ashes of the industrial revolution.

The building has a real presence to it in the town, as all civic seats should, instead of being intimidated by neighbours of glass and steel. A glorious wrought-iron balcony sits atop the central arch of five that form an arcade along the building's ground floor, and a clock tower capping the building brings a perfect symmetry to the structure. Reinforcing its importance to the town and its history, it also holds Llanidloes's war memorial, which is a dignified stone plaque added to the leftmost arch and lists the fallen of the town.

The building also now hosts the superb Llanidloes Museum, which gives real respect to the Chartist movement, and has some excellent documents and artefacts that remind visitors of the importance to the town of the textile industry, and the huge part it played in people's lives here.

After the decline of textiles, the town had an economic rebirth later in the nineteenth century when lead deposits were discovered at Y Fan just outside it. Within twenty years the mines here were some of the most lucrative in the world, leading to an economic resurgence for the town, and in the last fifteen years of the nineteenth century and the first fifteen of the twentieth, many new chapels were funded, rows of shops were built and some restorations of the timber buildings such as the Market Hall were undertaken.

What I see now, a hundred years after the lead mines dried up, is a relatively unchanged town from that time, but beautifully kept and something that Powys can call a genuine treasure.

As I walk around, I can't help but notice how brilliantly tree-lined it seems. There's no doubt that Llanidloes has charmed me. I know I've been here before, but only on the route through it, and to stop and take it in now has been a delight.

I stop for a coffee at a place that I fall in love with: the Hanging Gardens Café. It's a courtyard-style café that acts as a real hub for the community here, with a calendar of events over the next few months that suggests it could be the busiest café in Wales. Harp recitals, French conversation groups, art groups, book clubs, repair shops, bereavement support, baby music groups and many more gatherings are held in this fabulous space surrounded by myriad hanging plants and greenery. If there is one place in Wales that takes community seriously it must be this one.

A friend of mine who used to live in nearby Newtown told me with some dark humour that Llanidloes was where the last hippies came to die, but my experience already in the town, and at this brilliant community hub, is that it's where they thrive. No wonder Llanidloes has this slightly ethereal bohemian vibe: it's actively promoted. And not just here in the Hanging Gardens Café, but more generally, with real care taken in shop window displays, real attention given to its textile history and a general sense of wellbeing throughout the town.

I start up a conversation with David, a tall and gentle chap who fits the criteria to be called a hippy. Not excessively so; for example, he wears trainers instead of sandals, branded polo instead of a cheesecloth shirt, and I start getting angry with myself for making such stupid assumptions. One of the tallest men I've met in a long time, he sits cross-legged across from me at the communal table I've settled on, rolling a cigarette while we chat.

David has long silver hair very neatly pulled into a ponytail and talks very quietly. Not a whisper, but sometimes I must take a chance and nod and smile at what he says, hoping that's the right response, rather than ask him to repeat himself three times.

David worked in IT in Leeds for many years and then decided one day in work that it wasn't for him and gave it up. Just like that. Walked in, sat at his desk, decided enough was enough and walked out.

Being a musician, and single, he took to moving around Yorkshire trying to find work in bands or recording studios, but was having no luck and so decided to go all-in, sell his house, buy an old UPS delivery van and take to the road. Sixteen years on, he's still doing exactly that, although the UPS van is now a very neat mobile home (he shows me a picture), and the work is as a musical instrument repairer. He's in Llanidloes regularly for no other reason than 'Llanidloes gets me' and is here today to pick up a cello.

'I have a lot of people who know me, and they put people in touch with me, so I turn up with the van, get to work and move on, but I love it here, so I come back a lot.'

He asks me what I do and I take a long sip of coffee while I think of something he might be impressed by. Call it a desire to please.

I want to say I do something really cool, but I don't. I can't.

For some years after leaving the magical world of selling music, I worked a sad job selling something intangible that people didn't really seem to need, in an organisation largely run by bullies who had the people skills of a spoilt child. Some people with far more patience and tolerance than me did the exact same routine task at the same desk for over thirty-five years. Their feat was astonishing, impressive and yet, to me at that time, deeply demoralising too. For me, for too long, the place I worked and the work I did was soulless.

Like David, one day I'd just had enough. I left later than I should have and escaped a depressing inertia by taking my limited skills that the job required to far happier working environments elsewhere around the world and, thanks to wonderful friends I made in far-flung places, I came to enjoy and even be proud of the work. But it's still nothing to boast about. It sure as hell isn't music.

'Insurance,' I say with a barely audible sigh as accompaniment. 'Nothing sexy, I'm afraid.'

David is joined by two other friends, Livvy, who indeed *is* wearing sandals, and Magnus (it's either that or 'Magnet' but I can't tell, as

David is barely murmuring) who *is* wearing a cheesecloth shirt. Between them we have the grand slam. They're a friendly bunch and I notice how much they laugh while they converse and how much they smile at each other. It's not carefree, it's *with* care. There's a real sense that these people are in exactly the right place for them at the right time. Something I've sensed while working in Hong Kong, Tokyo or the US. That other things become what we do, but this is what we are, and where we should be.

Maybe that's part of why I have fallen out of love with Cardiff. It's only ever been where I did what I had to. What I wanted was light years away and it was only when I left that I saw that.

Livvy has a velvet bag full of jewellery that she has made and David starts to look through. As he puts things down, I see a long necklace that instantly makes me think of my wife. A long, black strip with small discs hanging from it. It's complete hippiedom and I ask if I can buy it. 'Sure,' says Livvy, 'how much do you want to pay?'

'How much is it?' I ask.

'Just say,' she says with a wide smile.

I'm in a very awkward position. I literally have no idea what to say. I'm going to look like an idiot if I go high, and I'm in danger of annoying the seemingly least annoyable people in Wales if I go low.

'I really don't know, honestly.' I'm grasping now and begin to wish I hadn't asked.

It's strange, but over this necklace, with these rather lovely, friendly people, I'm beginning to wish the ground would swallow me up.

David doesn't help. 'It's nice, man,' he says, and the hippy quotient has been turned up to eleven. 'Real nice.'

Livvy tries to ease the situation for me. 'You want to think about it? No problem. I'll be here for a while.'

I blurt out like an idiot, 'Ten pounds.' I just want the moment to end, and these incredibly laid-back, relaxed, smiling people have without any effort made me a ball of tension.

'Cool,' says Livvy, and while they carry on talking amongst themselves, I still feel as though I'm burning up. I learn that it's not easy taking life easy.

I still feel awkward ten minutes later, as though I've rained on a parade a little, but they give nothing of that away, and while I drink another cup of coffee, we talk about life in general, Llanidloes and why I'm riding an old scooter the length of the country.

'That's *such* a good idea,' says Magnus. 'I love that.'

Livvy, too, is excited for me and after my spell wondering what the right way to behave in front of hippies is, I'm starting to feel much more comfortable in my routine white-collar skin. David very kindly offers to take a look at Gwendoline for me and, as he's ready to smoke one of his roll-ups, he suggests we do both at the same time. I get a nice cheerio from Livvy and Magnus, and David and I head out.

'Do you think I paid enough for the necklace, David?' I ask as he sits astride Gwendoline and rocks her gently back and forth.

'No idea, man,' he answers. 'I'm sure it's all good. You offered and Livvy took it. Nothing to stress about for either of you.'

I don't feel any less unsure about it, but I do get a sense that in the grand scheme of things it's nothing to get hung up about. And maybe that's the hippy ideal. Everything is easy until it's important. If it's not important, it's easy.

David starts Gwendoline up and tries a few twists while drooping a rolled fag from his mouth as he speaks. 'Seems OK,' he says, and then adds suspiciously, 'you might make it.'

He gives me a rather too heavy-handed pat on the shoulder and laughs. 'Be good, man… it's all good'.

As he heads back to the Hanging Gardens, I push away and wonder if, when he gets back, they'll laugh about the stiff collar who overpaid for a cheap necklace, or whether they'll shake their heads in dismal reflection at the cheapskate who underpaid. And then, as I ride out from this pretty town into the beautiful green countryside that embraces it, I realise that actually none of that matters. It is indeed, as David said, all good. All good indeed.

*

And things do feel good after my morning in Llanidloes. I have a positivity about the trip that was recharged there, and it only increases as I ride out of Llanidloes alongside the narrow River Severn, nodding at the many sheep grazing between the rocky banks and who look up as we buzz past.

Ahead of me, a grouse runs across my path and into the wooded area that lines the opposite side of the road to the river, and is joined rapidly by another who plays chicken with me as I approach. He obviously feels avoidance is the better part of valour and, as I arrive, he scuttles back to the side of the water, which dashes against the stony bed and rushes on to its destiny as our biggest river. I could literally step across it here. And it stays like this for the next five miles until we reach the punchiest little village in Wales, Llandinam.

Not many places in the country with a population of less than six hundred have punched so far above their weight, with starring roles in the stories of the birth of the industrial valleys of South Wales, World War Two and, believe it or not, the prohibition-era gangsters of Chicago.

I stop at the entrance to the village and, in just the ten minutes it takes me to walk through it and back, I'm filled with a sense of the tiny hamlet that made a big noise.

Firstly, for such a small population, it is well served by two significant churches. To the southern end, a Presbyterian church with lovely gardens including a host of rhododendrons that must blaze in the summer, and to the north, the pretty St Llonio's church on a site that has been consecrated since the sixth century.

Putting my head through the door of St Llonio's, I see an immaculate length of pews that line up in and around a row of mathematically stunning arches and columns, to a neat altar underneath a rather lovely stained-glass window.

It's a silent, orderly, architecturally gorgeous little place, that would have meant a lot to one of the most significant figures in British, let alone Welsh, industrial history.

David Davies, the man who exported coal to the world from the docks of South Wales, was born here in 1818. The first man to build a bridge over the Severn here at Llandinam, he went on to build the railways that linked so many towns across Wales.

Not content with building one of the most important transport networks in the nation, which carried people and goods from sources of employment and production to destinations of commercial profit, he went on to own collieries and became an important figure back where we came from a few days ago in the Rhondda.

Realising the hold that Cardiff Docks had on the export of his coal, and the struggle the Taff Vale Railway had in carrying it in such volumes as he was producing, he did what any impatient industrialist would do and built his own railway from the Rhondda to Barry, where he built his own docks.

In fact, the statue that I'm stood under here in Llandinam, just along from the church, is of him standing tall and studying the unfurled blueprint plans of Barry Docks. Another statue of Davies stands today down at that very same Barry Docks, making him one of the very few people besides monarchs or military generals to have two statues erected in their honour.

There's no statue of Murray Humphreys, however, unsurprising though that is, due to his expertise being not in the development of the fabric of the nation, but in fixing for the Chicago mob during the fateful prohibition period of Chicago's history. His parents were from here in this tiny part of the world and emigrated to the US as the nineteenth century was coming to its close.

Murray 'The Hump' Humphreys was born in the US as Llewellyn, and in his youth in the tough neighbourhoods of Chicago he built a reputation of a hoodlum able to manipulate the law to suit his agenda, and bribe officialdom when manipulation failed. All the stereotypes fell into place one by one when he met the mob, starting with jewel robberies, liquor production and distribution, grand larceny and (although never tried for it) killing.

His rise through the Chicago organisation meant eventually he would come to the notice of one Al Capone, who took a liking to Murray and elevated him to a fixer for the chair of the board. 'No one hustles like Murray the Hump,' Capone is said to have uttered with some respect.

While Murray himself never saw the village his parents left behind, the privileged great-and-good schoolboys of Gordonstoun, alma mater of British Royalty, did when they were evacuated here for a large part of World War Two. While any ill-informed Nazi attempt to destroy the future British elite and privileged by bombing the school might have succeeded, they were never going to think tiny Llandinam would be of any great import.

Not long after Llandinam disappears from the rear mirrors, the A470 does that infuriating thing again where it takes a sharp left turn and becomes a different road altogether if you stay straight on.

Purists would say this next stretch is not the A470 but the Welsh government, in their desire to say how well the road links north to south, say it is. Either way, that sharp left turn takes us into the village of Caersws.

The only thing that immediately seems of note to me here is that it forms the median point between Aberystwyth and Shrewsbury. That will no doubt seem a little unfair to the local residents who at least kindly wave to me as I pootle through. Gwendoline has done that. I'm getting attention from the locals, friendly for sure, but I know it's because of her, not me. I've reached the point in my life where I gain popularity only by association. In this case, association with a machine with mood swings.

While I don't necessarily see some of the character in this town that I have in others, it does, however, just yards after that stupid left turn, host a petrol station and I take the chance to fill Gwendoline up, give her a bit of a spruce-up and drink a machine coffee. After Llanidloes which I fell for, Caersws seems a little like somewhere people live rather than a place filled with life. I don't intend to denigrate it, but I get the response I'm expecting when I ask the girl behind the petrol station counter if there's anything for me to see here.

She says no. A very, very firm no. Her bored demeanour suggests she means it, so after a ten-minute break it's off up the Carno Road (as the A470 seems to be known here) and away past some rather lovely stone houses. They're of some size, too, suggesting there was at least *some* Victorian or Edwardian money and interest here once.

The local football team briefly had a moment in the sun as competitors in the grandly named UEFA Intertoto Cup back in 2002, when they faced the Bulgarian side Marek Dupnitsa over two legs in that competition's opening round.

Quite what any travelling Bulgarians who made the journey from the ancient and busy town of Dupnitsa thought of Caersws, I can't be sure, but they would at least have had a grand night after at the Red Lion which, like many small-town Welsh hostelries, looks like a fine place for the coming together of strangers and locals.

However, they might not have easily realised they were in Wales, because yet again there's little to advertise the fact, and in fact several of the houses along the road here are flying Union flags and not Henry Tudor's grand dragon.

The road from Caersws to Carno doesn't offer much else to excite me, even though the hills in the distance seem to be beckoning.

A run through the villages of Pontdolgoch and the fabulously named Clatter paints a picture so sleepy that all I can do is wonder who lives here and what jobs they do. I'm fascinated by small places, distant from busy towns. Do people come here to enjoy a quieter life, or are these quieter places because of the people who live there? It's something I think about as I glide (thank you, Gwendoline, for an unpredicted moment of ease) through the place looking to see what the attraction may be.

It's then I realise that there once *was* something here. Now long gone in its importance and influence, but still holding its shape as a ghost of the past.

The Laura Ashley company, of Jane Austen dresses, country cottage décor and vicarage tableware, spread out all over the world from this town, creating hundreds of jobs supporting many of the families who made their lives here. At its peak, thousands upon thousands of dresses were sold each week in countless worldwide stores, all designed and stitched in the enormous factory here and all carrying a label saying 'Made in Carno, Wales'.

Women hoping to look like Princess Diana, who in the early years of her romance with Charles, Prince of Wales, wore the company's clothes regularly, would walk into shops in Tokyo, New York and Milan and walk out with a tiny bit of Mid Wales in a racing-green bag that in itself was a fashion statement and evidence of taste.

Laura herself was a hell of a lot more than a businesswoman, though. She was passionate about the power of women in the workplace and went to great lengths to make sure her employees had the benefits of work–life balance long before it became something corporations turned to when they were compelled to. She insisted that women's working hours fitted around the family and expected them to put the school run ahead of the sewing machine.

She was also one of the first industrialists, certainly in the UK, to understand the impact of manufacturing on the environment and invested heavily in natural-fibre research and development. Well before it was a buzzword, she understood the significance of sustainability in production processes.

Laura Ashley was the quintessential self-made woman, who moved from hand-making headscarves at her kitchen table in London, ultimately to worldwide sales of hundreds upon hundreds of millions of pounds during the company's most successful period. The girl from Dowlais, near Merthyr in South Wales, lived in an elegant home in Pimlico, London, but never forgot her Welsh roots despite the trappings of success. The private plane was an extravagant personal luxury, as was the yacht and the French chateau, but the commitment to Mid Wales was genuine, and whilst she had travelled some distance from where she started in life, she couldn't fairly be accused of not giving something back.

She would have been sad to see the shadow that the now-empty factory places over the small town.

As with many corporations, expansion when not controlled became an unmanageable nightmare, and the over-extension of licences to distribute the product around the world brought a weight of problems. After the tragic death of Laura Ashley in 1985, her husband Bernard and various board members and investors could never seem to steer the ship without chaos.

She and Bernard, who was her partner throughout her time leading the company, are now buried here in Carno's St John's church with a very simple headstone, in typical retiring style, no different to the others of this parish buried here.

It's not a surprise that when a major employer leaves town, the spirit of the place descends into gloom, but there is fight in this town. While the chance of another seven-hundred-job employer arriving to lift the mood is unlikely, the residents of this small Welsh town are at least not giving up the ghost and continue to push hard for the re-opening of a rail station here that was shut in the Beeching cuts in 1963.

The least far-sighted of individuals, Richard Beeching was appointed by the Conservative government of the time to make Britain's railways into a model of futuristic transport efficiency. He did this by recommending the slashing of thousands of miles of track and more than fifteen hundred stations across the country. If he had had his way, rural locations such as Devon and Cornwall, and indeed most of Wales, would have been stripped of almost all inter-town lines, leaving connections only to the larger urban locations. While Beeching's report wasn't implemented in full, hundreds of countryside villages and towns were deprived of the connections they needed.

While there was a major employer in town, the impact on Carno was negligible, the population after all was barely a thousand, but now with a need to lift the rural economy here, the lack of a rail connection becomes a restraint on attempts to regenerate the place.

'Carno Stop Now' the hand-painted signs say on the road out of the town past the factory, or 'Restore Rail to Carno' says another as I cross the rail bridge to the north. Trains run here, they just don't stop, instead passing through at speed with scant regard for yet another Mid Wales village that needs economic support.

If we look at the number of people employed in Wales, with data supplied by the Welsh government from 2020, only 4.5 per cent of jobs are here in Powys, the Welsh heartland. That's around just sixty thousand from a pool of one and a half million jobs across the nation. Cardiff and Swansea together swallow up one-fifth of all the jobs in Wales.

No surprise, then, that connecting places like Carno more easily to the national network, such as the university town of Aberystwyth to the west and Shrewsbury in England over to the east, more opportunities will likely arise.

Just as with Builth Wells, Rhayader and other such places we've passed through on this journey, the jobs that are here are largely dependent on the agriculture industry; and the huge green space I ride through on the A470 suggests that most of that farming is dependent on sheep.

The one field I stop next to – to take a breather from the wind whipping at my face – seems rammed with them and so I decide to count. Assuming the field is about two-thirds of the size of a football pitch, as almost everything seems to be measured by these days, there are over fifty of them grazing or dozing away. One just the other side of a wire fence is thoroughly uninterested in me.

According to the 'Meat Promotion Wales *Industry Statistics Report of 2021*', bedtime reading for anyone with an interest in such things, Wales has one-third of the United Kingdom's entire flock, and in any one year that could mean almost five million sheep grazing away at Welsh hillsides and marshes. If you add in the lambs they produce, that figure grows to over nine million, or three sheep for every man, woman and child in the country.

Perhaps the sheep owns a far greater claim to be our national animal than the red kite or the mythical dragon.

CHAPTER 13

WALES AT LAST?

Gwendoline and I start clocking up more and more tiny Welsh villages as we head on. Most of these are made up of a few cottages, two or three farms and, perhaps, out of nowhere a row of terraced houses, once a home for the many labourers who worked the land, now amongst the cheapest properties in Wales.

Inexpensive, but isolated.

Places like Talerddig with its deep railway cutting, the deepest in the world at the time of its creation. A train passing through would be shaving past near-vertical rock faces. Another station closed in the mid-sixties, and its old signal box lies away in the trees as I ride by.

Or Dolfach, whose only claim to fame seems to be that it lies near Talerddig.

Or Llanbrynmair, another hacked away from its umbilical rail connection to the rest of the country. In fairness, Llanbrynmair has more to it than its nearest village neighbours and acts as a central point for the farming community around here, almost all of whom would be Welsh-speaking and in many cases are fifth- and sixth-generation farmers.

Llanbrynmair is the edgeway to the Cambrian Mountains here, the exact nature of which seems to be something of a debate as I sit quietly looking out at them, nursing a warming coffee from the Wynnstay Arms.

The debate is about how widely we can attribute the name Cambrian Mountains. Effectively uninterrupted, these beautiful, steep-sided, harsh-edged slopes are the uplands that reach from the Brecon

Beacons all the way to the North Wales coast, and Cardigan Bay to the west. In other words, one large range covering almost half of the country. But over time we've adapted our vocabulary to separate Snowdonia from this, at least figuratively, and so the Cambrians as we know them today stop not far from here, and it's another set of mountains that I'll be skirting shortly.

This is mountain country for sure. Some of the hardest land to make a living from but the communities around here continue to strive with it. They do so with immense pride, but also with a sense of being 'other' when regarding their place in the nation's twenty-first-century demographic. Here, there is literally no connection to Cardiff, the capital. It's chalk and cheese. Or rather, it's white collar and overalls.

But here we *do* see the evidence of Wales the nation. The language is the one I hear in the pub and in the conversations around me, the flag is flying nearby at the old railway station, now a private home, and the whole feel of the place, richly green and edging onto the slopes of the Cambrians, is classically Welsh in nature.

This is the first time since leaving Cardiff that I get a sense of the country itself, not of its past, its castles and its beauty, but of its very soul. I don't want to get all '*Men of Harlech*' and 'down with Edward's men' about it, but yes, truly, sat here I do feel as though this is indeed the heart of Wales.

Geographically that's true, we are indeed in the centre of the nation, but more than that, I'm getting a sense of what Wales is.

It's small, but with a wide panorama. Tough but with a warm welcome. And prepared to live apart, but decent and inviting.

I don't say Cardiff isn't Welsh, that would be plainly ridiculous, but it sure as hell isn't *this* Welsh. If I walk through St Mary Street in the capital I could be in any merchant city in the United Kingdom, with my back to the castle anyway, but here you are most definitely in Wales. For good and bad. For the hard-earned living and the grace it's worn with.

Suddenly, I don't want to move on, I want to feel a part of this for a bit longer. My own Welsh is purely at school level, but I deliberately order another coffee using the language, and I even exaggerate my accent, and I'm delighted when I'm thanked in Welsh, too. Just for this short while, I feel more Welsh than I have in ages.

Back outside I sit down next to the road and take out a map. Looking at the distance I've travelled and the distance to go, I decide to hang around and just watch the day go by for a little longer. I really don't want to surrender this for another hour.

Llanbrynmair is, to be rather direct, just another small place on the road, with a pub, some farms, a school and a church, to all intents the same as many villages that sit away from the bustle of a large town or city. But right now this is physically and spiritually the best representation of Wales I've had on the journey, and it wasn't even trying.

When I do finally head out, Gwendoline's irritation is recorded once more by the return of the clicking noise I had coming out of Rhayader.

She also feels sluggish, as though we're carrying more weight than before. Knowing that some of our steepest climbs are to come, I'm beginning to wonder if this will be a long haul on to my stop for the night in Dolgellau, about twenty miles away but on a road that will make the journey seem endless.

By the time we reach the deathly right-angled turn at the village of Commins Coch and cross the narrow bridge over the River Twymyn, positioned here by a road planner with a murderous streak, Gwendoline is almost rasping.

As we leave this steam-era postcard model village, I'm determined to get to Dolgellau before she gives up the ghost completely. This is a fundamental mistake on the hill in front of me, which almost signals a seizure on her part.

The noise changes as we ride. Up the undulating road in front of me she coughs and wheezes, and then down the hill she whistles and clicks. It's like a John Cage piece. The flatter strips such as the one that takes us through the picturesque village of Cemmaes feel like some respite.

Cemmaes offers another sense of Welshness, too, with more red dragon flags waving in the breeze than even Llanbrynmair could offer. Some of the lovely grey stone cottages here prettify the place, and the tree-lined road through offers a change from the bare strip passing between sheep fields and hedges.

Some of the bends in the road now intensify and the A470 takes on a little of the rollercoaster about it, and some of the bends become terrifying as massive tractors or trucks and trailers wing their way towards us at speeds far too dangerous for blind curves such as these.

At Cwm-Llinau I take a moment at the side of the road and give a wide berth to a massive truck coming through filled with sheep. One of those enormous eight-wheelers with two tiers in the trailer, sheep on the top, sheep on the bottom. It slows down as it passes me and I get a wave from the driver and an autotuned bleat from one of his passengers.

As I crest the hill out of Cwm-Llinau, the view is spectacular as the sun makes a last-ditch dart through the clouds in bright rays further up the valley, and I'm in awe. Looking north between the interlocking slopes, I get such a lift to my spirits that it literally takes my breath.

What a position to be in. West and south are the Cambrians, north is the great Snowdonia range and the sky is turning a late afternoon blue where until now it's been a watery grey.

I'm begging Gwendoline to make the next dozen miles or so and I freewheel down the next hill, which is yet another mistake as, even with her engine engaged, her steering can be a little stiff, but without it, all I can do is use my weight to lean her out of the way of the huge tractor that I hear before I see it. The Welsh accent has been said to be guttural, phlegm-spitting, coughing and other totally unfair accusations. It can also be poetic, clipped and sing-song depending on the message. The one I get from the tractor driver as he slows to berate me is largely vile and abusive and sounds like 'Yoofakkingprig'.

It takes me three attempts to get a burst from Gwendoline, and after the adrenalin from my near miss starts to calm, I focus on some very sensible, keep-to-the-left, highway-code style of riding.

Mallwyd is the next marker as I count down the miles to Dolgellau, and I note here that I've left Powys behind and have entered what was once the ancient county of Montgomeryshire. Mallwyd is a short distance from Machynlleth, which lies away from my route and so gets by-passed by me on this occasion, but I remember days in the town some while ago at the annual comedy festival there, and I make a mental note to go back some other time.

Machynlleth lays claim to be the ancient capital of Wales, and the home of the remarkable Owain Glyndwr who had his Welsh parliament there, and the people of the tiny village of Mallwyd play the Machynlleth card very keenly. That association between the nearby hamlets and the ancient history of this Celtic land is very close to the hearts of many of Machynlleth's satellite villages, and certainly there's an 'otherness' here, grounded in rebellion and being an underdog.

It's in the Brigands Inn in Mallwyd that the sense of that becomes real, with the history laid out here of the Red-Headed Bandits who were the murderous gang that stalked these parts, stealing cattle and killing those who stood in their way, including the local sheriff. It's said that the custom of putting sharpened scythes in the chimney well to deter burglars comes directly from the farmers who defended their property from the bandits.

Certainly, there was a lawlessness to this region in the sixteenth century and, as far as property and livestock was concerned, you had to be prepared to defend it, because the arm of the law was barely present across the region outside the market towns. The Brigand's Inn has been here since the late fifteenth century – albeit with less dramatic names – and *possibly* was the meeting point for the bandits to plot their antisocial activities, but all is quiet for the moment as I interrupt my ride with a swift half and look around the ancient walls and timbers.

The next village along is Minllyn and now we really are in southern Snowdonia, and the mountainsides have become fierce in their slopes, and jagged in their crests. Minllyn has a rather dramatic, twin-arched packhorse bridge, covered in moss, which would look at home in any of *The Hobbit* movies, but little else to capture my interest, although it can certainly boast a location of high drama, as the mountains start to enclose the road here.

Away to the east of the A470 is the village of Dinas Mawddwy, which I can see as I ride through, but which doesn't feature on the journey. I could take ten minutes to head over to it across the water that flows alongside the road here, but in truth it looks like it mainly comprises caravan sites and camping grounds, and I really do feel a need to get Gwendoline tucked up for the night.

I also know that at this stage of the journey I'm leaving one very distinctive part of Wales behind and entering another.

From when we left Merthyr and rode north through Brecon, we have been in Mid Wales, the poorest part of the nation and yet also unique in its beauty. Throughout my ride, the same few characteristics have been ever-present.

The vital nature of the agriculture industry here, and the way it is clearly taken for granted in the administrative centres in the north and the south, have been with me since departing the Beacons. These aren't rolling plains of rape, wheat and barley; they are the steep hillsides, hellish to farm and populated by millions of sheep, with hill farms of massive acreage punctuated by smallholdings struggling to thrive, and producing some of the finest foods and plants anywhere in the United Kingdom.

The people are uncomplaining in the economic difficulties they face, wanting to stay and prepared to fight for the economically disadvantaged communities they have spent their lives in. They ask for nothing more than a fair shot. Transport connections where there are none and job security where it wavers. There is a whole generation of Gemma and Ross's age who see a future only possible outside their home towns, and an increasing number of people who want to buy a piece of this beautiful part of the world for only the occasional visit.

But most of all, Powys, the largest administrative county of Wales, all two thousand square miles of it, has been the place where, for me, Wales opened and revealed itself. I was able to leave an anglicised, commercially dominated south behind and find another nation amongst the heavily rolling Cambrians.

Mid Wales appears to be sandwiched between the two most demanding areas of Wales. The urban south and the dramatic north. Throughout my life I have loved them both and skipped the middle of the nation as the bit you must cross to get from one to the other, but

I realise now what a dreadful disservice I have given this heartland. Whether it's the historic entrance to Powys at proud Brecon, or the laid-back, bohemian dropout at Llanidloes, these are places that are so much more than just somewhere in between.

Now as I head down a steeply sloping A470 towards a stone-grey Dolgellau, sitting amongst the green forestry and parklands of the foothills of Snowdonia, I'm about to enter the north, and everything changes from here again.

Part Three

THE
NORTH

CHAPTER 14

A LAND OF KINGS AND A TOWN OF DISAPPOINTMENT

There's something wilder and harder about the north and yet its beauty is probably unsurpassed in the entire United Kingdom.

The economy of Gwynedd, the county Gwendoline and I are motoring into, is born from industry as hard and uncompromising as that of the Rhondda, and still it maintains a glamour that draws tourists and travellers here from all over the world. How the north pulls off this incredible balancing act so successfully, of harshness and grace in harmony, is something that has puzzled me for years.

It is so clearly both, and yet manages a separation of the two characteristics so cleanly cleft that, even in the middle of it, you wonder how it pulls it off. One or the other, and yet both at the same time. Industrial historians and expert climbers. Naturalists and wild swimmers. Railway enthusiasts and bird spotters. All completely different and yet all satisfied by what they can find here in this corner of the world.

A coach party of Chinese photographers will view Gwynedd, and Snowdonia, as much a perfect destination for them as will a minibus full of potholers. At times in the summer, the county is like a film set with all the extras waiting for their scene.

'OK, darlings, we'll have the motorcycle tourers next please, and if the geology students could wait over by the burger van with the hang-gliders and the church architecture group, that would be lovely.'

The north will give me towns built on slate mines, a nuclear power station, pine forests, little railways, stunning castles and Victorian tourist towns all vying for the tourist buck that keeps it bustling. When we're not faced with a pandemic, North Wales hosts almost four million overnight visitors a year, over twenty million day trippers and takes in a tourist spend of around one and a half *billion* pounds.

And the gateway to all of this, from the south and east anyway, is the town of Dolgellau.

Waking in Dolgellau and throwing back the curtains as though I am starting a fitness montage from a *Rocky* movie or feeling the opening bars of ELO's 'Mr Blue Sky' does not have the desired effect. It's very grey, very wet and very demoralising.

The town sits away from my window as a collection of grey tiled roofs, grey stone walls and a grey sky sits above it all. In case I haven't made the point clear enough, Dolgellau is grey.

That doesn't mean it's a sad and gloomy town – in fact, walking around looking for somewhere to breakfast, there's a heck of a lot of smiling people here and I get a few *Bore da*s as well as some nods of acknowledgement.

It is, however, a cramped little town, with very narrow streets, paths and passages linking towards a town square that seems as though it was built and then squeezed like a sponge just to get a couple more in. It's unabashedly a town of its age too. Contemporary is not a word that gets used a lot here, but its history has worn well and the bustle of modern life in no way appears incongruous in its setting, as perhaps it does in parts of Dorset or Cornwall. Just as the classic Dior 'little black dress' can be accessorised with a touch of modernity but still holds its place as the main feature. If a Lamborghini pulled up here, it would embarrass itself in its crass, self-aggrandised status in front of the neat butcher, the undertaker, the men's outfitter and the generational hand-me-down businesses that still proudly operate around the central square.

Dolgellau is the gateway to North Wales, but perhaps of more note, it's the door through which we enter the ancient Kingdom of Gwynedd, land of high mountains, sweeping ocean and valleys rich in history and blood.

Gwynedd is one of Britain's most invaded lands. After the Romans had their go, various warlords from the south and east tried their best until the Saxons took their turn, but the Kingdom repelled all comers until Edward the First finally landed killer blows through both military might and diplomatic connivance.

This is the country of Llywelyn the Great who united the Welsh princes in 1216 and who is still revered as the true hero of those seeking an independent Wales today. It was Llywelyn's namesake grandson who finally succumbed to English conquest sixty years later, and so ended the line of Welsh Princes of Wales. It's a title that receives a mixed bag of opinions here in Wales, with views being slung around from three distinct camps.

Firstly, there are those who see the title as one the wider world recognises so it elevates Wales to a position of notice, particularly across the Commonwealth but also in further-flung places. This view became embedded at the investiture of the then Prince Charles into the title at Caernarfon Castle, further north in Gwynedd, in 1969. Then, some years later, his wife Diana became the Princess of Wales and the country's profile remained low in political and economic circles but massive in fashion magazines, celebrity profiles and global paparazzi gatherings.

Then there are those who think the title should not follow the royal line at all, and that there is no legitimate reason why a family whose heritage is German and whose tentacles reached out to the thrones of Belgium, Bulgaria and Portugal as well as the United Kingdom should have any right to adopt themselves as sons or daughters of Wales. This group says the only legitimacy the title can bear is to Llywelyn, who ultimately surrendered it on his death to the English crown.

The final players in this argument are those who sit in a lukewarm mix of the two, who will accept a Prince of Wales in the British line if the child was born here. Something that conspiracy theorists say Diana wanted for her first boy, William, but which was prevented by her in-laws. Maybe far-fetched, but the Welsh never hold back on feeling slighted. Indeed, it's said by some, my father most often, that a Welshman would drive a hundred miles to get insulted.

Whatever the answer to this seemingly never-ending slight in the eyes of many, the history of Gwynedd is inextricably linked to the history of the British Isles.

And as I walk around Dolgellau today it could be a film set for a nineteenth-century British murder mystery – the marketplace where the gossip about the murder at the big house is rife, and the many with motives go about furtively avoiding the famous international detective inquiring in their midst. I must keep walking in a loop passing the same shops over and over as my breakfast place isn't open until eleven, so the good shopkeeper of a local outfitter eyes me suspiciously as I stop at his window for the third time today and finally, with no little embarrassment, feel the need to at least step in.

It's an immaculately curated, long-established shop and I get a sense of that amongst the stock as I walk slowly around. The mannequins in the window are dressed in that 1950s idea of smart casual, the gent wearing a zip-up cardigan and brown slacks, the lady an A-line skirt of no discernible colour but topped with a round-neck jersey in the most chocolate shade of brown possible.

Around the shop are rows and rows of trousers, jerseys, hats, church dresses and fleeces that seem to shout, 'These are not for *you*' and it's difficult to not feel a little sombre as I consider a pair of mesh-backed leather driving gloves.

The problem is that none of this is meant to be disparaging towards a family business that has been here on Queen's Square for more decades than it's possible to even consider, but even in just reporting what I see there is a sense of a past that will never be again. It's not as though fashionable modern clothing isn't found here; it's as though it never happened.

But maybe I'm not the intended customer and the lady who walked in just now, and who gets the wonderful warm welcome that I didn't, certainly is.

A very friendly chat between them is prompted by the starting line from the lady that 'Fred will be in later with his foot' and gets the response from the shopkeeper that he 'will have something ready but it might not be to taste'.

Putting down a tweed cap I picked up just to show willing, I notice the time and head out for breakfast at the Royal Ship, probably Dolgellau's most well-positioned pub, which gives me a window to look out on the town while despatching a bacon sandwich the size of a whole half-loaf of bread which will set me up until Christmas. It's fabulous. As is the pub hotel which has been here for over a century and has become a feature for the regular traveller starting a holiday in the great Snowdonia National Park.

Regular travellers such as Jenny and Vince who are here for a few nights away from their Staffordshire home, back in the Royal Ship for a couple of nights. In talking and swapping the usual 'where are you from' etc, Jenny tells me how much she loves Wales.

'We've got great friends in Merthyr, and we house-sit for them from time to time when they go off to Spain for the winter. We're known by the locals in the pub there because they think we're murderers.'

What follows is a bizarre tale of Jenny and Vince, who for some reason only known to them, created a character called Dafydd who they said they were friendly with, but who they never introduced to anyone. Over time people would ask where Dafydd was and they would answer that he was staying in, or was ill, but then one night in the pub after a few beers too many, Vince took one of the locals aside and told him that they had murdered Dafydd.

In fairness to the good people of Merthyr, while the story of Dafydd had been so carefully curated over time to be undoubted, on the news of his murder they reported nothing.

'They didn't change towards us at all,' said Vince, 'they carried on welcoming us into the pub, and Dafydd was only talked about again if we ourselves mentioned it, which we sometimes did if we'd had too many. How we killed him in the bath and then took him up to Dowlais Top to bury him.'

Jenny takes note of my incredulous face.

'Exactly! That's what they look like when we talk about it! It's such fun.'

'Anyway, been lovely to talk to you,' says Vince, and with a pleasant smile and warm shake of the hand they're off, either to plot another murder or take in the sights of Snowdonia.

It's a five-minute walk in complete shock back to my lodgings of last night, a rather good B&B which advertises itself with a humorous sign in the window as 'dog friendly, people tolerant'. It's here I meet up again with Gwendoline, who I'd love to share my weird morning with, but who instead just sits in silence, slightly tilted to one side, as bored with the trip as she has been all along.

The friction between us on the ride has grown and, as I climb on, I already feel that the pleasure in our relationship has subsided. We've only been in a partnership for a few weeks, and she's someone else's altogether so I shouldn't take it personally, but there's no doubt the initial thrill has gone, and the last few days have turned into a chore.

The parts of this journey I have enjoyed the most are when I have been able to park Gwendoline and walk around. The rides have gone from being fun, moving slowly to not fun, then rapidly to unpleasant and, on the roads in the north of Mid Wales, downright bloody awful.

I spend ten minutes trying to coax her into action – after all, there's so much beauty north to see and I'm anxious to get going – but she's not playing nice. Finally, after a thorough shake and a lift and drop I get something out of her, and after a rasping, metallic, shearing noise she rolls into a throaty roar that causes pedestrians near me to jolt.

She feels as though she's got something of the chase in her and, pulling away, the ride is smoother than it has been for days. Being suspicious in nature, I ride back to where the scooter was parked to see if something that had previously bothered her had been shaken loose, but there's nothing to see and so, while the ride seems the best it's been for a while, I make hay and twist out of Dolgellau, heading north back on the A470 and deep, deep into the mountains.

Cader Idris is visible from here. Although not quite a thousand metres, it has its place in mythology as the mountain home of bards and it is said that if you sleep on its slopes you awaken as a 'Poet of the Ages'. This area was a kingdom within a kingdom, with rulers of the smaller land of Merioneth sitting within the realm of the Kings of Gwynedd. King was a title bandied around freely in the fifth and sixth centuries and although written records of many don't exist, the stories of the fabled continued into legend.

The overwhelming sheep population on this stretch and around the village of Llanelltyd gives a nod to the history of this area being so tied to that of the woollen industry. In fact, the development of

Dolgellau into a market town is based on its role in distributing the produce of the mills that grew up around it.

Nowadays the area gets a large amount of income from its position at the southern end of one of the richest hiking and climbing areas in Europe.

The tourist spend across all of Gwynedd and all points north is crucial to the rural Welsh economy and represents a third of all Wales's leisure income. Batting well up the order, North Wales is also host to almost 40 per cent of all British visitors to Wales, many of whom come for some of the best and most varied outdoor sports available.

The A470 here takes us past many camping sites, outward-bound centres, water-sports facilities and of course climbing schools. It's almost impossible in the summer to drive a hundred yards or so without seeing a gaggle of rope-swinging climbers in luminescent gear walking to their next challenge.

For the authorities and local officials there's a fine line to walk, if you'll excuse the pun. The money inflow to these low-employment areas is vital, but the roads and villages are getting clogged between May and September with numbers of thrill- and pleasure-seekers way beyond anything the road and the environs were designed for. There are stories of rescue vehicles being unable to get onto the low slopes to provide medical aid for climbers due to the sheer number of vehicles blocking the road. This autumn day, though, it's much easier, although even today I pass at least six or seven groups of outdoor-lovers venturing to the wilds for the next hit of the outdoor drug.

I pass Ganllwyd with its neat row of shepherds' cottages and on to Bronaber, with its low plain stretching out to the left as a relief from the slopes.

Bronaber is the last village before you arrive at Trawsfynydd. The land between was used by the War Office in the early part of the twentieth century for military training, artillery testing and in both World Wars was the site of camps for prisoners of war: Germans in the Great War and Italians in the World War Two.

Effectively a shanty town of temporary buildings, the area became known as 'Tin Town' and, from the later 1950s, housed construction workers building Britain's first atomic power station here on the side of Llyn Trawsfynydd, a reservoir previously built in the 1920s.

Trawsfynydd Atomic Power Station has been doing the incredibly sensitive task of decommissioning since 1991 but has dominated the vista across the lake here since its completion in 1965. I could go into some detail here about Magnox reactors and massive Westgarth turbines, some of which is genuinely fascinating to those with an engineering bent I'm sure, but for me the fascination lies in its massive but simple twin grey-box shape, appearing as something arrived from the depths of space that we're waiting to work out how to communicate with.

You will pick up the theme from previous parts of our journey, but after twenty-five years of generating power for the national grid and creating as many as six hundred jobs in the area, on its cessation of operations the economic decline that followed hit the place hard. Some jobs remained to assist with decommissioning, which has now been going on longer than the plant was actually in operation, but a career with a future here is impossible.

Conversations about how the site can be transformed to generate green power continue while the debate about the lasting scars and waste of atomic power are dealt with without confidence by Welsh and national governments. Trawsfynydd village waits while its fate lies in the hands of bureaucrats, engineers and environmental scientists, but no one is holding their breath.

From the side of the huge artificial lake, the road north winds through steep undulations, and the rugged nature of the slopes increases. By the time we enter the historically important town of Blaenau Ffestiniog in late afternoon when the light is failing, the jagged mountainsides lurch only yards over the roofs of the houses that line the main road through town, and cast a darkness at the end of the day way ahead of sunset.

My immediate thinking is that Blaenau Ffestiniog is so bleak at this time of day, with its sheer slopes tunnelling the darkness through the town, that I would be giving it a better chance to impress if I saw it in daylight, so I head to my accommodation to rest Gwendoline after her much better performance today, and find a shower and something to eat.

This becomes the first of many disappointments in Blaenau.

The hotel is just off to the north edge of the town, a large, modernised building that services the many tourists who come here in the summer. In the autumn and winter, it's clearly something of an empty, echoing chamber.

It is perfectly located for one of Wales's newest tourist attractions, Zip World. Already known across Europe, and just outside the hotel grounds, this is the UK's fastest and longest zipline, taking thrill-seekers from on high and sending them like boilersuit-clad bullets across the Llechwedd quarry below.

This is my intended fun for tomorrow, so tonight checking in and settling down to a few drinks and a bite in the hotel's well-reviewed restaurant gives me the wonderful sense of a treat.

As I walk in, one girl of student age is staffing the bar. On telling her I'm looking to check in, she takes me to an office the size of a stationery cupboard. In fact, I think it is the stationery cupboard.

'Just to let you know that we're not doing food,' she announces as though I've offended her in some manner.

I say that this was the reason I chose to stay here, and she gives an exaggerated American-soap-opera shrug of the shoulders and a sigh. And nothing else.

We have that moment when one of us needs to add something and yet neither of us does. It's as though she's run out of script and I'm just a bit weirded out, especially when looking back across the entrance to the restaurant I see many tables all dressed for dining.

'It's only me tonight,' she announces, 'so we've got no one in the kitchen.'

The hotel is massive. It's like the hotel in *The Shining* and this poor student is running the whole show on her own.

Looking back at my online booking, the hotel boasts twenty-four rooms, luxurious dining and a stylish bar and terrace. I even walk back outside and look around to gauge if this is all some elaborate practical joke and when I walk back in with slumped shoulders, a

TV crew and twenty-four staff will shout 'SURPRISE!' and shepherd me to a table for the 'Best dinner in Snowdonia' that one (clearly preferred) customer described on Booking.com.

After explaining I was really looking forward to eating, the student performs the service of giving me a photocopied list of other places to eat in the area. The area being anything from Porthmadog, another twenty minutes ride to the west, to Dolgellau back to the south. The very few places to eat in Blaenau are rapidly whittled down as she points at the paper for me.

'The Chinese is closed on a Monday, sorry… and the Indian is closed full stop. Not sure why but he hasn't opened for weeks. Shame. Was a *massive* onion bhaji they did.'

She steps back at this point and creates a ball shape with her hands as if to twist the knife into my hunger.

After her recommendation that the fish-and-chips place back in town was 'OK-ish', emphasised by the rocking of her flat palm at her eye level, I succumb and at least I'm told they deliver, so I crash out on my bed after a shower and then enthusiastically dial the chip shop.

'We don't deliver,' is the answer.

Gwendoline thought she was done for the day, but she's back into action and rolls me down the steep hill from the hotel back into Blaenau. Thankfully, there's a supermarket next door and so, intending to drown the disappointment that my four-star hotel is taking a one-star approach to service, I pick up a six-pound bottle of wine, the cheapness of which seems appropriate given the circumstances, and join the queue to pay.

I say queue to pay, but in fact I think I've joined the queue for some sort of help centre.

The man in front of me is helped to the till by a friend where he puts down two bottles of vodka so hard that I wince. The next few minutes are straight from Laurel and Hardy. One pissed-up bloke in filthy clothes tries to wrestle the money out of his friend's pocket, while the fellow with the money grips onto the counter bracing himself. At one point the grabbing hand is so far down his mate's trousers that it looks like a ferret looking for the way out. As this is going on, a group of trackpants-wearing boys of no fixed sense are embroiled in an argument at the next till about their age as they seek excitedly to buy two bottles of cider and a packet of Haribo sweets. You know the classy combo. Six-per-cent store-brand cider and sour chews.

Laurel and Hardy finally find the cash, although it was an exhausting bout for one who drags himself out and sits on the ground outside while his mate shovels random coins at the lady behind the counter. I want to applaud her patience as she watches on as though contemplating her own death as some sort of release.

The boys eventually seem to accept that looking fifteen and claiming to be twenty-one is a step too far and so move out, pushing each other and jostling for physical seniority in the group.

When I at last get to pay, I walk out past the boys who are negotiating with the Oliver Hardy figure, currently lying prostrate on the ground, for his services in going back in to pick up their cider for them.

One lad, the smallest, wearing full American basketball gear from head to toe, has the bright idea of asking me, but as I decline to act as his alcohol broker he instead offers me a pound for my own wine. Again I decline. It's not the snob in me who thinks these boys might not be heading for an economics degree that dampens my mood, but the dad in me hoping that the drunk on the ground isn't foreshadowing the life of any of the boys in a few years if, with so little work in the area, the prizes of jobs and futures may be beyond them.

When I wake up the next morning, in a room that absolutely stinks of fish and chips, it's with no little gloom that I head into Blaenau for the full picture of the town that was raised up proudly on slate and now relies on tourism and its undoubted potential within that sector to keep itself relevant.

Gwendoline can be left in the damp car park just across from the railway station. The town is in its damp grey and black shroud after a heavy rainfall last night and the air is 'thick with the fog of disillusionment' as Dashiell Hammett might have said if he'd walked through here.

Typical of many Welsh towns, this isn't built around a square, but instead has thin arteries of terraced cottages branching off a high street which is lined with the houses, shops, hotels and civic buildings which once would have given Blaenau the characteristic of a well-to-do place, thriving on its slate-mining exports around the world.

I'm hoping the tourist office, signposted from back at the car park, will help me fill in the huge gap between busy industrial town and empty streets of no real conviction. The problem is I can't find the tourist office at all. I walk from one sign pointing south down High Street all the way to the one pointing back north, but there's no sign of anywhere that may provide the information I'm wanting.

Now I'm walking back and forth so many times that I'm starting to draw the attention of the locals sat in bus stops to avoid the thin wet mist that hangs over the street. I can sense their eyes on me and the whispers at the 'stranger in the village'.

If you've spent your life here it must have impacted upon your bearing. The town is swallowed up by massive banks of slate waste heaps and the high, overbearing slate faces that appear like sheer walls at the rears of tiny gardens behind tiny cottages. It's impossible to see Blaenau as anything but grey, and the clouds that sit overhead don't help to redraw the image as I walk back looking for something, anything that might give me a hook to understand the place better.

Just like in the Rhondda, the community only exists here because of what lies beneath.

There were many smaller seams of slate found on farmland here in the eighteenth and early nineteenth centuries, and workers gravitated to them away from the harsh farming land and the low standard of living it provided.

Before the nineteenth century, miners were living in small rows of cottages at each small slate mine, and it was the arrival of the railway that created a boom in workers and the opening of wider seams until Blaenau effectively was the nuclear centre of many pocket quarries and one or two much larger ones.

Also just as in the Rhondda, the huge surge in industrial activity stirred the imaginations of some of the nation's greatest engineers, and one of the most impressive features of slate-inspired growth here was the 'gravity run'.

All the slate was loaded onto simple, railed carts and literally pushed down to Porthmadog just over twelve miles away, picking up speed and eventually travelling the whole distance by the power of gravity alone. One such cart sits at the car-park end of the high street now as a monument to our ingenious use of science and engineering in the nineteenth century.

Of course, the carts had to be pulled back up and so, until powered railway solutions came to prominence, that duty fell to horses and there are some wonderful images of these and the gravity carts in the Welsh National Library at Aberystwyth. Even now during the summer tourist season, enthusiasts can experience the thrill for themselves as re-enactments of the gravity run take place on occasion, steered skilfully by experts who keep this small piece of British engineering history alive.

The onset of steam rail was the other element that gives Blaenau such an important page in Welsh history. Replacing those rattling gravity carts and giving horses respite from the long trek back up, steam trains arrived here in the mid-1860s, and that continuation from gravity through steam means that the Ffestiniog Railway Company, established in 1832, is the oldest independent railway company in the world today.

Nowadays running tourists around southern Snowdonia, these little trains of Wales form a very important part of selling Welsh heritage as a commodity and bringing vital tourist spend to an area which was so dependent on slate that, at one stage in the early nineteenth century, the quarries employed over 80 per cent of all workers in the town. Slate's decline triggered Blaenau's decline. And the economy here, and indeed in much of non-coastal Gwynedd, is almost wholly dependent on a combination of tourism and farming, with the spend of domestic and international visitors outstripping agricultural income by almost four to one.

There is still one working quarry here at Llechwedd and it's there I head now. I'm looking forward to flying over it strapped to a wire but as I approach, things aren't exactly looking positive.

Maybe it's my paranoia, but when the fellow tells me I won't be 'zipping' today, he does so in front of a sign that says I shouldn't be embarrassed if the controllers need to discuss a customer's weight. My immediate shame is curtailed, though, as the line is closed due to the wind.

When I suggest I can't feel anything beyond a breeze, he explains that where I'm standing, surrounded by huge peaks of slate, piled up like a freakishly never-ending drystone wall, I won't feel anything, but flying high above the quarry it would be like battling a wind tunnel. There are other activities available alongside and even below the quarry, but I'm a little put off by the almost eerily empty surroundings and don't fancy being a lone bouncer on an underground trampoline course.

In the summer, Blaenau is filled with fliers, bouncers and clamberers travelling from as far afield as all points in Europe to enjoy the extreme activities here, but I don't get a sense that they are staying here. Aside from the ghostly manor from *Scooby Doo* that I stayed in last night, Blaenau doesn't look as though it's geared up for much more than providing vodka and fish and chips, although I'm sure by the summer the Indian restaurant will be back open. The old Queen's Hotel still wears itself with some dignity, but it's a lone point of elegance in a town that wore toil and dirt with pride and never tried to present itself as the cream-tea capital of Gwynedd.

Unemployment across the rest of Gwynedd isn't such an issue. Bangor, further north, is a busy university city, and there are many jobs in the public health sector in the county but the tourist spend, so vital to the area, doesn't focus here, lifting the town beyond its post-industrial torpor, but rather is spread much further afield in the more beautiful parts further into Snowdonia, and along the pure rivers that flow out to the stunning coastline.

Blaenau relies on two specific types of tourists: the thrill-seeker and the railway enthusiast, and neither stay for long once they've had their fix. With Trawsfynydd Power Station dried up back to the south, the town does appear to be waiting for something. One can live cheaply here – in fact many houses are at prices so far below the national average that some holiday cabins a few miles to the north can often be more expensive – but low-price housing is a sign of a declining neighbourhood, not a measure of a high quality of life, and the population of the town has halved from the days of the height of slate mining.

The extent to which that quality of life has fallen can be measured by the Welsh government's reaction to pleas for assistance. In 2013, on receipt of requests for investment, the formal response was the provision of just £36,000 to upgrade a playground and renovate a café. In the closest of examinations of what is required to inject promise into this grey town, that was barely a sticking plaster. Local charities and community organisations strive hard here but the town remains one of the poorest in Wales, with some of the lowest average wages in the whole of the United Kingdom. That UNESCO determined the Slate Landscape of Northwest Wales worthy of World Heritage status is crucial. Not necessarily for what that brings to Blaenau Ffestiniog – one of the specific areas named in the certification – but more importantly for the flag it raised to the Welsh government to pay far more attention to what it has here.

To reach this status, the area had to comply with at least one of ten selection criteria, and the slate beds met two. Firstly, that it exhibits an important interchange of human values: in other words, it formed a connection with architecture, community and social development. And secondly, that it was an outstanding example of a landscape that illustrates a significant stage in human history.

UNESCO has woken the area from the dormancy of its past, and it now lies with the Welsh government to realise the contemporary value of the slate beds' history and social legacy. As I walk around, there's little evidence that they have woken up to that responsibility, and any aspirations of the people of Blaenau Ffestiniog to grow beyond its history sit rather still in a grey, damp slumber.

I stop in a rather low-stocked newsagents to pick up a snack for the ride north and try to raise a little optimism in the chap serving. His large sideburns and comb-over already suggest I've stepped back twenty years, but he is a cheery sort and I hope to get something from him that speaks positively about the town, and he doesn't let me down.

'You know Kylie Minogue?' he asks me, pointing my tenner back at me as though it's a test.

'Came from here, she did,' he says, putting my money in his till and forgetting my change.

There's a lull between us. He is waiting for me to be impressed, which I won't be because it's not true. I am, however, waiting for him to re-open the till and give me at least a fiver back.

'Well, her grandad did anyway. Hard bugger, by all accounts.'

I finally give up my polite patience and suggest I'm due some change.

'Oh yes! Sorry about that. I'll have to wait for another customer now though, so I can open the till.'

While I'm convinced that the skill to open his own till isn't as far beyond him as he suggests, I do attempt to reassume the patience that had faded from me, and listen to stories of his own grandfather who may or may not have known the early maternal line of the diminutive Aussie superstar. On the sale of a *Daily Mirror* to a lady in almost entirely home-knitted clothing aside from her house slippers, I'm finally freed and head back to Gwendoline.

The journey out is through stack after stack of piled-up slate waste. Often many metres high and looking as though, if the wrong slab was pulled at, the whole pile would come crashing down. The other way of looking at it is as the world's biggest stock of cheese boards.

I've found Blaenau Ffestiniog a depressing stop. Fascinating in its way, and worthy of interest to many I'm sure, but considering I'm in one of the most beautiful national parks in the world, this corner of it has not revealed itself to be any more than a post-industrial town in decline, and I'm eager to be back amongst the gorgeous slopes and fast-flowing streams of Gwynedd as the A470 takes me north again towards the end of my journey.

CHAPTER 15

THE GREAT OUTDOORS

Riding on, the journey becomes less about covering the distance between sea and shining sea, and far more about the stunning world around me. I've already used perhaps too many superlatives when describing the beauty beside the A470, but now I'm looking for new ones.

The slopes that interlock and file ahead of me present a glory that yes, OK, is a continuation of what I've passed before, but beyond that they create a new sense of wonder arising from the sheer scale and drama of the road cutting high across the mountains.

In places it narrows to just a car and a half's width, and some of the zigzag turns and belly-dropping humps create a competition between the physicality of the ride and the visually demanding landscape beckoning your attention just when you should have it on the road and the minibus hurtling at you.

I can drift so easily here.

One moment I'm maintaining that sensible close-to-the-verge consistency as the road straightens between two sheep-covered slopes, and then correcting myself violently out of the path of a tractor.

Rays of sunshine draw my focus to an escarpment and the icy blue stream chasing along it. The water reflects the light as it winds its way heroically from the waterfall high up the sheer side of a mountain previously unnamed to me, but forever now known as bike-crash hill in my mind.

In fact, it's only a scrape against a fence post and, due to the nature of the hill, I wasn't doing much more than jogging pace anyway, so after checking Gwendoline over I crack on to the village of Dolwyddelan.

We've entered Conwy County now, an administrative borough that will be the last of our trip. Dolwyddelan is the village that sits astride the border with Gwynedd, which we are leaving behind, although the ancient sons of Gwynedd, celebrated as the true line of Welsh kings, still hold their place ahead.

Dolwyddelan Castle is a fascinating glimpse of what Wales was because, unlike the ceremonial and palatial castles at Caernarfon and Conwy, built by the English king Edward the First, this towering fort, high on the wildest and most rugged slopes of Snowdonia, was built by Welsh princes. A stronghold like no other, not only did it serve the purpose of securing the seat of Llywelyn the Great, but it was also built only a spear's throw from where he was born, and so was rich with the symbolism of the true Welsh line.

Leaving Gwendoline to cool off after our narrow scrape, I take the walk up to the fortress and try to imagine the wild people of North Wales defending their land from the organised English army that would have been seen from here, gathering a mile away.

Edward had been here once before, subduing the skirmishing Welsh on behalf of some of his barons who had taken land locally but, clearly irritated by Wales's refusal to take such trifling matters as land and herd confiscation on the chin, he returned to conquer. Building settlements and, of course, massive castles – at this time the equivalent of a full nuclear arsenal – Edward moved many more of his barons and their entourages here and ultimately subdued Welsh resistance.

When the Scots sing with pride how they stood against 'Proud Edward's army' at rugby internationals, they can also add how they 'sent them homeward tae think again', but Wales instead eventually capitulated to English invasion and the economic and military destruction of local communities.

Most of North Wales at this time was a loosely arranged society of far-flung villages, often miles from any form of organised defensive structure, and so the English army, thousands strong, were able to subdue gatherings with ease, and despite continued sporadic resistance (especially around the villages high up the steep slopes),

Wales was ultimately taken as Edward's wider fiefdom and its status as an independent nation, ruled by native princes, was lost.

Today, as you walk around some of the busier towns and cities of Wales you will occasionally see stickers placed on civic buildings, lamp posts and signposts that just say 'YES'. These are communications from YesCymru, a movement in its own words 'dedicated to the goal of an independent Wales'.

As Britain has become less significant on the world stage, and as its economic and cultural connection to Europe has been severed, the movement for an independent Wales has risen from the middle pages of newspapers to the front once more, and whilst the immediate possibility remains unlikely, the noises asking for an exploration of the idea are increasing.

Historically, the independence movement has been unable to break through 25 per cent approval for the principle of Welsh independence, and the economic decline of the UK post-Covid has only hardened public opinion against it, with many people believing that, unlike Scotland, our relative economic hardship as a nation is a blocker.

There seems to be a cul-de-sac in intellectualising the argument. It can't just boil down to whether Wales is economically able to sustain itself as an independent nation. Wales's GDP in 2020 was around seventy-five billion pounds, putting it ahead of independent European countries such as Croatia, and well ahead of Estonia, Latvia and others. To me, if independence is a cultural and social goal, the pound signs are a distraction, and the real issues that prevent such a momentous step are far more structural, and yet rarely debated because of the noise created around the nation's wealth.

In their report *Economic Futures for Wales*, the Economic Research Advisory Panel commissioned by the Welsh government throw other concerning factors forward for consideration, such as the lack of manufacturing and technological impetus, a declining birth rate in an ageing population, and the lack of a key major city of a scale such as Manchester, Birmingham, Sheffield or Leeds.

Whichever way future generations think about Wales, whether to be an independent nation or a continuing part of the Union, it can't only be down to how much money we have, else without investment in new jobs, new technologies and greater, more equitable social constructs, independence is a completely moot point anyway.

And as I stroll back away from Dolwyddelan Castle, with spots of rain turning into a downpour for the first time on the journey, it seems fitting that the fort stands as a metaphor for Wales as a whole. Once significant, then stolen, now lying in need of some intensive care.

The village itself is another reminder of the slate industry around here. It effectively was the housing for the workers at five slate quarries that surrounded it, and now the A470 pushes through it, with some splendid stone walling separating fields rich with sheep from the few buildings that line the road.

On through Dolwyddelan and making good time, we come to Pont-y-Pant, which is little more than a railway halt. A request stop, to be precise, if you're heading from Blaenau Ffestiniog up towards Llandudno.

The question as to why there would be a tiny single-platform halt here is answered very easily just by looking around. The mountainsides that slope down and form the Lledr Valley at this point, with the fast-flowing waters of the Lledr itself rushing by, make for superb walking, and along the road there are several hostels and camping grounds that suggest walking the numerous paths on a sunny day would be a joyous experience.

Following the Lledr, we start to meet several bridges as we're arriving soon at a confluence of three rivers and the picturesque town of Betws-y-Coed that sits where they meet.

You could be forgiven for framing it within an alpine setting as you ride in from the A470, with the huge Gwydir Forest surrounding it on three sides. The air is so fresh on this autumn morning, and the waters of the River Conwy flowing so clear and fast through the town, that such parallels with Swiss mountain villages are not just available but quite overpowering.

As Betws-y-Coed is another town that claims to be the 'Gateway to Snowdonia', it's no surprise that the people milling around the place today are largely walkers. Groups ranging in size from three or four to as many as twenty, stepping off coaches near the tourist information office, look well-equipped for some of Wales's most stunning hiking trails.

Some look as though they have arrived expecting to climb Annapurna, gripping two walking poles, carrying rucksacks of blinding luminescent colours, and chatting excitedly about the afternoon ahead.

One couple, Richard and Tessa from Bristol, are here on an annual weekend spent hiking over the Snowdon range, and always enjoy time in Betws before setting off on one of their day's walks.

'It's perfect for us around here because we can choose how tough a walk we want to take,' explains Tessa, 'you can do a few miles relatively flat if you've had a tough night before, or you can push yourself up some seriously steep sides.'

'But today is just a quiet ramble as we're going to walk Snowdon tomorrow,' Richard throws in.

Richard and Tessa have been coming here for the last seven years and although they've walked the Lake District and many beautiful parts of Scotland, Snowdonia wins out for them every year now.

'There seems to be a camaraderie here that we don't see everywhere,' Tessa suggests, while searching through her backpack for something either miniscule or invisible. 'Everyone acknowledges you with a smile as you pass, swapping thoughts on the weather or how tough the track ahead is, and it restores some faith, you know?'

Richard has been retired from the world of supermarket management for almost a year and Tessa has one more to go as a supply teacher, and already they're looking forward to much more time spent in the Snowdonia National Park, or as they are kindly and politely trying to call it, with the Welsh language receiving greater consideration, Eryri.

In total, the footprint of the Snowdonia National Park is over eight hundred square miles and, far from being just the Snowdon range, has eight others that link here, creating the valleys, rivers and streams that cut across almost the entirety of north-west Wales, and allow for well over a thousand miles of walking routes. Some simple, some undulating, some challenging and some downright treacherous.

'We tried Crib Goch once,' says Richard with a dry chuckle, 'but that was way beyond what we would call enjoyable,' referencing the most infamous route up Snowdon, and the one which requires the most nimble and courageous of hikers. Or really, I should say climbers, because some of the route is a real scramble.

'We saw someone being carried down on a stretcher that day,' Tessa says, 'and I think that gave us enough to think we should stay well clear next time.'

'Perhaps when we were younger?' Richard leaves the question hanging as Tessa finally finds the troublesome item in her bag and drops it straight onto her tongue.

'Antihistamine,' she announces. 'I love the walks, but the trees don't like me. The fellow that was stretchered down from Crib Goch had had an anaphylactic shock, so I take one every time we walk. God knows I'd die of embarrassment if rescue had to be called out for me.' She nods to the couple of men thirty yards or so away, dressed all in red, standing beside a Land Rover equipped for almost anything including armed insurrection.

I've never seen such a loaded vehicle before and the two men, all gym-shaped and aviator sunglasses, look as though their holding back a gang of armed and angry walkers would be fun. I get the feeling that if nothing happens on the mountains today, they might stage an accident for something to do.

That disservice I do them crassly understates their importance and the huge skills they bring to bear on some of the toughest terrain in the UK, under some of the worst possible weather conditions.

David is a volunteer amongst the rescue crew who base themselves here out of Betws-y-Coed, and who rely wholly on donations for the magnificent emergency service they provide.

'It's quiet today, not as many out as could be, but a couple more coaches will come in yet for sure,' he tells me while sipping tea from a mug which suggests he is not only a rescuer of some bravery but is also the 'Best Daddy in the World'.

His partner, Andy, is making himself a cuppa from the tailgate of the Land Rover and rummaging around what looks like enough equipment to start a whole new society if this one breaks down.

A crackle of the radio in the cab starts up and a voice rattles off a sentence I could never possibly understand.

Andy, David and I are silent, letting the crackle of the radio dominate.

While I wait for the duo to throw down their cups and leap into the cab for the next rescue, they instead relax and swap a line in Welsh I don't fully understand but contains the words *'glaw'* and *'cwmwl'* telling me that rain is heading in, and things may get a little tougher on some of the trails later.

The rescue teams in Snowdonia are the busiest in the entire United Kingdom, with hundreds of operations taking place in the national park each year, ranging from helping someone with a twisted ankle, to airlifting a climber with a life-threatening injury, or even bringing down a body.

'You'd never be surprised anymore by how unprepared people are for the mountains here,' David says with a wry glance up and down at my jeans, trainers and baseball cap.

'I'm not walking!' I say, too hurriedly and defensively.

'Good thing, too,' Andy chips in, 'you won't like it later when the rains come.'

In fairness, everyone I see heading off for the trails seems well, equipped. No one stands out like the fellow David tells me of, who attempted Snowdon in flip-flops. Actually made it up, too, to everyone's amazement, but then broke his leg on the way down and was featured on Welsh national news as a warning to others, and a major embarrassment to himself.

Other walkers are coming back into town after a day on the trails and head to one of the many hotels that line the town here, all of them designed to cater for the outdoor-lover.

Many of these are fine Victorian double-fronted buildings, built to capitalise on the improving links between Britain and Ireland since the early eighteenth century, which meant the main artery between London and the port of Holyhead passed directly through here.

To improve the road and make it the fastest method of carrying mail from Ireland to Britain and vice versa, superstar engineer

Thomas Telford erected the Waterloo Bridge over the River Conwy here in 1816, and it stands now as a marvellous example of our iron heritage, so important throughout the early nineteenth century.

Betws-y-Coed knows exactly what it is, and has become expert at capitalising on the economics of outdoor activities. Seemingly every other shop is catering for the walker and mountaineer, some of them almost superstore size, with every possible accessory you'd need for a day in Snowdonia. From compasses to cagoules, from haversacks to hats and from maps to mountain emergency kits.

You'd genuinely think that one small outdoor shop for a village with a population of less than a thousand would be a business gamble, but here I count five within sight of each other and every one of them is busy, even on this autumn day, months after the tourist season peak.

The large green at the heart of the village forms a triangle with the main road through, one side running along the fast-flowing waters of the Conwy and the final side lined opposite with myriad gift shops and places to eat.

If you're looking for a full-on breakfast to load the tanks before you set off for a ten-mile hike, or a glass of something celebratory with your boots off on your return, you'll find ample choices for both here.

At the car park I can see Andy and David jumping into the Land Rover and heading off, finally getting some action, unwanted or otherwise, and I settle down in the nearest café for a pot of tea and a Welsh cake at the disturbingly grand price of seven quid.

'The Original Welsh Cake' says the sign above the counter.

It sounds like a hell of a boast to make about the most ubiquitous of food items in the country. Shops selling nothing but this one style of cake are everywhere, and in Cardiff alone I know of four that sell only the small round cake.

Imagine a shop that sells a ham sandwich and nothing else, or going into Starbucks and they only sell Americanos. Now imagine a shop that only sells one type of cake, and you're likely in Wales.

Like the cawl I discussed in Rhayader, the Welsh cake is incredibly simple but argued over. At this point I will put my stepdaughter forward as the best Welsh-cake maker I know. My mother will read this with some fury, but even though both use the same ingredients, somehow there's a difference. My nan would have said 'the secret lies in who makes them, *not* what they're made from'.

Either way, to make one properly, you need a piping-hot cast-iron bakestone. Ours have been in the family for almost two centuries, passed down from generation to generation, and the recipe is unchanged.

Flour, mixed spice, baking powder, an egg, a splash of milk, butter *and* lard. Traditionally, while you start looking for the family defibrillator, you could also add currants.

All mixed up, you roll out the doughy mixture and cut it into rounds which you then place on the bakestone and turn once one side is a glorious golden colour. Once the other side is equally golden, sprinkle with sugar and you have the perfect accompaniment to a cuppa.

The supernatural occurs when two people using the same ingredients, cooking for the same length of time with the same equipment get two totally different cakes. It's bizarre. My attempts often result in two things: a stiff biscuit resembling a dog toy, and the polite shrug of my stepdaughter. The one I'm eating here beside the green in Betws-y-Coed is clearly OK, but not up there with my family's best.

As with all things twenty-first century, the Welsh cake has been re-interpreted, and the trendier shops in Cardiff Market or in the old Edwardian arcades there will sell you white-chocolate flavour, raspberry or something wilder like miso. There's probably an app for them or a social media platform called 'Cakeo'.

I digress.

The point I make is that many places claim their cakes are the 'one' and yet of course the origin lies not in one place, but in the thousands of households throughout Welsh history where the matriarch of the family remembers how a grandmother with only a few things left in a cupboard could fill a family's stomachs until the next time there was money. It's the same with cawl. Whatever was available you'd use. Like the best peasant cuisines all over the world, from paella, to pasta, to goulash, none of these were born as treats; they were all born as acts of survival.

Well, perhaps the Welsh cake was always a treat.

As with the 'original recipe' claims, many villages and towns around Snowdonia claim to be its gateway. You could access it from many points around its edge and yet Betws-y-Coed's claim would seem to be a very legitimate one.

Once the railway came here in 1868, it became the stop-off point for tourists and visitors who would base themselves here when touring the region. To Porthmadog and the glorious beaches to the west, to historic Conwy to the north and to all points mountainous and glorious in between. It became a gathering place for some of the great artists of the nineteenth century, such as Henry Whaite or Thomas Collier who would meet at the Royal Oak Hotel in the heart of the village here.

Landscape artist David Cox was a regular visitor throughout the mid-nineteenth century, and with like-minded fellows founded a local colony of painters that thrived, taking inspiration from the natural world that closed around the village, and his work can be seen on the walls of the hotel today.

But art and artists are not confined to history here and a movement still flourishes. One of the most touching works visible is by Alison Bradley, who still takes her inspiration from Snowdonia, and whose quite brilliant huge charcoal drawing of a Welsh Black bull takes my breath away as I nurse a beer under it.

Betws-y-Coed appears, on arrival, to be a place you come to, to start a day out away from it, and yet there is so much more here than you would notice at first glance.

The church of St Mary, built after the railway as the visitors to the town multiplied year-on-year, is a dramatic architectural interlocking of shapes and angles and has a rust-red outline to its grey stone walls and its Trumpton-style clock tower. Grade Two listed now, it sits remarkably serenely as a meeting point for groups of trekkers setting out, perhaps hoping it will bring a little divine intervention to them as they walk and render the Davids and Andys of this world unnecessary for one more day.

The row of hotels and restaurants that line the road have a real sense of history about them, and of course the landscape that hugs the village close is bound to be the main draw. And yet, finding art and history here, you get the sense that this small place is a guardian of something also. A sense that, while Wales is well represented by its geography here, there is something else of the Welsh soul within it, too.

I get that sense as I stand beside the River Conwy which flashes by me at breakneck speed, crashing into the rocks and boulders that sit within it. It's clean, it creates a freshness to the air that exceeds even that of the heart of rural Powys, and it's with a rush of joy that I see a kingfisher – flashing all blue and orange – dart into the roots of a tree sat at the bank.

If you were to build a new village from scratch that reflected the gentle yet powerful heart of Wales, its natural beauty and its welcome to those who want to witness it, you'd use Betws-y-Coed as its blueprint.

People come back here. They could access the national park from a hundred different points if they chose to, and yet Betws has become its gateway for more than just the convenience of its position. It offers a real 'good luck' as walkers and climbers set off for the day and a very warm fireside 'welcome back' on their return.

CHAPTER 16

LLANRWST, LANGUAGE AND LLYWELYN

As Gwendoline and I head back out on the A470 north of Betws-y-Coed, in only a few miles the scenery changes again. The Snowdonia National Park starts to fall away here and we're heading north-by-north-east out of the shadows of the mountains and the tree-lined slopes that previously beckoned. Now, just like when riding through the Rhondda, I have a river as a partner, running parallel to the road.

The River Conwy is one of Wales's least-talked-about waterways but for drama has no equal. Later, in its old age, it will open into a splendorous estuary providing the backdrop for one of the nation's most stunning postcard views, but here as we skirt the last foothills of Snowdonia, it's a fast-flowing wide stream that slices across a glorious vale.

The tourist authority here describes the vale as 'where Snowdonia meets the sea' and while the coast still lies twenty miles away, the sense that we are coming to the end of the ride is accentuated by the changes to the slopes that were once jagged and steep and now roll slowly to the water in a low arc.

This part of the journey is the one I have been looking forward to the most, as the road becomes flatter and straighter, and the landscape changes from demanding and intimidating to something far more comforting. Gwendoline prefers it too and is running nicely, even quietly, as though not wanting to disturb the scene.

It's strange how the vale and the estuary that it leads to get so little attention in the great sale of Wales to the world.

I can see the adverts now: a bass beat with three-second flash images cutting between Cardiff on match day and surfers chasing into the sea at the Gower. Cut then to a group of laughing friends in a nightclub or high-end restaurant – again, probably in Cardiff – and then a retired couple on the little train that runs up Snowdon. In comes a scorching guitar chord as a family run hand in hand across Portmeirion Beach, chased by the family dog – probably a corgi for consistency – and as the buzz of the band rings out to low feedback – nothing too coarse – we finish with a couple on a hillside, embracing and staring at the stars. Then a slogan that cost sixty thousand quid will come up as the images fade, something like:

'Wales... Come be yourself.'

It's been done to death, and yet rarely features this beautiful part of the nation, which in the next twenty miles will provide some of Britain's loveliest villages, a green plain with blue water chasing through it as prettily as in any European valley, and finally a coast that rings with the best that the UK can offer.

I've been lucky enough to live in many parts of the world, but if the chance ever came up, this may just be where I would want to be.

We've all done that thing where we go on holiday and, after a sunny day in a white-walled Greek village, paddling in a crystal-clear sea the colour of sapphires followed by a lazy evening in the friendly taverna, we start looking at house prices and imagining a life where it could always be like that.

But as I enter the small, historic town of Llanrwst, I'm thinking the same thing. Why doesn't everyone in Wales live here? OK, the commute would get tough if you're still banging out numbers on a screen while your life ebbs away at a job in Cardiff, but if we look past that with rose-coloured glasses on, this place could be the one.

Llanrwst already looks like something from a fable as we ride in. The lovely stone bridge, the Pont Fawr across the River Conwy here, has the look of the ages, with its three low arches and a wall rising to meet at an angle above the centre. You can imagine knights on horseback riding out from the town here.

At the end of the bridge away from the town sits a unique stone cottage that appears as though it has arrived from another time altogether. Owned by the National Trust, this twin-chimneyed cottage, straight out of a fairy tale, is covered wall to wall and ground to roof with beautiful Virginia creeper plants, turning now at this tail end of autumn into a glorious red and orange.

With nothing else in the eyeline other than the stone bridge and the cottage at its far side, you could be in the Conwy of any pre-industrial century. I'm not usually one for the 'doily brigade', as my wife calls the members of the National Trust, and I'm far more impressed by our magnificent edifices of engineering than I usually am by a country house or a historic tea shop, but this scene has really hit me hard in the heart.

I have a favourite view in Wales: the one looking south from Anglesey across the Menai Strait to the mainland and over the beautiful Menai Bridge. If you're stood in the right place, you can look at it from the lay-by at the main Anglesey Road high over the strait, framed through trees carrying spring blossom, and with wild roses edging the fields. It's a very full scene that on the right occasion challenges anywhere else in the United Kingdom for the overused descriptor of 'Awesome'.

But here with just a single stone bridge and a leaf-covered cottage, I think we have a competitor. The word that comes is 'tranquil'. Another is 'grace'. And finally, as I'm taking in the last slopes of Snowdonia in the mid-distance behind, I think 'perfect'.

The cottage, once Llanrwst's courthouse, is now a tea room, but sadly for me a very busy one, and with 'no room at the inn' I leave Gwendoline here and walk over the bridge towards the historic town to find out how it maintains its status as one of Wales's prettiest best-kept secrets.

There's been a community here since the twelfth century when the first church dedicated to St Grwst was built. Grwst would have been a missionary, likely down from Cumbria, and would have benefitted from a grant from the King of Gwynedd – at the time wanting revered Christians to set up community parishes within his fiefdom.

'I'll look after you, if your God looks after me' would have been the general gist of the conversation, and from the sixth century onwards, the area would have been a particularly God-fearing one.

Grwst, of course, doesn't hold a candle to St David in Welsh legend. He remains the saint we honour on 1 March each year, wearing our daffodils, and holding eisteddfods in all our schools. Those of us with friends abroad send and receive cards celebrating the day, and yet here in the nation itself it's just another day.

No national holiday for us on our national day, unlike the Scots who take St Andrew's day off school and work. I can't even blame the Welsh government for this, as the power to designate a public holiday lies in Westminster, but I'm very happy to start a campaign if you're with me?

St David in legend was a remarkable individual. Not content, it is mythologised, with conversing with dragons, his miracle was in being able to raise himself above the ground so that his congregation could see him preach from the back of the crowd.

The flag of St David, a bright yellow cross on a black field, flies here in Llanrwst from some of the windows in the village, alongside the red dragon flag, and there is a real sense of civic pride in the town as I walk through. It's spotlessly clean today, and the locals chat amiably around the place and greet me in the friendliest of fashions as I dip in and out of various shops and take pictures of the town.

One of the most impressive buildings here is the Eagles Hotel, a fortress-tower-like building that sits alongside the River Conwy and just yards from St Grwst's church. As I walk in and settle in the rather lovely lounge bar, there is a real calm that comes over me, and I realise that it's probably to do with the music playing.

'Lovely, isn't it,' says a watery-eyed old fellow struggling to stand but too proud to do it with help. He seems out of breath gathering his things together but still finds enough to tell me about the instrument we can hear drifting gently around the cosy room.

'Beautiful, the harp, I think,' he says, in that glorious Welsh way of rearranging the structure of a sentence into a maze that still says what it's meant to.

'I don't know who it is,' he says in an almost disappointed tone, and looks around him as if the answer lies somewhere on the walls, 'but the tune is "Bells of Aberdovey", I think.'

He looks up to the ceiling as if that's where he'll find his affirmation.

He's such a smart man. Crisply creased trousers, shiny shoes, and a military tie knotted perfectly under a V-neck jumper with a club badge on the breast.

'From away, are you?' he asks as he picks up his walking stick ready to leave.

When I reply, he responds with, 'Cardiff! Oh, never mind. You'll get over that one day, I'm sure.' He smiles.

'Lew', he kindly says I can call him, has opinions on Cardiff. 'It's England, isn't it?' he says as a fact, not a question.

He's more cheerful when talking about the harp music and, despite looking a bit fragile 'on his pins' as my nan would have said, he shuffles over and places a hand on my table to balance himself before brightly listing his favourite tunes. I daren't shut off as his wet eyes are staring me down so I mix it up with the occasional raised eyebrow and sound interested with an occasional, appropriately timed 'Oh'.

I don't want to sound unkind, but Lew has no 'off' switch. A trait of the Welsh senior. Gaps that allow a deep intake of breath sit between each tune he lists, many of them in Welsh and almost all of them unknown to me. I start to think he wants me to write them down.

Lew wanders over to the bar and looks around for the cover of the CD that's playing, and when he gets some attention from the barman, a hunt through every cupboard and shelf begins, while Lew clearly starts to flag.

Once the hunt is given up with a shrug of the barman's shoulders, Lew makes his way out, but not before slowly coming back to my table first to wish me well. As I watch him walk out and then pass the window outside, the tune that starts up is the 'March of the Men of Harlech' and I smile at the happy coincidence.

The harp is a fascinating instrument and Llanrwst has a very deep connection with it. The town became the focal point for harp-making after the instrument came to Britain from Italy in the 1600s. The 'triple harp', with an almost impossible-sounding one hundred strings, became a major export of the town from the eighteenth century onwards, and today remains the centrepiece of many a special occasion in the nation. Outside of their natural concert habitat, the harpist will most often be found at weddings, corporate events and the launch of any Welsh government initiative, with the gentle and plaintive strings attempting to rise above the clinking of glasses and the murmurs of a largely ignoring audience.

There's always music in Wales. I don't mean to reinforce a stereotype here, but I do think it's so deeply notable that nothing in Wales seems to happen at all without the accompaniment of music. This thought stays with me as I walk around the village after leaving the Eagles Hotel.

It's of course a nonsense that we are all singers. We're not. On the vocal front, we're no different to any other nation, but we do seem to have adopted this image of having the voices of angels. The reason I think we get away with that is because we have such a rich choral history and, in a crowd, the occasional tone-deaf participant can be covered up. I know that's how it's always worked with me.

'Listen to the singing,' says the rugby commentator as the Welsh anthem gets belted out by over sixty thousand people, and yet believe me, I know that most of those singing are under the influence of alcohol and are shouting rather than beautifully following a melody. But in sixty thousand voices, you really can't pick out a bad one, and so the myth of the voices of angels continues.

That's not to denigrate the many superb singers who have taken Wales to the world. They *are* the representation of the point I made earlier that music is always there, and they all would have grown up with music starting and ending each day in school, or hearing those choirs on radio and television throughout their youth. Wales, in fact, very much *is* a musical nation, and a nation of poetry too. The significance of the arts here, and of poetry and song, is not an overplayed card but a very real element of the country's rich history.

The National Eisteddfod is the shop window of that musical and poetic heritage, taking place each summer and featuring over a week of song, spoken word and poetry competitions. Sometimes over five thousand individuals compete and celebrate with an audience attendance of around thirty times that.

Llanrwst has a special place in Eisteddfod history, having held a poetry festival event here first in 1791, but it also hosted the modern

National Eisteddfod in 1951, receiving its ring of stones known as the Gorsedd Circle that all National Eisteddfod hosts are granted, and which I am walking around now with the sound of the rushing River Conwy behind me. Aside from being the principal celebration of Welsh arts, it's also the most important event in the Welsh language calendar.

This journey and my record of it is no place to discuss the importance of the Welsh language as I could never do it the justice it deserves, and many incredibly deft writers have already performed that task quite brilliantly. But I do think it's fair to raise a couple of points that have frustrated me over the years in the way it is sometimes regarded, not just by visitors, but often by Welsh people themselves.

Firstly, the rather stupid comment that I occasionally hear that Welsh is a dead language is the unjustified claim for the sake of attention, usually made by those in the south-east of the country who barely ever encounter it.

It's true that in Cardiff and Newport it is not heard everywhere unless you've got S4C – the Welsh-language broadcaster – on for the rugby or are mixing with the fluent elites in Pontcanna, a suburb of Cardiff known primarily for its outrageous house prices and its overpriced delis. But the lack of the language's dominance in those cities reflects the anglicised nature of them, and is not in any way a reflection of the desertion of the language in the nation as a whole.

The statistics are easily skewed by the major conurbations of the south that are in themselves the most international of Welsh towns, and the ones in which Welsh will be most diluted. We do know that in Gwynedd, 66 per cent of people speak the language and on Anglesey, over half do.

In smaller, isolated communities such as many we have ridden through in Gwynedd and Powys, the language is spoken by over 80 per cent of the residents, and across the country, while there have been decreases in the popular use since 2001, it remains a language compulsory in most schools and encountered daily in one form or another by a significant proportion of the population.

My stepdaughter was taught wholly in Welsh, whether it be physics, mathematics or art, and went to a school in the heart of the Rhondda.

My own two daughters were schooled in industrial Gwent and barely encountered it. The eldest of those, though, has a deep pride in it and uses it in snippets whenever she can.

Clearly, the Welsh government wants to establish a lifelong learning of the language, but to do so must somehow bridge the gap between those for whom it is a lifeblood and those who do not or maybe never will need it. Attempts to do that have so far been to create dual signage for almost everything, and to change the names of some of our most well-known locations to Welsh primacy.

For example, from 2023, the Brecon Beacons, as I have been calling them throughout this journey, are to be officially known henceforth as Bannau Brycheiniog. However, changing the name does not immediately change the common usage, and neither Luc 1, nor indeed Luc 2, will give that due regard yet as they rumble through it on their mega-bikes. Throughout Wales for a while to come, it is likely many people will still call that area the Brecon Beacons. But language and culture evolve, and if we plant a marker now that we want to give more power to the language, then I certainly cannot argue against the strategy of giving Welsh place names primacy. However, in itself, to me at least, this is not the answer to greater adoption of the language at home.

The continued spreading of economic and educational opportunity throughout the Welsh-speaking nation beyond the anglicised cities of the south could well be. But either way, the language remains a crucial element of contemporary Welsh life; it is neither dead nor diminished by the fact that it is not the most dominant one.

The second aspect that really aggravates me is the pathetic 'isn't it funny' approach that many in South East Wales take to the vocabulary, which has sadly spread into a common theme. It's self-harming when we join our English friends in mocking the language.

'Sounds like phlegm, mate!' HAHAHAHAHAHAHAHAHAHA-HAHAHAHA.

Or the genius, 'Welsh for microwave is POP-TY-PING!' HAHAHA-HAHAHAHAHAHA.

It's cringe-making when I hear Welsh people denigrate the Welsh language for the sake of laughs.

Once when I was working for a national record chain, the London head office refused to use Welsh-language signs for the musical genres because 'it looks stupid'.

'What do you mean, Welsh for children is "plant" – are you leek-eaters taking the piss?' was the less-than-witty reproach.

Don't get me started on their approach to place names.

If a BBC newsreader can't be bothered to get a Welsh place name right but will die in a ditch to get any Ukrainian town spot on, we have an issue. I have an in-law who regularly laughs at the places he drives through, deliberately mangling Tonyrefail, or Maesycwmmer, but would never dream of laughing at French or Greek town names when he's holidaying.

And just for the record, the Welsh for microwave is meicrodon. Grow up.

Apologies, rant over. But the point is important: that the language is in no way dead and is as rich a cultural source of pride for the Welsh as is the music, poetry or natural beauty that we boast of to the world. Maybe it's time for all of us, from the first-language user in Dolgellau, to the Cardiffian who never lets Welsh fall from their lips, to at least have a single unifying respect for it. For the user to acknowledge that not everyone does speak Welsh, and that's OK, and for the non-user to at least champion it and not turn it into a music-hall gag.

Here in Llanrwst it's heard in most of the places I walk, and as I do so I also think that the town is looking like it may punch above its weight on wealth. Some of the houses here are very impressive, and the town has that smart edge to its shops and restaurants rather than the reliance on cheaper-end living that maybe others on this journey had. It certainly looks smart today, and the group of schoolchildren that snake across the pavement in front of me are all proudly wearing their neat uniforms and holding hands in orderly fashion as the teacher calls them around the corner.

Llanrwst gives off the appearance at least of being one of the towns of Mid to North Wales less in need, so to speak. There is a real sense of community, largely generated by the town's shopping heart being almost entirely independent and having a very non-homogenous feel. There's an excellent poster in the newsagent's window that speaks volumes of the approach here:

Live totally, shop locally, say something good and invest in your town.

Many places sing it, but not many know the tune. Llanrwst seems to have the melody, the arrangement and successfully sells the tickets, if I haven't battered you with the metaphor enough yet.

Llanrwst always was 'better off', if I can use that phrase, largely due to its importance in the wool trade. It even dictated Britain's wool price many centuries back, as the scale of the market and the sheer number of merchants trading in it was so significant here.

When Edward the First (yes, him again) conquered Conwy and fortified it, about fourteen miles downstream, he also banned any Welshman from trading within a ten-mile radius of it. As Llanrwst sat just outside that red zone, Welsh merchants gravitated here to buy and sell so much product that the town grew rapidly and wealthily to support them. By the end of the thirteenth century, Llanrwst was North Wales's richest town and was seized and protected by Llywelyn ap Gruffydd in the last years of the Welsh Princes before the capitulation to the English line.

His grandfather, Llywelyn the Great, was interred in a mighty stone coffin on his death, and that coffin, empty now, sits within St Grwst's church in the Gwydir Chapel, which to me is one of Wales's most precious little treasures. The chapel looks nothing more than a stone box from the outside, but once inside the seventeenth-century room, its full beauty hits you.

The walls are beautifully polished wood, and the carvings on the pulpit are exquisite, but the glory is in the ceiling painted in the most daringly rich autumnal colours.

'Look upwards to lift the spirits', the National Churches Trust leaflet says, and they're not wrong. A dramatic collection of brightly outlined cherubs, angels robed in fiery red, and Christ surrounded by the rays of the sun, form a neck-aching artistic endeavour worthy of far more attention than this little chapel in a faraway market town in Wales can truly afford it.

Llywelyn's empty coffin may be the most politically potent and symbolic artefact that Llanrwst possesses, but it doesn't have anything more spiritually creative than this, and it may be the most beautiful and simple celebration of Welsh humanity found outside any of our nation's museums.

Walking back over the wonderful stone bridge to reunite with Gwendoline, I'm filled with positivity. Llanrwst has woken something in me that Blaenau threatened.

It is easy, given the economic and social difficulties that Mid and North Wales face, to believe we are a nation split to form divides, and that the south-east can irresponsibly cast other parts of Wales adrift. I found this in Blaenau Ffestiniog and it created concerns that I am a part of that negligence; however, Llanrwst has reminded me that the spirit and community that being Welsh engenders, wherever you are in the nation, or indeed world, is a richly nurturing thing. I find peace, pride and the resonance of art and culture here that causes an optimism, and as I ride out it is with a smile on my face and an extra twist of Gwendoline's throttle to get a celebratory roar.

I'm also encouraged by the sense that I'm approaching journey's end as I ride through Maenan, which effectively is simply the site of a hotel, and then on to Tal-y-Cafn, which is where I find another North Wales treasure: Bodnant Garden.

Gwendoline is at her best here, purring now as we ride through Llansanffraid Glan Conwy and that glorious Conwy Estuary opens up to our left. Broad, wide, glistening in the last late-afternoon light, the reed beds that line the banks sway gently and create a scene of such idyll that it's impossible to ride on without stopping.

At this northern end of the River Conwy, the settlements here were all once making their subsistence living from the river and its estuary mouth. The inhabitants of fifth- and sixth-century hamlets would have fished here, tying up simple flat craft in the reeds at night, whereas now the estuary is dotted with sleek yachts and other signs that the waterway is at the heart of the North Wales coast's tourist attractions.

To get the best view, though, and perhaps the most dramatic entry to any town in the country, Gwendoline and I sidle briefly off the

A470 to ride across the 1958 road bridge that straddles the estuary towards the town of Conwy.

This bridge replaced the Thomas Telford one that, at its time in 1826, was one of the first road suspension bridges on the planet. But even though that has been superseded, the view of the magnificent Conwy Castle waiting at the other end of the bridge is unchanged from the last century and still makes the excited traveller gasp.

CHAPTER 17

THE CASTLE
AND THE FAB FOUR

Make no mistake, this right here is the Welsh town that people who've never been to Wales expect.

The massive stone castle still retaining most of its original design, sat high above an estuary of incredible beauty, and the narrow streets protected by those high, strong, mediaeval walls that circle it.

I'm going to lay my cards on the table. I love Conwy.

Not for any great nostalgia or for a clinging onto a magical, mythological Wales of princes, poetry and passionate pride. I love it because it represents itself as a town of independent character, of great history and of a social climate that just appears, from the bustling streets late this afternoon, to work.

Parking Gwendoline at the rear of the old Castle Hotel and strolling down High Street towards the harbour wall, I pass a fabulous row of independent stores, cafés, galleries and chip shops. If there's a centre to the world of chips it could well be here in Conwy.

What I love is that every chip shop, and I count five within a potato's throw here, declares itself as purveyors of the best chips in Wales. Certainly, if the jury of seagulls at the side of the estuary is to be believed, the chips are damn good.

It's a British thing, isn't it? Eating chips out of paper, sat by a harbour wall, being strafed by seagulls. To avoid losing an eye, however, I decline the chips for now and walk along the wall past the boat-trip adverts towards Wales's smallest tourist attraction.

There's a tiny queue outside but it turns around quickly, as the time spent admiring 'Britain's Smallest House' is about as long as it takes to look around a room. The terraced cottage is painted a bright red to distinguish it from the Tudor black-and-white terrace it bookends, and it's impossible to imagine how anyone would or even could live in it, but live in it they did up until around 1900.

The lady who takes my one pound fifty is dressed in that Salem Chapel garb of shawl, pinny and stovepipe hat, and asks me to wait while the couple ahead of me enter. I count to thirty before the man and his wife are back out, making it not only Britain's smallest tourist attraction, but likely its quickest, too.

When I go in, I look around a tiny room with a wooden bench and a fireplace and poke my head up to a second floor with a single bed. It's dressed as it would have been in the late eighteenth century with an iron fireplace, and colourised sepia prints give some extra character, but that, so the saying goes, 'is all, folks'.

Stepping back into the room on the ground floor, I knock a metal thing off a shelf and the clatter on the floor sounds like a shopping trolley emptying a set of cutlery onto stone. The lady in the Welsh garb comes in and obviously has some sympathy.

'Oh, don't worry,' she reassures me, and I can tell that this is a routine happening in this cell of a place. 'We get all sorts bumped around in here,' and then spectacularly adds, 'it's so small, you see,' as though I had failed to notice its only unique attribute.

Actually, the lady is very friendly and helps me select a place for a beer, back up in the town – that's about all of fifty feet from the quayside – within a pace or two of the incredible castle that dominates Conwy.

As I walk towards it, a train rushes through almost directly under the stunning high towers and I imagine that must be one of the best views from a moving train in the country, with the walls of the mighty fort falling away behind and the huge estuary opening out to your left as you rail onwards to Llandudno only minutes away. I play with the idea of leaving Gwendoline in Conwy and taking the train for the final leg, but the scooter has already had her bad days, and with improvements in her behaviour since Dolgellau it might seem churlish of me to deny her the final yards.

Without wanting to turn this into a geography lesson, it is worth pointing out that Conwy Castle not only looms over this lovely town, but also dominates the skyline for a huge distance all around. From all directions it rises high above the ground, and benefits from seeming to look complete still, unlike many which seem to be hanging on by a thread or exist now simply as a ragged wall – I'm talking to you, Newport.

'Exceptionally well preserved', Cadw (the Welsh government's historic sites organisation), calls it. And they could be talking about Conwy itself, which is basically a settlement that is protected by the walls of the castle to one side and the wide waters of the River Conwy to the other.

No one in their right mind could see this and the others built by Edward in the north, the last wild and free area of Wales, as anything other than the final word of a conquest. Harlech and Caernarfon castles formed a western and northern defensive point and, along the eastern coast, Conwy created a triangle of might that was overseen by a succession of English kings until becoming the subject of a rebellious Welsh siege led by Owain Glyndwr at the turn of the fifteenth century. This was the last time that Wales could declare itself a free state, with Glyndwr benefitting from recognition from France and Spain for a brief reign as a recognised Prince of Wales.

Glyndwr is a fascinating character, not in any way to be done written justice by me here, but one worth further reading for sure, and who retains legendary status in Wales as the last leader of a free Wales, even if only for less than a decade, and who was never captured.

In the last years of his life, he led guerrilla actions against Henry the Fifth's forces in Mid and North Wales, and despite the offer of pardons upon surrender, and ultimately a price on his head, he eventually disappeared. He was never found, his burial place is unknown, and he remains to this day a man of mythological status and a symbol for the Welsh independence movement.

It's tempting to walk backwards down the hill of Castle Street to keep the incredible stone monolith in view but, of course, in the busy, narrow streets that just makes you a nuisance. Especially with the tourist numbers being what they are, even this late in the year.

Lionel and Sarah are two such tourists, and we share a tiny table in the crowded Blue Bell pub, almost overrun by a coach party from the United States.

It's so nice to be able to chat with Americans about Wales and not have to start with either Diana, Princess of Wales, Tom Jones or castles, even though I'm guessing the latter is the main draw for them this day.

'Actually, we're here on a Beatles tour,' says Lionel, a retired dentist from Dayton, Ohio.

Not wanting to point out the difficulties of tying the Fab Four to Conwy (although Ringo used to drum at the Butlin's forty miles from here in Pwllheli – I should say in *pre*-Beatles days, so as not to suggest his career hit a freefall in 1970), I let him carry on although I'm *really* hoping there is a connection I'm not aware of.

'We've done Liverpool for three days and the tour has a day out in Wales as an addition, so we thought why not?'

It turns out Lionel and Sarah want to know more about Wales, and I want to know more about them, so we gel well over the next hour as the night falls outside.

Lionel and Sarah have been to the UK only once before, for a golfing holiday in Scotland, and Liverpool is a bit of a pilgrimage for them both as they became such huge Beatles fans in their early days of courting. I'm plainly overcome with excitement, as they are the only people I have ever met who were at the now-legendary Shea Stadium concert in 1965. I joke that it puts them as courting two weeks before I was born, and I'm genuinely astonished as Sarah in particular looks nowhere near even possibly that age.

We swap questions between us and as I write them now, it looks like the strangest conversation possible.

'So do you speak Welsh?'

'Did you hear John talk or was the screaming as loud as it seems?'

'But you're governed by London, right?'

'What songs can you remember?'

'How are the Welsh different from the Irish?'

'How far were you from the stage?'

'You have your own police but not your own defence force, right?'

'How long did the show last?'

'Where does the money in Wales come from?'

'Did they finish with "I'm Down"?'

'So, you feel different to the English?'

'Did you come away with a favourite Beatle?'

At this last one, Lionel feels a need to give it some serious thought and says he'll come back to me.

It's a fabulous conversation and I think we all gave what the others wanted. Lionel is a big man, not big as in wide, but big as in everything. About six three and solid as Ohio's Campbell Hill. He's one of the few Americans in the pub not wearing a baseball cap or something that identifies him as a veteran, but he did serve, and Sarah glosses over my interest in that quickly.

She's immaculate in that 'Ralph Lauren' way and has a wonderful calm to her voice, straight from the blue waterways of Appalachia.

'We'd love to come back,' she says, 'what else should we see?'

This poses me a difficult question, as of course I want to give the best possible take on the country I come from, and yet after my ride of the last few days I find I can't put a coherent response together. You know what it's like when you've been out for the day and someone asks you what you've done, and you always miss out something no matter how recent it is? I feel like that. There is so much to tell them about the wonders of Wales, the cities, the villages, the beauty and the people that I end up murmuring something about the sea to the north, the mountains to the centre and the city to the south.

Clearly unimpressed by my advert for the Welsh tourist authority, Lionel asks me what the golf is like and we end a wonderful conversation skirting around something I can't help with.

I think Sarah notices my struggle and gently puts her hand on my arm, smiles kindly and says, 'I guess there's just so much, you just don't know where to start?'

I don't want to let them down, so I start over-talking to them about my journey. About what I was hoping to find, and how I hoped a Wales I hadn't known would reveal itself to me. The arrogance of the capital, the beaten-down communities of the Rhondda that don't give up, the paucity of investment in Mid Wales surrounded by its natural splendour, and so on and so on until I bring them figuratively through Snowdonia, to here in this marvellous town on the edge of a beautiful estuary.

Lionel and Sarah are silent for a moment and then she says a sentence I'll never forget. 'Wow! Lionel, we must tell people about this; it sounds like Ohio.'

Minutes later, a loud American voice announces that the coach is loading, and Lionel and Sarah stand to leave. I notice Lionel helps Sarah up from her chair and see for the first time that she walks with the aid of a stick. They hold hands as they leave and through the window I can see Lionel carefully guiding Sarah up onto the coach step. A couple who were screaming kids at Shea Stadium, who within a couple of years were separated by war, and after a life together with its ups and downs wanted to come and see Wales.

A moment or two later, Lionel comes back into the pub and hands me a card.

'I just wanted to settle Sarah into her seat but thought I'd give you my card before we head out… just in case you want to compare Ohio to Wales yourself and want somewhere to stay when you do.'

Normally, we throw these things into conversation as if they're meaningless, 'Oh you must come and see us if you're passing', but Lionel has gone to his bus, picked up a card and come back so he obviously means it, and before leaving finishes a previous conversation we had a while back.

'In answer to your question, I think it was George,' he says, before adding with a huge smile and a wagging finger: 'Was never going to be Paul because Sarah fawned over him.'

He laughs so hard at this that he starts to wheeze. A fabulous memory from the ages that catches up with his age.

I walk out with him and wave them off imagining (if you'll excuse the pun) Sarah as the sixteen-year-old girl who saw the Beatles, and it gives me a broad smile that I don't lose until I get to my hotel for my last night on the journey.

CHAPTER 18

TIDDLY-OM-POM-PROM

Let me nail some colours to a mast before I go on. The spirit world is alien to my personal experience. I'm not one to take too much interest in the ghostly, and the 'undead' remain simply the dead to me. I've always thought that if there was any evidence of an afterlife, we'd have heard about it on the news at least. But those of you with a different experience may well give a nod and a knowing bow to a reported phenomenon called timeslip.

Timeslip, at least as far as the theory goes, is a paranormal occurrence where a person can be in one time (our present) yet experience by vision or sound another time (the past) happening around them. A brief look on the internet will give you thousands of examples of this, with people all over the world passing on their own stories and experiences. Those of a flexible mind suggest it can be evidence of time travel or the supernatural, whereas scientists will tell you it's evidence of nonsense.

Either way, the tales are entertaining at least. The lady in France who stayed in a modern B&B but woke up in an eighteenth-century inn, complete with horse tracks outside where the night before a busy road was. Or the young girl who fell asleep on the seafront at Brighton and was woken by the sound of hundreds of 1920s bathing belles splashing in the water, and horses and carts winding along behind her.

In these and other cases, the experience is temporary and the evidence non-existent. If the above has piqued your interest, I direct you to the podcast (and now TV show) *Uncanny*, hosted by Danny Robins who examines the phenomenon brilliantly. But for those of you who just fancy the idea of experiencing timeslip once in your lives, I recommend you visit Llandudno.

In fairness, the town is looking its best as I enter it, with the sun high and golden over the Great Orme. This headland creates the western end of the glorious, sweeping shore that runs for two miles in a breathtaking arc to the eastern headland, less imposingly named the Little Orme. Between the Great and Little Ormes, that seafront is calling me to make it my first stop in the town, and I can't resist.

I give Gwendoline a pat. It's been a strange relationship and I guess I should be celebratory, but she's not mine and I feel my attitude towards the scooter is simply one of 'mission over'.

I'll have to get Gwendoline back and already I feel as though riding the whole length of the A470 in reverse will be just an arse-aching chore so, while I give that some thought, I leave her to cool down in the wind tunnel that the seafront creates.

Looking to my left as I stand on the wide promenade that runs along the whole shore, I see under the sheer face of the Great Orme a long Victorian pier jutting out on its thin legs to a calm, grey sea. That grey water doesn't understand its role here. It should be blue, or a shimmering aquamarine, but instead it stubbornly takes in the glorious sun and reflects a pale grey with the whitest of dots as gentle waves break in the distance. This lack of adherence to the centuries-old colour palette rules of the sea doesn't detract from the view, which is of the calmest water stretching out widely to a distant horizon littered with wind turbines spinning deathly slowly in the barest breeze.

Behind me begins a two-mile stretch of uninterrupted Victorian buildings following a perfectly parallel curve to the promenade at the waterfront. Many of these are the grande-dame hotels that welcomed wealthier Victorian visitors in the latter days of the nineteenth century, and dotted only occasionally between them are the smaller boarding houses that allowed the working classes and their families a day or two of parity, and a respite from the mills and factories of the industrial north-west of England.

H. V. Morton raised his game when writing about Llandudno in his book *In Search of Wales*.

He writes that 'there is no finer situation in the whole country for a big holiday town. It has all the virtues of an island', and then goes on to add, with no hint of overstatement whatsoever, that 'the sweep of its bay is as fine as that of Naples'.

That is some Tripadvisor review!

Not a single shop or pub disturbs the row of hotels on that front. If you look above the cars parked along the road, and only at the buildings arcing into the distance towards the Little Orme, and you listen to the sea making its arrival onto the pebble shore, you can have that moment of timeslip. You're in the present, but you're looking at the undisturbed past.

This happens a lot in Llandudno. Close your eyes and you can hear the same old sounds of the approaching water, or the feet treading on the wooden-slatted pier, or the gulls in their gang-fights for dropped crumbs.

Even the eyeline looking out at the sea through the iron legs of the pier is unchanged over a century, and the Great Orme itself, looming large and seemingly threatening the very existence of the western end of the promenade, gives you a sense of time holding still.

Beyond the pier and under the sheer face of the Great Orme sits Llandudno's landmark Victorian hotel: the Grand. Incongruous with the neat surroundings below, and the elegance of the other hotels on the sweep, the Grand stands apart both literally and metaphorically. Detached from the town's heart, it sits high above the sea's edge, staring down at the pier below like the Bates Motel in *Psycho*. It's far more a threat than a welcome. Where the elegance of the promenade hotels appears, from a distance at least, to be of great charm, the Grand has only it's overbearance to announce itself.

It's still early in the afternoon but perhaps the journey is taking its toll as I sit on a bench at the entrance of the pier and just enjoy being still.

The autumn sun is finally, after the chills and dank of most of the journey, warm on my face, and the holidaymakers are gathering on the wide promenade in front of me. The gulls are madly on the prowl. One sits further along my bench and looks at me for a moment before realising that the book in my hand isn't a sandwich-theft opportunity, and then blanks me, giving an occasional 'Waah' to his mates.

I notice the group of people gathering in the space in front of me seems to be getting bigger, and there's a chatter now that signals something will be happening. Why I hadn't noticed the tall, striped, wooden box only yards to my left is a wonder. It's about eight foot tall or more, garishly painted in bright stripes, and clearly is the focal point for the gathering families.

From where I sit, I can see a flurry of activity behind the box, a swish of a curtain, then a combination of confused children, chatting parents and smiling grandparents are arrested into a sudden silence. It's another timeslip moment as Professor Codman's Wooden Headed Follies Punch and Judy Show announces itself.

The performances have been entertaining the good holidaymakers of Llandudno at the promenade since 1864, making it unquestionably the United Kingdom's longest-running Punch and Judy show, and one of the many things in Llandudno that cling onto a past while operating in a very different present. My instinct is to sigh and prepare myself to witness a car crash. I'm expecting people to bear up for a moment or two, perhaps looking abstractedly at their phones while their kids reach boredom point within minutes, but that's not how things seem to be panning out.

After ten minutes of puppetry, the crowd has grown to about twenty or more, and clearly most of the phones have been put away, and the kids sat cross-legged under the makeshift theatre are engaging with the action. Huge laughter as Mr Punch suffers the angry attentions of his wooden wife and anticipatory silence as the puppets disappear below for a moment, ready to bounce back up into their playful dispute.

The show is billed as 'wholly traditional' and while that means Judy and her baby suffering a plotline that would have the scriptwriters for *EastEnders* thinking twice about appropriateness, there is something that remains rather charming about a group of children almost wetting themselves at the antics of the crocodile hell-bent on sausage theft.

Closing my eyes again, I could once more easily be in the time of Victoria. The sounds of the children laughing, and the old puppet-play script being shouted from inside the box, are as unchanging over the century as the grey sea rolling in and out.

The show has been in the Codman family for five generations and sticks rigidly to its original format and themes. The Codmans recognise it won't be for all, and I watch more than one family move away with a concern in their eyes and more than just a tut under their breath. To counterbalance that, though, and considering the show runs for about half an hour, when I stood up to leave just about halfway through, there was still a decent number rapt in the story. But then I left before the bit with the hangman and the devil.

This whole area, the prom, the pier and the sweeping front, are part of the Mostyn estate. The Mostyn family are the owners and guardians of a huge swathe of this corner of Wales and therefore place many controls on how Llandudno, and other areas in the region, develop. Rules on how the buildings can look, rules on what businesses can operate, and rules on how the land is used, can be seen as what retains Llandudno's appeal or what holds it back. Either way, to keep delivering the Codman family's Punch and Judy show, the performance must have the backing and support of the Mostyn family, and after 160 years that's clearly still the case.

It's only a short walk from the antics of Mr Punch to another prime example of the Victorian age, the famous Llandudno pier. Jutting out from under the Great Orme headland, this is Wales's longest pier, the fifth longest in the UK and the second at this site. The first, a much shorter wooden version, was storm-damaged frequently and was subject to a cycle of repair, use, repair and use again until it was given up on in 1859.

This pier that I'm walking out on to today is a far grander and longer design, trimmed with exquisite and elaborate ironwork and housing several ornamental kiosks and huts along each side. These are turned now into typical seaside stalls, offering the customary cockles and whelks, buckets and spades and, for the income-generating hen parties, penis key rings and pink cowboy hats.

I don't intend any snobbery by this; the Victorian seaside resort was always designed to cater to our unleashed holiday selves, not our at-the-coal-face, discipline-at-all-costs selves, and the saucy postcard was a popular souvenir over a hundred years ago, so an update for the Tik-Tok generation seems only reasonable. I draw the line at the strawberry breasts on a stick, though. I'd feel less of a fun-seeking holidaymaker and more of a creep on some sort of list, walking along with that raised to my face.

When I started this journey back at Cardiff Bay, it was a grey morning with a cool wind blowing in hard off the water and some of that pointless fine drizzle was dotting around me. Here on the pier at the end of the long unwinding road, it's a glorious blue-and-gold afternoon and the sun is warm on my face.

Strolling on the boardwalk of the pier past the various typical seaside entertainments, I can get a clear sense of being in Llandudno, with its huge and impressive sweeping seafront to my right, but what I start to realise I *don't* get is that sense of being in Wales I picked up on the last couple of days in Llanrwst and Conwy. In fact, this town has a very generic seaside feel to it, particularly here walking on the pier, dodging the dive-bombing gulls and listening to the amusement machines blasting space battles and bells out into the sun from their shady arcade.

The Ocean Bar at the very end of the pier's seven-hundred metre length is a very welcome place to look back at the town from. Sat at the most distant bench, I get a real sense of this North Shore of the town. The Great Orme lurches high over the Grand Hotel and the pier in front of me, and then over to my left is the dramatic sweep of the bay with its almost uninterrupted row of hotels and boarding houses running for two miles east.

The only break to the row is the incongruous Venue Cymru, the town's pre-eminent concert hall and theatre complex, which to my eyes has the appearance of a refurbished communist-era bus station.

Sitting back with a cold beer and the sun on my neck, I have a moment of real satisfaction. I've travelled the length of the country, right up through its heart, and really started to understand both how disconnected and fragmented the country and its inhabitants are, but also how so many vital themes run as consistent threads through us all, giving us real opportunity for unity. Work, family, the environment, quality of life, patriotism, internationalism, all rang loudly while I was on the long unwinding road.

Sitting here watching the simplest of pleasures being enjoyed by so many along the pier and the shore gives a touching moment of joy. A moment almost immediately shattered by the loud bass thuds of 'Pokerface' by Lady Gaga delivered by a stuffed monkey in a pram pushed by a Roman centurion.

Sam Peters walks, or should I say dances and shuffles, the promenade and pier on a regular basis. After a series of health problems over the last few years, not least during the Covid pandemic, Sam finds a release from tension in his persona as the 'Monkey Man' pushing his soft-toy chimpanzee in a buggy to the accompaniment of classic dance grooves belting out from a boom box.

It's loud, it's completely imposing if you're wanting a quiet spell to yourself, but more than anything else I've seen since I've been here, it's creating laughter and smiles in everyone around me. Sam gives everything else on the pier, from slot machines to karaoke, and from photo booths to candy floss, a real lesson in conveying simple pleasure.

We chat for a few minutes, during which time he doesn't turn the volume of the music down, and over 'SOS' by Abba I shout out a few 'Why this?' and 'Why now?' questions but the whole point isn't in the 'why', it's in the 'what', and Sam simply pushes a monkey around the pier to music and it makes people smile. Sometimes you've just got to accept joy when it comes, however it looks.

Sam is far more widely known that I would ever have imagined. You'll find him online under his Monkey Man moniker, and there's a real uplifting tale to be told of his recovery from the lowest of lows. He's battled loneliness, fatigue and depression and resolved many of his internal anxieties by externalising happiness. It's something to behold as he walks off being waved at by everyone, fixing a grand smile across his face and watching it spread like joyful fire across the holidaymakers.

And there is no doubting the value of the holidaymaker here and how important it is to keep them content. The whole town survives and to an extent thrives because of the power of the visitor.

Many of the visitors come here for the simplest of vacations. The pier, the seafront, the hotel entertainment, which is invariably a singer with a backing tape, and the chance to take in the views from the Great Orme after a steep walk or a tram journey. The average visitor knows what they're getting here but it's not particularly Welsh. It's the classic British seaside weekend.

However, away from the grand high-fronted hotels steeped in decaying or shabby Victorian façades, there's a group of people doing everything they can to modernise Llandudno's holiday image. While they don't have the capital to transform the massive seafront properties that loom large, further down the front and away from the pier they are buying smaller three-storey properties to create classic British B&Bs with a twenty-first-century twist. If anyone is going to take Llandudno from timeslip to today, it's them.

A great example is the small, terraced Glan y Môr Hotel, elegantly proportioned and stylishly designed by a couple who see Llandudno less as a sleeping giant of the vacation world, and more as a here-and-now destination just crying out to be noticed.

Stepping inside, there is a real sense of home about the place. Modern in its décor yet very much traditional in its service. The bar at the rear is promoted as a gathering place where all guests are welcome to share time together over a finely mixed G&T before heading out to enjoy the Llandudno evening. This informal get-together is enhanced by the owners joining us themselves and encouraging stories between the guests of where they've been and where they're going.

These B&Bs are not, as some of the older and grander hotels are, a destination in themselves, with breakfast, lunch, dinner, bar and entertainment all thrown in, but are much more a place to drop your bags, meet others of a like mind and then head out for an evening knowing that you've got high-end comfort and service to come back to.

Mark and Liz have run Glan y Môr since Mark's early retirement as a policeman, and between them they represent the best of Llandudno's embrace of a future state that will beat a path away from an underinvested Victorian museum resort to something far more contemporary and alive.

'I think we just wanted to do something a little different,' Mark says while we share a G&T served from his cool bar in the lounge at the back of the B&B.

'Most people come to Llandudno thinking they will get a break from the normality of their lives, but aside from the beautiful shore there's often a disappointment, particularly out of season.'

He's got that right; on my stroll around the streets that run behind the town's famous Victorian façade later, I encounter more than a few closed establishments, restaurants and bars shutting once the few remaining tourists have headed back to the kiss-me-quick karaoke and scampi-in-a-basket at their hotel.

'We just thought,' he goes on, 'what if we made people feel at home instead, and so we try to create a place that feels like going to a friend's house. You can hang around as much as you like, and we'll join you.' He smiles and raises a glass at this, and I clink back feeling exactly like he suggests. At home.

There's more to the modern B&B he and Liz have created, though. Liz has a superb eye for detail, and as she joins us looking elegant in her evening wear, she talks about how she wants to keep going with her design project.

'Each guest is different, so we give a variety of designs to the rooms and make each evening a pleasure,' she says. A few like-minded B&B owners are also starting to punch above their weight against the more traditional, and declining, tourist experience, but Mark and Liz's dedication to representing Llandudno in a more contemporary style will only be a drip of colour in an ocean of beige unless many more take up the baton.

The bar in the Grand, for example, on my arrival seems to have all the celebratory atmosphere of a poorly attended office leaving do. My stay is punctuated by two arguments in only ten minutes. One between two members of staff who clearly resent being there, and one with a guest who far too graphically describes the welcome they found in the toilet bowl in their room.

I'm told by another lone guest nursing a flat-looking beer that in season this place is 'buzzing' and is a popular location for some of North Wales's bigger wedding celebrations, so it's sad that I've caught it on one of its 'off' nights.

On more than one occasion, someone walks in, stands still for a few moments and then changes their mind and leaves, adding further to the stagnant atmosphere. Each entrant to the bar becomes a person of great interest to the few of us sat within, and on their receding, we seem to give a collective sigh and turn back to our drinks. It's as though the next one that stays will get a round of applause and an embrace.

Without wanting to linger, I head back outside and start a walk up the Great Orme, the huge headland that looms over the town and offers a view out over the ocean to the north, but also gives fabulous vistas of Anglesey and Snowdonia. You can get to the top by tram if you wish, in similar style to the little train that would take you up Snowdon, but the walk is breathtaking. Literally.

This is the oldest I've felt in a long time and reminds me of my age, but by the time I get to the top it's worth every struggled step, every cough and every splutter. Night is falling, but the last light away to my left over the Irish Sea gives a glimmer of reddish silver, and looking back over the promenade well below me I get a sense that the town has far more to offer than I've given it credit for.

The lights along the prom have come on and the hotels are lighting up to create a fine arc of gold and white spots that reminds me of a Mediterranean town, perhaps in southern France. The wind is picking up, too, much to the irritation of some of the town's famous goats who seem to have taken ownership of the Great Orme and who wander with purpose across its grassy top. Their company makes me feel that maybe I've been a bit hard on Llandudno, with my suggestion that it will take far more people like Mark and Liz to change the atmosphere, and instead I'm wondering, as I try to thrust a handful of grass at an uninterested goat, if actually it can thrive it can thrive quite paradoxically as two places in one.

For the group of people who want a throwback holiday, to have everything served to them on a plate, and to live a few days away from the distractions of home without being challenged. Perhaps take in the singer at the Grand and share chips with the strafing seagulls.

Llandudno serves them well.

But also travellers who have been across North Wales, climbed, walked, hiked, ziplined and, hell, even scootered from glorious location to glorious view, and now want a touch of modern elegance and individualism to finish their trip. It would be good to be able to say that Llandudno was perfect for them, without having stepped into the past even for a minute.

I'm taken out of this evening daydream by increasing bleats around me and find that my handful of grass is the focus of at least four or five goats, but none of them want to introduce themselves closely.

Thinking fondly of Lionel and Sarah, whom I met back in Conwy, I name the goats John, Paul, George, Ringo and Goat, say my cheerios and wander back down off the great headland to Mark and Liz's, for a nightcap and a welcoming chat about the future of Llandudno and how it would look if Liz had the town planner's pen.

I've got a lot of time for Llandudno and a lot more for what it could be. In fact, its potential seems to far outweigh its aspiration. Perhaps part of that is the ownership of much of the land lying with a single family.

Because the Mostyns own the freehold of most of the commercial town centre, after being the main driving force for its transformation from mining outpost to Victorian destination resort, as I've already mentioned, they also control how the area looks and, to an extent therefore, how it feels.

Their control stretches as far as Mark and Liz who need to present requests for permissions first if they want to change any aspect of the façade of their B&B. Change the windows? Sure. Change them for those ones there? Not a chance.

If that sounds as though I have a downer on the Mostyns, I'm not sure that's wholly fair. The fact that Llandudno retains its character as a resort with history is down to that level of authority over detail, but the fact that this maybe presents a hurdle to a full MOT could be a developmental issue, even if Booking.com, the hotel-booking website de rigueur, makes it one of the finest resorts in Europe.

Maybe I'm deaf to them, but I hear no complaints about the Mostyns on this night in Llandudno and, over a last beer with Mark while he rifles enthusiastically through Joy Division tracks in his excellent house bar, I'm able to get a sort of review of where Wales is from someone who came to it late.

'We seem to get more people over from England than we do from here in Wales,' he says, while asking politely if I mind him switching the music to New Order – undoubtedly *not* what they're listening to in the Grand.

'I think what Liz has done here must work,' he says with a low note of real affection in his voice, 'because we're booked up for the whole of next year already. You'll always get a room in one of the cavernous places down the road, but we're heaving.'

So, Wales is still a draw, then?

'Oh aye,' he says, in a gently rising Mancunian lilt, as if it's a daft question. 'It's bloody marvellous! Ain't it, Liz?' he calls over to his wife, who's sat at the end of the bar on a high stool and raising a glass in confirmation.

He's right.

Throughout this journey, I've found the low points, the shameful moments in history, the poor communities, and the poor conditions that many lived in, and in some cases still must, but it's always been punctuated by the breathtaking nature of the land and, in most cases, a welcome of real warmth.

The point of this journey was exactly that. To see what Wales looked like across its many divides, social, economic, geographic and cultural. To that extent, Llandudno at the northern end – or start, depending on where you are – is completely different to Cardiff at its south.

Both born of Victorian principles. The capital out of the nineteenth-century boom in industry and engineering, and Llandudno out of the increase in leisure time as a legislated break from the working week.

Wales will never be wholly united as a single people despite the cosmetic attempts to do so at the next rugby international, but that's *because* of our wonderful differences. The sheer arrogance of white-collar Cardiff isn't a lie – there is plenty to be boastful about – but it won't win friends in Mid Wales where the land still gives of itself to those who work it. Likewise, the future of the nation as an economic force will partly depend upon the internationalisation of those southern cities, and the rest of Wales should want that to be successful.

Socially, we are not, as many would think, divided by the language but the fact that it remains a political issue needs to change. It lives well where it is the first, and should be proudly acknowledged by those where it is either second or not spoken. We as Welsh people do not do ourselves any favours when, as we have done for so many years, we turn in on ourselves much to the amusement of others, especially those over Offa's Dyke to the east.

We still, even so many years after Llywelyn the Great and Owain Glyndwr, need to understand that there is a point to rebellion. No longer by the sword or siege, but certainly through the ballot against institutional damage to our wellbeing. I'm talking of the desperation many people feel about not having their own home in the community where they were born, while those from many miles away buy up property as a sheer act of selfish vandalism against communities in the west and north. Permitting this is as much an act of self-harming as it is to consider Cardiff and the M4 corridor the only relevant investment locations in the country.

Likewise, there are aspects of institutional Wales we need to be prepared to protect. Agriculture in the mid and north reaches of the country gives life to many communities and enables us to think about a new relationship with the environment that is not fully understood in Swansea, Cardiff and Newport.

A new relationship between these commercial centres and the Wales north of Merthyr needs to be fostered, and the Welsh government should take the lead in creating a vision of Wales for all and not just for those on St Mary Street on match day.

For that is what this whole trip has been about: what does Wales look like? And the sad fact is that it only scores one out of three if we tick the boxes.

Yes, it looks beautiful. From the grey and green roll of the Rhondda, up through the reservoirs and steep hills of the Beacons and out to the rugged lands of Powys. Into the blue lakes and mountains of the Snowdon range and out through the Vale of Conwy alongside the beautiful estuary flowing to the sea, Wales has a glory and grandeur to be proud of at home and envious of abroad.

But only occasionally did I get a sense of being *in* Wales. The dragon flag is often an afterthought, and in some cases is buried beneath a weight of Union flags. Maybe it's because north of Merthyr the towns are so strung out, so separate, that a unity behind a single culture becomes a chore, and certainly when I was in the larger towns there was more of a Wales coming through, but it did so often very quietly.

And finally, we Welsh ourselves. I was hoping for some sort of brotherhood, I guess, and I never found that, but I did find welcomes, the desire to talk, to share and to give words to what we thought. Never afraid to venture an opinion, we are best in company, we give our hearts to the underdog and we take very little lying down.

Being Welsh means being in a minority. In the United Kingdom there are only around three million of us. We would fit into London three times. Perhaps because of that underdog sense, we are accepting of those who need us. Cardiff is a multicultural city because it took in the nations of the world, and a small corner of it remains almost wholly cosmopolitan to this day.

We gave the world the energy and the power to build itself. The Eastern USA, Europe and Southern Africa were developed using the riches of the minerals found under the Rhondda, and the world's greatest engineers tested their theories and their designs here.

Whilst I didn't 'see' Wales, or at least the Wales of my loose imaginings, I became far prouder of it than I ever thought I was. The incredible stoicism and sheer class of the residents of the Rhondda is something that will stay with me for a long time, and the profound feeling of being 'from here' that hit me at various points of the journey, such as in Pontypridd and Conwy, is something I think I want to carry far more loudly than I have before.

Now, on my last evening in Llandudno, a ramble along the prom-enade gives me a chance to reflect on whether my own discovery, or perhaps rediscovery, of my country has been worth more than the sum of its few days, and clearly the answer is yes. I'm abuzz with more plans for journeys to make here: Anglesey, the Gower, Snowdonia itself, Cardigan Bay, all places I've been but perhaps none that I've seen. I mean *really* seen.

Gwendoline won't be making the journey home, after 187 miles – a number perhaps allowing for the odd deviation – as Clem, her owner, explained with much kindness in a short phone call that he will pick her up here on his way to a scooter show in Liverpool.

She has been a partner of varying degrees. At times noisy, other times, such as riding past the River Conwy, barely giving a whisper; she has veered – literally – from useful to would-be killer. I think Gwendoline is as much done with me as I am with her.

I'm certainly not done with Wales. What this journey has taught me is that the nation has a million stories to tell, and I'm ready to discover the next. That River Taff, you remember from an earlier chapter – the one that died and came back to life, the one that shaped the entire economic and social fabric of the south? That might be worth looking at again. And as Dusty the golden retriever needs the exercise, perhaps we'll do it together. I hope she's comfortable in a canoe.

SUGGESTED READING

Throughout this account of the journey that Gwendoline and I took in the autumn of 2022, I refer to several books that revealed more detail to me on the places we saw, and the themes relevant to Wales both historically and today.

The most-thumbed was of course *In Search of Wales* by H. V. Morton, which is written with such vivid colour and style that it felt like a friend on the ride. Not all of Morton's terminology resonates with twenty-first-century sensibilities, but my goodness he had a good eye.

Other books that I turned to while writing may also be worth your interest, and some of them are listed below.

Jan Morris's *Wales: Epic Views of a Small Country* is a terrific narrative from arguably our finest writer on place.

Gaynor Madgwick's incredible book on the Aberfan disaster, *Aberfan: a Story of Survival, Love and Community in One of Britain's Worst Disasters*, is both distressing and yet incredibly uplifting, and remains for me one of the most important books on Welsh social history.

In fiction, Alexander Cordell's two novels *Rape of the Fair Country* and *Hosts of Rebecca* give great colour to the incredible harshness of the lives of working families, and his descriptions of the landscape are indisputably brilliant.

For history, a number of books were invaluable: John Davies's *A History of Wales* was my definitive choice, but also Jon Gower's *The Story of Wales* filled in many cracks for me, particularly on social history, and Marc Morris's fabulous *A Great and Terrible King: Edward I and the Forging of Britain*, his biography of Edward the First, took me vividly back to a time when Wales was a wilder, almost lawless place.

Suggested Reading

Labour Country: Political Radicalism and Social Democracy in South Wales, 1831–1985 by Daryl Leeworthy was a mine of information on the socio-political history of the Rhondda, as were Richard King's quite brilliant *Brittle with Relics: a History of Wales, 1962–1997*, and Joe England's *Merthyr: the Crucible of Modern Wales*.

ACKNOWLEDGEMENTS

I need to take a few lines to offer huge thanks to those who put up with me during the researching and writing of *The Long Unwinding Road*.

Firstly, to Andrea and the girls, Georgia, Izzy and Ashley, my thanks for not thinking this was a whim and for pushing me to the finish with all their questions.

Thanks also to Amy Feldman of Calon for inviting me in, and to the wonderful Abbie Headon, my ever-patient editor, who seemed to know what I was trying to say far better than even I did. A huge debt of gratitude also to Catriona Robb who, in copy-edit, was both remarkably patient and forgiving of my excesses as were the terrific Anna Baildon and Caroline Goldsmith.

I owe a huge debt to Gail Simmons and Stephen Moss who spotted something and encouraged me all the way, and without whom you wouldn't have this book in your hands.

Beyond those, a huge number of friends all over the world from Asia to the Americas have kept me motivated, and there will be a cold beer in a foreign bar somewhere with you all soon. You know who you are. Very special thanks closer to home are owed to Clem Thomas, King of the Mods, who kindly put me on a date with the difficult Gwendoline, and my long-time friend Simon Matthews, who enjoyed some of the road with me.

Finally, there are a number of writers who, though completely unaware of me, have influenced and shaped the way this book reads, so to Stuart Maconie, Mike Parker, Monica Rajesh, Steve Silk, Tom Fort, Tom Chesshyre, Tim Moore, Rebecca Lowe, Simon Parker and Erika Fatland, thanks for everything.

ABOUT THE AUTHOR

Marc P. Jones was born in Cardiff and has lived and worked across four continents. From having the best job in the world in the music business, he eventually gave in to his passion for travel and writing, documenting the world at TravellersWrites.com.

Nominated for Best New Travel Writer 2021 at the Edward Stanford Travel Writing Awards, he has also written on cricket and on music for *Record Collector* magazine. Currently living in Hong Kong, he is married and is co-owned by a cat and a golden retriever who will figure in his next book.